Rain without Thunder

THE

IDEOLOGY

OF THE

ANIMAL RIGHTS

MOVEMENT

Gary L. Francione

TEMPLE UNIVERSITY PRESS *Philadelphia*

Temple University Press, Philadelphia 19122
Copyright © 1996 by Temple University. All rights reserved
Published 1996
Printed in the United States of America

⊛ The paper used in this book meets the requirements of the American National Standard for Information Sciences—Permanence of Paper for Printed Library Materials, ANSI Z39.48-1984

Text design by Gary Gore

Library of Congress Cataloging-in-Publication Data
Francione, Gary L. (Gary Lawrence), 1954–
    Rain without thunder : the ideology of the animal rights movement /
    Gary L. Francione.
        p.   cm.
    Includes bibliographical references (p.   ) and index.
    ISBN 1-56639-460-0 (cloth : alk. paper). — ISBN 1-56639-461-9
(paper : alk. paper)
    1. Animal rights movement—United States.   2. Animal welfare—United States—
Philosophy.   I. Title.
HV4764.F73   1996
179′.3—dc20   95-49676

For JVB and The Bandit, two very good friends indeed

If there is no struggle,

there is no progress.

Those who profess to

favor freedom, and yet

deprecate agitation, . . .

want rain without thunder

and lightning.

Frederick Douglass

Contents

Acknowledgments

I most gratefully acknowledge the assistance that I have received from Dean Roger I. Abrams and the faculty at the Rutgers Law School in Newark. In these reactionary times, Rutgers Law School under Abrams continues to encourage an approach to the law that is progressive and that has as its foundation the view that law can effect positive social change for disempowered populations. Moreover, Abrams's uncompromising support for academic freedom has reinforced the reputation of the Rutgers-Newark Law School as a place where progressive scholarship is encouraged. It is a true luxury for a scholar to be able to take controversial and often unpopular positions with the encouragement of an administration and faculty that take academic freedom and social justice seriously. I also acknowledge the efforts of the Newark Provost, Norman Samuels, who similarly takes an uncompromising approach to issues of academic freedom.

I am deeply indebted to my colleagues at Rutgers as a group for creating and maintaining an atmosphere at Rutgers that fosters and promotes stimulating and often provocative discussion on a wide variety of matters abstract and practical. I acknowledge in particular the assistance of Professors William Bratton, Alexander Brooks, Drucilla Cornell, Doug Husak, Howard Latin, Phil Shuchman, and George Thomas; Assistant Deans Linda Garbaccio and Marie Melito; and Rose-ann Raniere.

Our library faculty, especially Professor Carol Roehrenbeck, Margorie Crawford, Glen Bencivengo, Nina Ford, and Ronnie Mark, provided absolutely first-rate research support. Gwen Ausby prepared the manuscript for publication with her usual expertise and good cheer.

I also wish to thank the animal protection organizations that provided me with information about their various campaigns and positions on issues that are discussed in this book. I am also grateful to several individuals who have contributed enormously to my efforts. James Corrigan and Elisabeth Colville have been stalwart colleagues for many years, and discussions with them have helped me to clarify my thoughts about the character of the animal movement in the 1980s. Shelton Walden and Johnny Fernandez have also had a considerable influence on my thinking about the relationship between the animal rights movement and other social justice movements. Henry Cohen, Esq., of the Library of Congress, provided research materials.

Priscilla Cohn, Professor of Philosophy at Pennsylvania State University, provided invaluable feedback on virtually all areas of the book. I am particularly indebted to Dr. Cohn for her insights on the role of inherent value in rights theory. Alan Watson, Ernest Rogers Professor at the University of Georgia, also provided invaluable assistance as I thought through issues concerning human slavery and its relationship to the exploitation of nonhumans. Tom Regan, Professor of Philosophy at North Carolina State University, made helpful suggestions concerning my theory of incremental change leading to animal rights. I also acknowledge helpful comments from Leslie Bisgould, Esq., Cheryl Byer, Marly Cornell, and Lyne Letourneau.

Patty Shenker, Doug Stoll, Bill Crockett, Priscilla Cohn, Stephanie Schueler and Jim Schueler, Barb Reibman, and Amy Sperling have continued to be stalwart supporters of the Rutgers Animal Rights Law Center, of which I serve as Faculty Director. The Center allows law students from Rutgers and other institutions to learn about animals and the law while we work together on actual cases. Our cooperative efforts have helped me to understand better the ways in which current animal welfare laws simply do not work.

Once again, David Bartlett, Doris Braendel, Joan Vidal, and all of the marvelous folks at Temple University Press made the publication process as painless as possible and graciously extended their assistance and cooperation at every stage. I also wish to thank Keith Monley for the painstaking care that he brought to his edit of the manuscript. I am indebted to him for his excellent work.

Finally, I could not have completed this were it not for the support that I received from my life partner, Anna E. Charlton, Esq., Codirector of the Animal Rights Law Center, and our nonhuman companions past and present, Chelsea, The Bandit, Stratton, Emma, Hamidallah, Robbie, and Chelselita Tedwyn.

January 27, 1996

Rain without Thunder

THE IDEOLOGY

OF THE ANIMAL RIGHTS

MOVEMENT

Introduction
Animal Rights and
Animal Welfare

During the past hundred years or so, until the late 1970s, concern about animals had been limited to assuring that they were treated "humanely" and that they were not subjected to "unnecessary" suffering. This position, known as the *animal welfare* view, assumes the legitimacy of treating animals instrumentally as means to human ends as long as certain "safeguards" are employed. For example, animal welfarists argue that the use of animals in biomedical experiments and the slaughtering of animals for human consumption are acceptable as long as these activities are conducted in a "humane" fashion.

The late 1970s and 1980s marked the emergence of the *animal rights* movement, which "retained the animal welfare tradition's concern for animals as sentient beings that should be protected from unnecessary cruelty," but added "a new language of 'rights' as the basis for demanding" the end of institutionalized animal exploitation.[1] To oversimplify the matter a bit, the welfarists seek the *regulation* of animal exploitation; the rightists seek its *abolition*. The need to distinguish animal rights from animal welfare is clear not only because of the theoretical inconsistencies between the two positions but also because the most ardent defenders of institutionalized animal exploitation themselves endorse animal welfare. Almost everyone—including those who use animals in painful experiments or who slaughter them for food—accepts as abstract propositions that animals ought to be treated "humanely" and ought not to be subjected to "unnecessary" suffering. Animal rights theory explicitly rejects this approach, holding that animals, like humans, have inherent value that must be respected. The rights view reflects a shift from a vague obligation to act "humanely" to a theory of justice that rejects the status of animals as property and the corresponding hegemony of humans over nonhumans. The rights theorist rejects

1

the use of animals in experiments or for human consumption, not simply because these activities cause animals to suffer but because such use violates fundamental obligations of *justice* that we owe to nonhumans.

As a general matter, rights are, as Bernard Rollin writes, "moral notions that grow out of respect for the individual. They build protective fences around the individual. They establish areas where the individual is entitled to be protected against the state and the majority *even where a price is paid by the general welfare*."[2] For example, if my interest in free speech is protected by a right, my interest is generally protected *even if* the general welfare would benefit from my being deprived of that right.

The theory of animal rights maintains that at least some nonhumans possess rights that are substantially similar to human rights. Animal rights ensure that relevant animal interests are absolutely protected and may not be sacrificed simply to benefit humans, no matter how "humane" the exploitation or how stringent the safeguards from "unnecessary" suffering. Animal rights theory rejects the regulation of atrocities and calls unambiguously and unequivocally for their abolition. Rights theory precludes the treatment of animals exclusively as means to human ends, which means that animals should not be regarded as the property of people. And because rights theory rejects the treatment of animals as property, rights theory rejects completely the institutionalized exploitation of animals, which is made possible only *because* animals have property status.

Just as the theory of animal rights is fundamentally different from that of animal welfare, so, regrettably, is the theory of animal rights fundamentally different from its realization in the social phenomenon called the animal rights movement. Despite an ostensible acceptance of the rights position, the modern animal protection movement has failed to translate the theory of animal rights into a practical and theoretically consistent strategy for social change. The language of rights is, for the most part, used rhetorically to describe virtually *any* measure that is thought to lessen animal suffering. So, for example, a proposal to provide a bit more cage space to animals used in experiments is regarded as promoting animal *rights* even though such a measure represents a classic example of welfarist reform. Indeed, on a practical level, the modern animal movement still embraces the nineteenth-century theory of animal welfare, whose primary goal is to ensure that animals, who are regarded as property under the law, are treated "humanely" and not subjected to "unnecessary" suffering. For example, a leading animal "rights" advocate has promoted the use of a six-step "pain scale" for experimenters to evaluate the invasiveness of their research. At the lower end of the scale, level 2—which represents "laboratory experiments and field studies involving mild pain / distress and no long-term harm"—includes "frequent blood sampling," "intramuscular injection, skin scraping," "negative reinforcement" such as "mild electric shock" and "brief cold water immersion," "food deprivations that do not result in more than a 10% weight loss," "water deprivation slightly exceeding particular species' requirements (e.g., deprivation in rats of less than 18 hours)," and "procedures involving anesthetized animals with mild post-operative pain / distress and no long-term harm."[3] This same animal "rights" advocate is the editor of a journal that "publishes reports and articles on methods of experimentation, husbandry and care that demonstrably enhance the welfare of farm, laboratory, companion and wild animals."[4]

It would be simplistic, however, to say that the modern animal movement is *no* different from its classical welfarist predecessor. In this book, I argue that the modern animal "rights" movement has explicitly rejected the philosophical doctrine of animal rights in favor of a version of animal welfare that accepts animal rights as an ideal state of affairs that can be achieved only through continued adherence to animal welfare measures. I regard this hybrid position—that the long-term goal is animal rights but the short-term goal is animal welfare—as the "new welfarism" and its advocates as the "new welfarists." The new welfarists apparently believe, for example, in some causal connection between cleaner cages today and empty cages tomorrow. As a result, the animal "rights" movement, despite its rhetorical use of rights language and its long-term goal of abolishing institutionalized animal exploitation, continues to pursue ideological and practical agendas that are functionally indistinguishable from measures endorsed by those who accept the legitimacy of animal exploitation.

In my view, there are two simple reasons for this disparity between social theory and practice. First, many animal advocates believe that, as an empirical matter, welfarist reform has helped to ameliorate the plight of nonhumans and that these reforms can gradually lead to the abolition of all animal exploitation. Second, although many animal advocates embrace as a long-term goal the abolition of animal exploitation, they regard rights theory as "utopian" and as incapable of providing concrete normative guidance to day-to-day movement strategy and practice.

The purpose of this book is to explore these two assumptions. I argue that welfarist reform has not—and *cannot*—lead to the abolition of animal exploitation. Animal welfarism, especially when applied in an economic system that has strong property notions, is structurally defective and conceptualizes the human / animal conflict in ways that ensure that animal interests never prevail. Moreover, the assumption that welfare and rights are connected begs a fundamental moral question: if we believe that animals have moral rights *today*, it is wrong to compromise the rights of animals *now*, by, for example, pursuing or supporting legal changes that facilitate supposedly more "humane" experimentation in the hope that these changes will lead to rights for *other* animals *sometime in the future*.

I argue that rights theory provides more concrete normative guidance for incremental change than other views relied on by animal advocates. That is, animal rights theory is not "utopian"; it contains a nascent blueprint for the incremental eradication of the property status of animals. The incremental eradication of animal suffering prescribed by classical welfarism—and accepted as the primary normative principle of new welfarism—cannot and will not, in itself, lead to the abolition of institutionalized exploitation; what is needed is the *incremental eradication of the property status of animals*.

Nevertheless, I must stress several important qualifications integral to my views and therefore to my analysis.

First, I do not deny that many people not only have a long-term goal of animal rights but also employ short-term strategies that are consistent with the rights approach. For example, some animal rights advocates have sought incremental change through the abolition of particular types of experiments that involve animals. I am also not claiming that organizations or individuals who tend to adopt welfarist means in an effort to achieve rights ends always adopt such means, or that they never use means that are consistent with their expressed goal of achieving rights for animals. My point is simple and limited: the modern animal "rights" movement—as exemplified by the large, national animal advocacy groups—has, by and large, adopted the position that it is permissible at least some of the time, under at least some circumstances, to pursue a short-term policy of animal welfare, which, they claim, will lead eventually to the recognition of animal rights. With very rare exceptions, national animal rights organizations have not explicitly adopted animal rights both as a guiding theory and as the criteria for identifying the *types* of short-term, incremental changes that are consistent with the realization of the long-term goal. Some groups and individuals promote this view more than others, but almost all national organizations accept this welfarist view on some level.

Second, and related to the preceding point, the views I criticize are, by and large, adopted by and promoted by national animal advocacy organizations. These national organizations are to be distinguished from local groups that are not affiliated with national groups and comprise mostly local volunteers. These grassroots groups usually take positions that are far more progressive than those adopted by the national organizations. As one political scientist who has studied the movement observed, "One of the key reasons for the sustainability of the animal rights challenge has been the roots it has grown at the local level. . . . The vast majority of these local groups are the products of the emergence of radicalism since one of its major characteristics is the emphasis on grassroots campaigning. By contrast, animal welfare groups tend to be far more elitist and cautious, relying on expert opinions and preferring to leave campaigning to their own paid staff."[5] The national animal movement in the United States has largely ignored the grassroots movement, and one national leader recently went so far as to label as "grassroots elitism" any criticism of the national organizations by independent activists.[6]

Third, I emphasize from the outset that my intention is not to criticize the good faith of those who are concerned about animal suffering but who do not accept animal rights theory. Considering the staggering amount of animal suffering in our society, I fully understand the desire of animal advocates to "put aside the theory and just get something done." The problem is, in my view, that the "something" that we are presently doing—namely, promoting animal *welfare* measures that we construe as providing *rights* to animals—is counterproductive on both theoretical and practical levels. In a nutshell, things are worse for animals than they were one hundred years ago; the present strategy is simply not working.

Some animal advocates feel that *any* criticism of "the movement" is unacceptable and "divisive" with respect to movement unity. I expect that many of these same animal advocates will think this book divisive even to question or criticize the strategies and tactics of the animal rights movement. Such a response is more characteristic of cults than of intelligent, progressive social movements, and I hope that those who are interested will approach the issue of animal rights and animal welfare with an open mind. We are part of a culture that has for centuries accepted animals as *things* that, at best, deserve some minor moral consideration as long as no humans are inconvenienced in the process. The notion of animal rights represents a radical departure from this hierarchical paradigm, and it should come as no surprise that the animal rights movement would experience certain intellectual "growing pains" that would cause reflection on fundamental issues and positions. Such examination is to be welcomed as part of the maturation of the movement and the necessary development of its ideology.

Fourth, I emphasize that in defending the need for rational discourse, I am not in any way diminishing the importance of an emotional response to the plight of animals. Indeed, I agree with feminist Marti Kheel that a "unity of reason and emotion" is important for animal rights theory, and with Tom Regan, who maintains that "'philosophy can lead the mind to water but only emotion can make it drink.'"[7]

Fifth, it is probably clear from the foregoing that I certainly do not regard the rights/welfare debate as solely or even primarily a theoretical or academic debate. The outcome of the debate will determine whether efforts on behalf of animals will effectively chip away at the property status of animals and move in the direction of establishing their personhood, or merely continue the status quo. In many respects, at least some animal advocates have believed—naively in my view—that animal exploitation can be eradicated by making animal rights a "mainstream" issue. But that approach truly is like expecting "rain without thunder."

CHAPTER One

Animal Rights

The Rejection of Instrumentalism

The Transition from Animal Welfare to Animal Rights

Theories of Animal Welfare

Throughout history, many people have expressed concern about the way in which we treat the other sentient beings with whom we share this planet. This concern has, in the past several hundred years, regularly given rise to efforts to protect animals through the adoption of laws. Although it is thought that laws to protect animals originated in England in the later part of the nineteenth century, the first such law can be traced to the Massachusetts Bay Colony, whose 1641 legal code protected domestic animals from cruelty.[1] In 1822, the courts of the State of New York held that wanton cruelty to an animal was a misdemeanor at common law. Efforts to improve legal protection for animals continued throughout the 1800s in the United States, and in the early part of the present century, efforts to regulate vivisection, or the use of animals in science, were many and vigorous. After World War II, "the institutional use of animals increased both because of the vast increase in animal research on both sides of the Atlantic and because of the advent of factory farming."[2] Concern about animals led to laws such as the federal Humane Slaughter Act in 1958, the Wild and Free-Roaming Horses and Burros Act of 1971, and the federal Animal Welfare Act of 1966.[3]

Nevertheless, in the United States alone, over eight billion animals are killed every year for food. An overwhelming number of these animals are raised in a system known as "intensive agriculture" or "factory farming": "Animals are treated like machines that convert low-priced fodder into high-priced flesh, and any innovation will be used if it results in a cheaper 'conversion ratio.' "[4] Hundreds of millions of animals are used in experiments in which they are burned, scalded, blinded, and

7

otherwise mutilated, often without anesthesia during or after the procedure.[5] Animals are also used for clothing, sport, and entertainment.

It is generally agreed, however, that the character of our concern for animals has changed dramatically in the past twenty years or so. Until the mid-1970s, the form of our concern for animals was, with few exceptions, generally restricted to standards that sought to ensure animal *welfare*. Animal welfare, although it comes in various shapes and sizes, exhibits four essential characteristics.

First, animal welfare theory, by its very name, recognizes that animals possess *some* sort of welfare. No one would be concerned about animal welfare if animals were exactly the same as stones or telephones. Animals are *sentient*, capable of feeling pain and experiencing pleasure.

Second, animal welfare holds that although animals are sentient, they do not deserve the moral respect and consideration that we accord to human beings. Human beings are viewed as "superior" to nonhumans in that the former possess certain attributes that supposedly are not shared by nonhumans. This animal "inferiority" often rests on theological superstition, scientific dogma, or cultural beliefs, all of which assume, in a very circular manner, the very animal inferiority that they set out to prove. For example, some people adduce from the "fact" that animals do not possess souls god's intention to create them inferior to human beings. Such normative assumptions are often present in "factual" assertions about animals, even if they are not as obviously theistic. When experimental psychologists seek to determine how closely an animal's intelligence approximates human intelligence, they employ methodologies that rely on a complex series of assumptions all of which implicitly assume that animal intelligence is qualitatively inferior to human intelligence. The data from such an experiment can only be understood through a paradigm that is unable to comprehend animal intelligence as anything *other than inferior* to human intelligence.

Third, animal welfare doctrine accepts that animals are the *property* of people and that any regulation of animal treatment must take into account (1) the property status of nonhumans and (2) the deference, greater or lesser, that must be given the rights of property owners.

Fourth, animal welfare maintains that it is acceptable to trade away *any* animal interest—including freedom from pain or death—as long as the human interest involved is regarded as "significant" and as long as any animal pain, suffering, or death is not "unnecessary." It is primarily in this respect that versions of animal welfare differ. The range of opinion regarding what constitutes "humane" treatment or "unnecessary" suffering or a "significant" human interest is considerable.

At one end of this range, animal suffering is considered "necessary" as long as it is a part of a generally accepted social practice, and "benefits" of animal exploitation may consist of nothing more than the enjoyment of those who, say, attend a rodeo or circus. Practices that are regarded as "cruel" are those—and only those—that "waste" animal resources through the imposition of "gratuitous" pain or suffering. For example, we permit farmers to castrate and brand animals without any sort of pain relief even though it is acknowledged without exception that these practices are very painful. These practices are part of our treatment of "food" animals. We do not, however, allow the farmer, without reason, to neglect the animals so that they starve to death. The suffering and death from such neglect is regarded as unnecessary because the treatment does not facilitate the institutional use of animals for food or other human benefit, that is, because the treatment serves no economic purpose and represents an overall diminution in social wealth.

On the other end of the spectrum, animals are still viewed as the property of people, but the interpretation of "necessity" is more restricted. For example, many animal welfare advocates are opposed to raising veal calves in confinement units so small they are unable to stand, turn around, or groom themselves. These advocates do not necessarily argue that people should not eat meat as a general matter, or that they ought not to eat veal in particular. What they object to is the way in which veal is currently produced, and they urge that alternative husbandry systems, such as group housing, should be used instead. Such a change in veal production would arguably involve higher prices for veal, and many veal producers believe that these higher costs could not be passed along totally to consumers and would have detrimental effects on the market for veal overall. Nevertheless, these animal advocates argue that this change in veal production is mandated by moral concerns that override the economic considerations.

These different understandings of what constitutes "necessary" suffering or "cruel" treatment serve to illustrate the essential differences between these versions of welfarism. Some welfare advocates maintain that animal exploitation is permissible as long as it can be cost-justified; that is, the conduct is acceptable as long as it facilitates the economic exploitation of the animals or maximizes the value of animal "property" for animal owners. If the conduct does not facilitate the exploitation of the animal within the context of a generally accepted social practice (e.g., the use of animals for food), then the use diminishes overall social wealth and constitutes "cruelty." Other animal welfare advocates seek changes that are not cost-justified, at least in the view of those who own animals and exploit them for financial reasons. These changes in animal treatment go beyond what is necessary to facilitate efficient animal exploitation and impose additional costs on animal owners.

In the United States (and in many other countries), there are various laws and regulations that ostensibly regulate many uses of animals. As I have argued elsewhere, these laws—especially in the United States, where there are very strong views about respect for private property— rarely go beyond the minimal animal welfare position.[6] They seek only to ensure that animals are used efficiently and are not wasted through the infliction of gratuitous suffering or death (defined as that which does not serve any economic interest and which does not constitute an integral part of a socially accepted institution). The law requires that animal interests be balanced against human interests, but in light of the status of animals as property, this is a balance performed on a rigged scale: virtually every human use of animals is regarded as "significant" (i.e., more significant than the animals' interest in not being so used) because the desires of human property owners always trump the interests of the property. And this is precisely why, despite general moral agreement that animals ought not to suffer "unnecessary" pain, animals are subjected not only to barbaric practices customary in the meat industry but also to trivial (and not necessarily any less barbaric) use in circuses, rodeos, and captive pigeon shoots. I refer to the version of animal welfare contained in the law as *legal welfarism*, which comprehends animal welfare as that level of animal care that will efficiently facilitate the exploitation of nonhuman property.[7] Legal welfarism reflects the view that animals are *only* means to human ends because they are the *property* of people, and to be property means precisely to be a means to an end exclusively.

Until the 1970s—at least in the United States—the discourse about animals was expressed almost entirely in terms of animal welfare. The only real question was whether the particular reform sought was one that could be characterized as promoting efficient animal exploitation (and should be endorsed by any rational property owner who wanted to maximize the value of her animal property), or whether the reform sought changes that transcended that level and represented a further cost imposed only to accommodate moral concerns about animal pain, suffering, and death. Indeed, there were some welfarists who focused effort on getting animal exploiters to accept regulations that would enhance the value of their animal property. For example, legislation promoted by welfarists concerning the "humane" slaughter of animals for food was often supported by claims that adoption of the legislation would benefit exploiters, who had not realized the negative economic impact, consisting of carcass damage and worker injuries, of an essentially unregulated slaughtering process. So, these welfarists were not arguing that exploiters ought to recognize that animals deserve greater protection than their property status merits, but only that the owners of animal property ought to behave more rationally toward their property in order to obtain even greater economic benefits from that exploitation.

There were, of course, some exceptions, and there were some animal advocates who early on grasped the difference between welfare and rights. For example, Helen Jones, of the International Society for Animal Rights (ISAR), and Alice Herrington, of Friends of Animals (FoA), argued that particular practices—most notably the use of animals in experiments—should be abolished and not merely regulated. Apart from arguments of these modern antivivisectionists, however, there was little discussion about anything other than refining the concepts of "unnecessary" suffering and "humane" treatment, though there was much disagreement about the meanings of these terms in different contexts. For example, in 1958, the federal Humane Slaughter Act became law. The law provided that animals whose meat was sold to the federal government had to be "rendered insensible to pain . . . before being shackled, hoisted, thrown, cast, or cut."[8] At no point in the legislative process did anyone express concern that the use of animals as food might itself be morally objectionable. On the contrary, everyone concerned—including the animal welfare groups that sought and supported the legislation—assumed that the purpose of the legislation was merely to ensure that animals were slaughtered as "humanely" as possible.

Although animal welfare theory takes many forms (depending on what criteria are used to determine necessity), no form of animal welfare has ever challenged the basic assumption that animals are somehow "inferior" to humans and that humans are justified in exploiting animals. More generous versions of animal welfare may accord to animals a higher moral status than the bare property status of legal welfarism, but all versions of the theory regard animals as means to human ends and without any rights to insulate them altogether from particular forms of exploitation.

In the mid-1970s, discourse about the human/animal relationship began to shift dramatically away from the welfarist position. This shift occurred in response to important changes in our thinking about the nature of our moral responsibilities to other animals, as well as the highly publicized actions of progressive animal advocates.

The Influence of Philosophers

Moral philosophy has played a major role in the development of the modern animal movement. Political theorist Robert Garner notes, "For the first time, those concerned about the treatment of animals have had the benefit of a sustained attempt by academic philosophers to change radically the status afforded to animals in moral thinking. The result has been the development of a 'new' ideology (or, to be precise, ideologies) which has had profound implications both for the movement which seeks to protect animals and for the way in which the debate about their treatment has been conducted."[9] Lawrence Finsen and Susan Finsen argue that "a major difference between the older humane movement and the animal rights movement" is that concern about animal rights "has earned a place both in the scholarship of moral philosophers and in the university curriculum itself."[10] Every major scholarly work—without exception—that discusses the animal rights movement contains a discussion of the philosophical ideas that animate the movement.

A number of philosophical theories concern our treatment of nonhumans, but the two that have emerged as dominant in virtually all studies and discussions of the movement are those articulated by Australian philosopher Peter Singer in his book *Animal Liberation* and by American philosopher Tom Regan in his book *The Case for Animal Rights*.[11]

Singer's Nonrights Theory

Peter Singer's *Animal Liberation*, first published in 1975, is important for two reasons. First, Singer presents a detailed description of the salient forms of the institutionalized exploitation of animals, together with photographs. For many people, this was their first exposure to the industries that produced the meat for their dinner or that subjected nonhumans to shocking, scalding, burning, and mutilation in the name of science. Second, Singer presents a *theory* that would provide greater protection for animals than has classical animal welfare.

In order to understand Singer's theory and the role that it has played in the modern animal protection movement, it is necessary to introduce some elementary notions used by philosophers to discuss ethical issues. In moral theory, a broad division separates those who do from those who do not believe the consequences of conduct determine whether the conduct is right or wrong. *Consequentialist* theories, as they are known, take different forms.[12] For example, an *ethical egoist* maintains that the moral quality of an act is determined by the consequences for the individual moral agent. A *utilitarian*, on the other hand, is more collective-minded and maintains that the right act is that which maximizes the best total consequences for everyone who is affected—positively or adversely—by the action. There are two primary types of utilitarianism: "Act-utilitarianism is the view that the rightness or wrongness of an action is to be judged by the consequences, good or bad, of the action itself. Rule-utilitarianism is the view that the rightness or wrongness of an action is to be judged by the goodness and badness of the consequences of a rule that everyone should perform the action in like circumstances."[13] So, for example, an act-utilitarian faced with a situation in which one option is to tell a lie will judge whether, on balance, the consequences of lying *in that particular case* weigh in favor of the lie. A rule-utilitarian, on the other hand, is not concerned about the consequences of lying in the particular situation, but looks to the consequences were everyone to lie in the same or similar circumstances.

Singer is an act-utilitarian; he believes that it is the consequences of the contemplated act that matter, not the consequences of following a more generalized rule. Of course, views differ over what consequences are relevant. For classical utilitarians, such as Jeremy Bentham and John Stuart Mill, pleasure alone was intrinsically valuable, and pain alone was intrinsically not valuable. Singer, however, claims to subscribe to a modified form of utilitarianism known as "preference" or "interest" utilitarianism, which provides that what is intrinsically valuable is what "furthers the interests of those affected."[14] These interests include the desires and preferences of those who are affected. Pleasure and pain matter because they are part of what humans and nonhumans desire or prefer or seek to avoid. In *Animal Liberation*, Singer argues that in assessing the consequences of our actions affecting animals, it is necessary to take the interests of the animals seriously and to weigh any adverse affect on those interests from human actions as part of the consequences of those actions. Humans fail to do this, Singer argues, because of a species bias, or *speciesism*, that results in a systematic devaluation of animal interests.[15]

Singer claims that speciesism is no more morally defensible than racism, sexism, or other forms of discrimination that arbitrarily exclude some humans from the scope of moral concern. When people seek to justify the horrific way in which animals are treated, they invariably point to supposed animal "defects," such as the inability of animals to use human language or to reason as intricately as do humans. But a number of severely retarded humans cannot speak or reason (or, at least, can do so no better than many nonhumans), and most of us would be appalled were such humans used in experiments or for food or clothing. Singer maintains that the only way to justify our present level of animal exploitation is to maintain that species differences *alone* justify that exploitation. But that is no different, Singer argues, from saying that differences in race *alone* or sex *alone* justify differential treatment.

Singer's approach is clearly more favorable toward animals than is classical animal welfare, which accorded little weight to animal interests. Singer's theory, however, is not a theory of animal *rights*. For Singer, the rightness or wrongness of conduct is determined by consequences, not by any appeal to right. If violating a rightholder's right in a particular case will produce more desirable consequences than respecting that right, then Singer is committed to violating the right. For example, although Singer opposes *most* animal experimentation, he does so because he thinks that most animal experiments do not produce benefits that are sufficient to justify the animal suffering that results. But he does not—and cannot—oppose *all* animal experimentation; if a particular animal use would, for example, really lead directly to a cure for a disease that affected many humans, Singer would approve that animal use. Indeed, Singer has acknowledged that under some circumstances it would be permissible to use nonconsenting *humans* in experiments if the benefits for all affected outweighed the detriment to the humans used in the experiments.[16]

Regan's Rights Theory

Although Peter Singer's *Animal Liberation* had an unquestionable impact on traditional animal welfarists, it was American philosopher Tom Regan who, in his book *The Case for Animal Rights*,[17] presented an argument in favor of animal rights.[18] For Regan, if a person or animal has a *right*, then that right may not be sacrificed or violated simply because the consequences of doing so are thought to be more desirable than the consequences of respecting the right. Regan's theory is *deontological*, which means simply that the morality of conduct is not dependent on consequences but, instead, is dependent on something else—in this case, an appeal to a moral right.[19]

Indeed, Regan's rights theory may be understood as a rejection of utilitarianism, all versions of which share the common notion that questions of right and wrong can be determined by aggregating the consequences of acts (act-utilitarianism) or the consequences of following general rules (rule-utilitarianism), and pursuing the course that maximizes whatever it is that counts as intrinsic value—pleasure, happiness, preference satisfaction, and so forth. Regan rejects utilitarianism in all of its forms for many reasons, but the most salient of these is his view that it is morally wrong to regard individuals as nothing more than receptacles for that which is of intrinsic value but as lacking any intrinsic value of their own. The utilitarian regards as intrinsically valuable, not the individual, but only some quality, such as pleasure or preference satisfaction or knowledge. The value of the individual is gauged by the extent to which the intrinsically valuable quality is possessed by the individual and provided to others by the individual. Regan rejects the notion that individuals do not have value in and of themselves and that human value is dependent on possession or generation of some quality thought to be intrinsically valuable by the utilitarian. Rather, he argues that individuals do have inherent value and that it is inappropriate to treat individuals solely as means to the end of maximizing that which is regarded as intrinsically valuable.[20]

Regan maintains that theoretical and empirical considerations indicate that at least some animals (normal mammals of at least one-year of age) possess beliefs, desires, memory, perception, intention, self-consciousness, and a sense of the future. The attribution of these mental states to animals also suggests that it is sensible to regard certain nonhumans as psychophysical individuals who have an individual welfare in that "they fare well or ill during the course of their life, and the life of some animals is, on balance, experientially better than the life of others."[21] Because animals have desires, beliefs, and the ability to act in pursuit of their goals, they may also be said to have preference autonomy.

Animals may be benefited or harmed; they have a "welfare."[22] Animals are not only interested in particular things, certain things are also in their interests in that these things contribute to the good, or welfare, of the animals. Benefits and harms are, of course, relevant to any discussion of animal (or human) welfare. Animals have interests in satisfying basic needs, but satisfaction of basic needs alone is not sufficient for well-being according to animal (or human) capacities. Rather, it is necessary to achieve a harmonious satisfaction of desires and accomplishment of purposes in light of different biological, social, and psychological interests. Harms can be either inflictions or deprivations.

Deprivations imposed on animals (e.g., restraining them from behaving in ways that are natural for the species) may harm even though there is no pain or suffering involved. Such treatment deprives animals of benefits necessary for their welfare. The death of a healthy animal (or human) is a deprivation because it represents an ultimate and irreversible closure to the satisfaction of further preferences. This is the case whether the death is painful or not. The "euthanasia" of healthy animals frustrates animal welfare because it is not in the interests of healthy animals to be killed.

The central part of Regan's rights argument begins with his postulate of *equal inherent value*. In a sense, this notion is an alternative to both the utilitarian theory of intrinsic value and the perfectionist view of value. According to the former, the value of individuals can be determined by totaling the intrinsic values of their experiences; according to the latter, individuals have value, but the level of value differs from person to person depending on certain favored characteristics possessed by the particular person. Inherent value theory holds that the individual has a distinct moral value separate from any intrinsic values and that inherent value is held equally, in part because of the difficulty of formulating criteria for differentiating amounts of value.[23]

The attribution of equal inherent value to both moral agents and relevantly similar moral patients is required because both agents and patients are *subjects-of-a-life*: that is, agents and patients are conscious, possess a complex awareness and a psychophysical identity over time. Agents and patients may be harmed or benefited and have a welfare in that their experiential life fares well or ill for them independently of any utility that they have for others or the interest that others have in them. Being a subject-of-a-life not only is a sufficient condition for having inherent value but is also a criterion that allows for the intelligible and nonarbitrary attribution of equal inherent value, whether the subject-of-a-life is an agent or a patient, human or nonhuman. Regan stresses that any separation of moral agents from moral patients must be arbitrary and that any differentiation of human moral patients from nonhuman moral patients must rely on some form of species bias or speciesism.

Regan introduces a moral principle that takes equal inherent value into account: the respect principle requires that we treat those individuals who have inherent value in ways that respect their inherent value. The respect principle states simply that no individual with equal inherent value may be treated solely as a means to an end in order to maximize the aggregate of desirable consequences. Regan's respect principle is both similar to and different from Kant's notion that we treat other persons as ends in themselves and never merely as means to ends. Rational agents, Kant argues, have value in themselves independent of their value to others—a notion very similar to that of equal inherent value. What is different is Regan's use of the subject-of-a-life criterion to identify in a nonarbitrary and intelligible way a similarity between moral agents and patients that gives rise to a direct duty owed by the former to the latter.[24]

Regan next distinguishes between basic and acquired moral rights, and between these rights and legal rights. Basic moral rights do not depend on voluntary acts or social institutions for their existence, as do, for example, rights created under a contract. In addition, basic rights are universal: "if any individual (A) has such a right, then any other individual like A in the relevant respects also has this right."[25] Finally, basic rights are equal in that those who have such a right have it equally. Acquired rights are subject to social conventions, institutions, and voluntary acts, and legal rights need not be (and are usually not) universal or equal. Relying on John Stuart Mill,[26] Regan argues that moral rights (whether basic or acquired) are valid claims. Relying on Joel Feinberg,[27] Regan analyzes claims as assertions that the rightholder is entitled to certain treatment and that the treatment is owed directly to the rightholder. Thus, the rightholder has a claim against particular individuals or against many individuals and a claim to what the rightholder asserts is owed.

Moral agents and patients possess equal inherent value, and this status entitles them to be treated with respect. Moral agents and patients have a right to respectful treatment because their claims to justice are valid claims in light of the respect principle. The basic moral right to respectful treatment is universal: all relevantly similar individuals have it, and they have it equally. Further, the right to respectful treatment is no stronger in the case of moral agents than in the case of moral patients. Both agents and patients have inherent value (based on the subject-of-a-life criterion), and both possess it equally. The right to respectful treatment prohibits treating subjects-of-a-life as mere "receptacles" of intrinsic values, as advocated by the utilitarians.

From the right to respectful treatment derives the harm principle: the prima facie right of the moral agent or patient not to be harmed. All those who satisfy the subject-of-a-life criterion have an experiential welfare that can be harmed or benefited and are regarded as having equal inherent value. As a prima facie matter, harming the interests of a subject-of-a-life is to show disrespect for the inherent value of the moral agent or patient. Regan argues that this is a prima facie right because the right of the innocent may be overridden in two situations that are derivable from the respect principle. First, when faced with a choice of harm-

ing the few or the many, Regan argues that it is better, special considerations aside, to harm the few.[28] Second, when faced with a choice to
harm the many or the few, and when harming the few would make
them worse off than any of the many, it is, special considerations aside,
appropriate to override the rights of the many.[29] Regan is careful to note
that these principles do not reflect the utilitarian notion that we ought to
minimize aggregate harm. That theory simply reduces people to mere
receptacles of value. For example, it is not morally permissible under
rights theory, on the rationale that harming the few will (supposedly)
benefit the many, to use animals in experiments, because the use of the
animals *presupposes* that animals can be treated instrumentally, and the
rejection of that notion is a fundamental part of Regan's theory.[30]

Finally, Regan discusses the implications of the rights view for a
range of activities in which nonhumans are exploited by humans. As a
prelude, Regan discusses the liberty principle, according to which innocent individuals have the right to pursue their interests and to avoid
being made worse off as long as all those involved are treated in accordance with the respect principle, even though other innocent individuals may be harmed in the process. This principle underlies the coun-
terargument to assertions that animal exploiters have some liberty to
exploit animals.

The position Regan takes is uncompromising: he unambiguously
condemns the use of animals for food, hunting, trapping, education,
testing, and research. According to Regan, the rights view requires the
abolition of all of these activities. Since humans and nonhumans are
subjects-of-a-life that have equal inherent value, the respect principle
requires that they not be harmed unless that harm can be justified *without* assuming that the fundamental interests of human or nonhuman
rightholders can be treated instrumentally. The use of animals for food,
sport, entertainment, or research involves treating animals merely as
means to ends, and this constitutes a violation of the respect principle.
Moreover, animal exploiters have no liberty to use animals, because the
liberty principle allows for harming innocent individuals only when
their equal inherent value has been respected, which is, by definition,
not the case when animals are treated solely as means to ends.

It is important to understand that Regan's theory does not provide
for the resolution of conflicts between human and animal rights *once we
assume that animals have rights*. In this respect, Regan is like the nineteenth-century abolitionist who argues that slavery should be ended
because, as an institution, it represents a systematic violation of the
most fundamental interests that a human being has in liberty and dig-

nity. Regan does not go on to tell us what specific rights animals should have in a world in which institutionalized exploitation has been abolished (other than the right not to be regarded solely as a means to human ends), or how to resolve conflicts between competing rights held by humans and nonhumans. That is, Regan does not argue against exploitation as such. For example, he talks about how we "use" other humans for skills and talents that they have and that benefit us. What Regan opposes is not exploitation per se, but *institutionalized* exploitation of animals exclusively as means to human ends.[31] Animal agriculture, vivisection, the use of animals for clothing or entertainment—all rest on the notion that the most fundamental animal interests in physical security and liberty may be sacrificed simply because an aggregation of consequences that is thought to represent human "benefit" justifies the sacrifice. It is this institutionalized exploitation, which represents the systematic and structural violation of a variety of animal interests, including, but not limited to, the interest in avoiding suffering, that causes the suffering in the first instance. Indeed, these institutions of exploitation explicitly maintain that the violation of these interests is *always* justified as long as there is sufficient benefit.

Though I cannot here examine the various criticisms that have been made of Regan's theory, I offer one general comment about Regan's identification of a key concept in moral philosophy. Some of Regan's critics claim that his theory is defective because it relies on "intuitions," and such things are somewhat mysterious and, in general, not taken seriously. Although Regan does argue that one criterion of the acceptability of moral principles as a general matter is conformity of those principles with our moral intuitions, he makes it clear that he is using "intuition" not as "self-evident truth" but, rather, as *considered moral judgment*. Moral principles should accord with our intuitions, but only after we have subjected those intuitions to a number of "tests" to ensure that those intuitions reflect considered, reflective moral judgments, not just our "hunches" or "feelings."[32] One such test requires that any moral judgment be impartial and treat similar cases similarly.

If there is any intuition, or "considered moral judgment," that each of us shares, it is that we each have a life that matters to us, however miserable it is and whether anyone else values it or us. Those who disagree have committed suicide and are not reading this anyway. Most of us would not volunteer for painful medical experiments, especially those that result in our death, irrespective of the benefit that we would bestow on others. That sentiment does not make us selfish. The root of the moral intuition is simply that we have value as beings and cannot measure that value by how much general happiness would result were we to sacrifice ourselves. The Marxist may eschew the notion of rights, but the Marxist needs some conception of the individual to make sense of collective notions. The feminist properly criticizes the patriarchal *use* of rights, but cannot deny that without some notion of nontradable interests there is no standard by which to judge rape or other forms of violence as wrong. Without some limits on what can be done to people, there can be no social organization. Every society must recognize *some* interests that are not tradable, irrespective of social cost. In our society, most people would regard as nontradable our interest in not being incarcerated without the state's first proving beyond a reasonable doubt that we have committed a crime, and they would regard this interest nontradable irrespective of the potential benefit from (intentionally) imprisoning innocent people. If every interest is to be treated instrumentally and sacrificed when some person or persons decides that the sacrifice produces "benefit" for some other person or group, then we had better have a great deal of confidence in whoever is entrusted to make decisions about what level of "benefit" will suffice.

Although we may be willing to make many personal sacrifices for the sake of the "common good," it is simply counterintuitive to view our life or liberty as something that can be traded away for consequential reasons alone. Indeed, the only time that our society tolerates the sacrifice of an individual's interest in life or liberty for the "common good" is in time of war, when conscription is used. But conscription is highly unpopular, has been known to cause massive social protest, and is avoided precisely because it offends many people's moral intuition that basic rights in life and liberty should not be sacrificed for the common good. Taxing people for the common good (the unpopularity of which is generally tied directly to prevailing norms about property ownership) is different from forcing them to fight against their will.

The Role of Animal Advocates

Until the emergence of the animal "rights" movement in the late 1970s, animal welfare was espoused for the most part by well-financed but highly conservative charities, such as the American Humane Association (AHA), the Humane Society of the United States (HSUS), and the Animal Welfare Institute (AWI). Although some of these groups were more aggressive than traditional humane societies and sometimes mounted political and legal campaigns to change certain practices that adversely affected animals, they advocated the *reform*, not the *abolition*, of institutionalized animal exploitation. As I mentioned above, some organizations, such as ISAR, promoted a more abolitionist agenda, and the antivivisection societies advocated the abolition of animal experiments in particular, but these groups had yet to have a significant impact on the direction of national discourse about the human/animal relationship.

In the late 1970s, a new group of animal advocates emerged, and the character of political and legal effort ostensibly changed. Those scholars who have studied the American movement are agreed that a crucial figure in the rise of the modern American animal rights movement is Henry Spira, a New York high school teacher and labor organizer who has been called an "inspiration for the movement" and whose early successes "perhaps even helped create" the animal rights movement.[33] Spira learned that the Museum of Natural History was conducting experiments funded by the National Institutes of Health (NIH) that involved particularly unpleasant mutilation of cats in order to determine how the sexual behavior of the animals was affected. Spira, working with other animal advocates, filed requests under the federal Freedom of Information Act and had the experiments evaluated by scientific experts. When the museum refused to meet with Spira's group, Spira wrote a detailed exposé of the experiments for a New York weekly newspaper. Every weekend—for eighteen months—Spira and his colleagues picketed and demonstrated in front of the museum. The museum acknowledged that "a broad section of the public—by no means limited to antivivisectionists—became involved in questioning the research."[34] The campaign generated over eight thousand letters and an "uncounted" number of telephone calls. Spira's coalition pressured NIH as well as the corporations and foundations that contributed to the museum. Congressman Ed Koch became interested in the matter and toured the laboratory. In the *Congressional Record*, Koch reported a conversation with a museum researcher who said that the federal government had paid $435,000 to determine that a male cat whose brain is damaged by researchers will mount a rabbit instead of a female cat. Congressional interest intensified; over 120 members joined with Koch in questioning the experiments. An influential science writer, Nicholas Wade, took Spira's side, and museum members began to cancel subscriptions. NIH withdrew funding, and the lab was closed and remains closed. Spira, together with Helen Jones of ISAR and others, went on in 1979 to bring about the repeal of the Metcalf-Hatch Act in New York, which permitted research institutions to take unclaimed animals from shelters and pounds for experiments.

There is no doubt that Spira's early, aggressive abolitionist campaigns served to animate a decidedly more radical attitude toward the human exploitation of nonhumans. The museum campaign was not an effort to reform the manner in which the particular experiments were done; it was an effort—and a successful one—to *end* the experiments altogether. Spira's objection to these experiments went to the merits of the experiments themselves. Spira's challenge cannot be underestimated; he challenged the substance of federally funded, peer-reviewed experimentation, and prevailed.[35]

In the early 1980s, Alex Pacheco and Ingrid Newkirk founded People for the Ethical Treatment of Animals (PETA), and they went on later to become prominent leaders of the emerging movement. The case that catapulted PETA onto the national scene involved the Silver Spring monkeys, "arguably the most famous experimental animals in the history of science."[36] Indeed, the Silver Spring case is regarded as the "cornerstone . . . for the emerging animal rights movement,"[37] and "many believe that [the Silver Spring monkey case] marked the start of the current combative animal rights movement."[38] Lawrence Finsen and Susan Finsen claim that the Silver Spring monkey case "helped create a mass animal rights movement."[39] One commentator stated that the case "served dramatic notice on members of Congress that things are not all they could be in the nation's laboratories."[40]

In 1981, Pacheco obtained a job in the laboratory of Edward Taub, who was the chief experimenter at the Institute for Behavioral Research (IBR).[41] The stated purpose of Taub's experiments was to understand why certain stroke victims were unable to move their limbs even though nothing was neurologically wrong with those limbs. Taub severed the nerves to the limbs of macaque monkeys through a surgical procedure called somatosensory deafferentation, and then tried to get the monkeys to use the deafferented limbs by "motivating" them with cigarette lighters, shocks, and other forms of painful stimuli.

Pacheco did not reveal to Taub his affiliation with PETA, and instead told Taub that he wanted to pursue a career in medical research. Taub, in turn, soon gave Pacheco considerable responsibility for caring for the animals and conducting certain phases of the experiment, although Pacheco had no prior training that qualified him to do the experiments. Pacheco began to document the conditions in the lab and the treatment of the animals. He brought various scientific experts and veterinarians through the lab on weekends and evenings, when no other lab personnel were around, in order to obtain opinions about the condition of animal care at IBR. Newkirk kept guard outside the lab and used a walkie-talkie to notify Pacheco of any possible intruders or disruptions.

The experts were generally agreed that the conditions at the lab were appalling and that the animals were being treated inhumanely. The lab was encrusted with mouse urine, droppings, and other filth; wire protruded through the cages, and the animals consequently had difficulty moving in their cages; the food supply was inadequate and unwholesome; and the animals' wounds had not been treated, with the result that a number of the animals had seriously mutilated themselves. The U.S. Department of Agriculture (USDA), which is responsible for inspecting facilities such as IBR, had not found any violations of relevant laws or regulations at the lab.

Pacheco submitted his evidence to police in Montgomery County, Maryland, who seized the monkeys. Taub was eventually prosecuted and convicted for violating the Maryland anticruelty statute, not because the nature of the research was per se unacceptable or immoral, but because Taub had failed to provide proper veterinary care to six of the monkeys. He appealed, and his conviction was upheld, but only for Taub's failure to provide adequate veterinary care to one monkey. The Maryland Court of Appeals eventually reversed the conviction entirely, holding that Taub's conduct was not covered by the state anticruelty statute, on the ground that the law prohibited only the infliction of "unnecessary" or "unjustifiable" pain and that the Maryland legislature surely knew the infliction of pain on animals used in experiments was "purely incidental and unavoidable."[42] Taub's funding was terminated by the federal government, which claimed that Taub had failed to provide adequate veterinary care to the monkeys. Following the criminal proceedings, PETA, together with other animal advocacy groups and individual advocates, sought to obtain custody of the monkeys in a series of civil proceedings that differed from the criminal prosecution. These civil efforts continued until 1994 and were unsuccessful. Nevertheless, the infiltration of Taub's lab by Pacheco and the subsequent criminal prosecution generated unprecedented publicity; the *Washington Post* carried the story on its front page, and Congress responded quickly by holding hearings on the matter as part of a general investigation into the use of animals in experiments.

In addition to the more confrontational approaches of people like Spira and groups like PETA, other developments at the same time indicated that human concern for animals was taking a very different direction from that it had followed in the past. For example, the clandestine Animal Liberation Front (ALF) and other such groups engaged in illegal activities on behalf of animals. In most cases, these activities involved removing animals or information from laboratories. In discussing the ALF "raids," science writer Deborah Blum states that "there were times when those raids changed the way science was done. The most compelling case—and undoubtedly the most influential—was the 1984 break-in at the laboratory of Thomas Gennarelli, at the University of Pennsylvania."[43] The ALF removed approximately forty-five hours of videotape, made by the researchers themselves, that captured experiments in which they had inflicted brain damage on conscious, unanesthetized baboons. On the tapes, lab personnel, including Gennarelli and other professional staff, mock the brain-damaged baboons. In one scene, a researcher lifts a baboon by the shoulder after he indicates that the shoulder is probably dislocated. In another scene, two researchers cut into the brain of a conscious, restrained baboon after they acknowledge that the animal is conscious, in pain, and in need of anesthesia.

Copies of the videotapes were provided by the ALF to a number of recipients, including PETA, which created a twenty-minute video entitled "Unnecessary Fuss."[44] The videotape was shown across the United States, Canada, and Europe; and the United States Congress became interested in the matter, numerous members demanding investigations into the treatment of animals at the Penn lab. The event culminated July 15–18, 1985, in an illegal occupation of the National Institutes of Health in Maryland by over one hundred animal activists from around the country. Margaret Heckler, secretary of health and human services, ordered that the Penn lab be shut pending an investigation. Later in 1985, the lab was shut indefinitely. In 1993, the lab reopened, though Gennarelli now uses pigs instead of monkeys. Nevertheless, the Penn case and other ALF activities served to distinguish the emerging animal rights movement from its welfarist predecessor.

Finally, the modern animal movement, at least in its initial phases, rejected the top-down, businesslike structure, with centralized control, that characterized the often large and always conservative animal welfare charities, such as HSUS. In many respects, the "radicalism" of the modern animal movement is connected with its grassroots orientation, and scholars distinguish the animal rights movement from its animal welfare predecessor based on the grassroots orientation of the former. For example, Garner argues that "one of the key reasons for the sustainability of the animal rights challenge has been the roots it has grown at the local level." Local groups are, according to Garner, "the product of the emergence of radicalism since one of its major characteristics is the emphasis on grassroots campaigning. By contrast, animal welfare groups tend to be far more elitist and cautious, relying on expert opinions and preferring to leave campaigning to their own staff."[45] Garner quotes Alex Pacheco, who claimed to form PETA in 1980 because of a need for a "grassroots group in the USA that could spur people to use their time and talents to help animals gain liberation."[46]

Rights and Welfare: The Opinion of Scholars

In the past several years, scholars from different disciplines have sought to describe this shift from traditional animal welfare concerns to the animal rights position. Although there are variations among these scholarly descriptions, all agree that the animal rights movement challenges what political theorist Robert Garner calls the "moral orthodoxy" of animal welfare: "that any significant human interest outweighs any (sum of) significant non-human interests."[47] Garner fails to recognize the broad range of positions that could be classified as "moral orthodoxy" based on differing assessments of what constitutes a "significant" human or animal interest, but he is certainly correct to isolate as the essence of animal welfare the notion that *any* animal interest can be sacrificed as long as the benefit for humans is regarded as "significant," however generously or narrowly interpreted. In order to avoid the ambiguity in Garner's notion of moral orthodoxy, I generally use the term "instrumentalism" to designate the view that animals are means to human ends, no matter what level of consideration to be accorded to animals is required by a particular instrumentalist theory. It is also my position that the law embodies the instrumentalist view in that animals are regarded as the property of people. According to philosopher Jeremy Waldron, property "cannot have rights or duties or be bound by or recognize rules."[48] Legal scholar Reinold Noyes claims that "legal relations in our law exist only between persons. There cannot be a legal relation between a person and a thing or between two things."[49] The fact that animals are property means that animals are regarded merely as means to ends, which means that the law embodies the instrumentalist view of animals.

All commentators regard Regan's theory as a rejection of instrumentalism that is supposed to characterize the modern animal rights movement and separate it from what came before historically and conceptually—the animal welfare movement. The animal rights movement, it is argued, rejects instrumentalism in favor of attributing to animals a moral status that includes their ability to hold at least some rights. For example, sociologists James M. Jasper and Dorothy Nelkin argue that although the modern animal protection movement "retained the animal welfare tradition's concerns for animals as sentient beings that should be protected from unnecessary cruelty," the movement "added a new language of 'rights' as the basis for demanding animal liberation." This vision of animal rights is, according to Jasper and Nelkin, drawn partly from feminism and environmentalism, which, they argue, embody a rejection of "instrumentalism," or "the confusion of ends and means," that reduces nature, women, and animals—"all with inherent value as ends in themselves—to the status of things and tools."[50] Animal rights advocates demand the "abolition of all exploitation of animals, on the grounds that animals have inherent, inviolable rights."[51] Rights are "accepted as a moral trump card that cannot be disputed. Justified in terms of tradition, nature, or fundamental moral principles, rights are considered non-negotiable."[52]

Anthropologist Susan Sperling claims that although traditional animal welfarists have "attempted to improve the treatment of animals in a variety of settings and to educate the public about humane concerns . . . adherents of the recent [animal rights movement] question assumptions about the human relationship to animals that have been fundamental to Western culture in the modern period."[53] Animal rights advocates, Sperling argues, do not want merely to reform institutions of animal exploitation; they wish to abolish that exploitation altogether. The modern rights position is, according to Sperling, conceptually related to the antivivisection movement of the nineteenth century in that both fear increasing technological manipulation of the earth and all its inhabitants.

Political scientist Garner argues that "the terms welfare and rights are indicative of the key division within the animal protection movement: between those who consider that animal interests should take a subordinate, albeit important, position and those who recognize a higher moral status for animals." Depending on the theory involved, this moral status may entail according consideration to animal interests equal to that accorded human interests, or it may involve something more akin to "personhood" status for animals, which would entitle them to be holders of rights. In any event, Garner contends that animal rights advocates, unlike their animal welfare counterparts, reject the moral orthodoxy that regards animals as "inferior" to humans and, based on the acceptance of this higher moral status for animals, seek the "complete abolition of animal use for science and / or food."[54]

Philosophers Lawrence Finsen and Susan Finsen argue that "prior to the emergence of the current animal rights movement, the aims of eliminating cruelty and encouraging a more compassionate attitude toward animals dominated the thinking of those who gave any thought at all to the treatment of animals in America." The modern animal rights movement "does not seek humane reforms but challenges the assumption of human superiority and demands abolition of institutions it considers exploitative. Rather than asking for a greater (and optional) charity toward animals, the animal rights movement demands justice, equality, fairness, and rights."[55]

The notion that animal rights means, at least in part, the explicit rejection of animal welfare has also found its way from academic scholarship to the media. In discussing the origins of the animal rights movement in Britain and the United States, a 1995 article in the *Economist* notes that the rights movement emerged in the 1970s and "spoke of 'oppression' and 'liberation' of animals, *and contemptuously attacked the 'welfarist' approach as favouring longer chains for the slaves.*"[56]

Rights and Welfare: The Opinion of Supporters of Institutionalized Animal Exploitation

Those who support various forms of institutionalized animal exploitation are very much aware that animal rights and animal welfare are wholly different philosophies. Although both the NIH and the American Medical Association (AMA) have consistently opposed the most moderate efforts to improve animal welfare, both groups endorse animal welfare as accepted by scientists and the public alike, and reject the notion of animal rights, which, they argue, is linked with illegal activities and ignores human well-being and superiority over nonhumans.[57]

For example, in 1985, NIH, which funds the overwhelming majority of experiments involving nonhumans, argued that in order to protect the use of animals in experiments, it would be necessary to draw a sharp distinction in the public mind between those who advocated traditional animal welfare concerns and those who claimed that animals, like humans, are holders of moral rights. The NIH plan called for the discrediting of animal rights advocates by linking the rights position with alleged instances of violence, terrorism, and a complete disregard for the health and well-being of humans. Chiming its support, the AMA in 1988 issued a white paper adopting the NIH strategy. The AMA claimed that animal welfare is "understandable and appeals to scientists, the public, and legislators." Animal rights, on the other hand, reflects a view that is "radical," "militant," "terrorist," and opposed to human well-being.

Similarly, Americans for Medical Progress (AMP)—a tax-exempt organization heavily supported by U.S. Surgical, which manufactures surgical staple guns that are demonstrated by salespersons on live dogs and whose president, Leon Hirsch, has long been a most vehement opponent of moral consideration for animals—in 1994 wrote to law school deans around the country to warn of a "dangerous philosophy that is quickly emerging as a popular course of study in our law schools."[58] AMP represents itself as a "grassroots" group whose self-stated goal is to "educate the public, the media and policy makers about the role of medical research in curing disease, easing pain and making quality medical care more affordable." AMP lists as members of its board of directors theologians, educators, researchers, politicians, business people, and lawyers. The "dangerous philosophy" referred to in AMP's mailing is the philosophy of animal rights, which, according to AMP, "goes beyond legitimate animal *welfare* issues."[59] The letter indicates that although "most Americans fully support animal welfare (the humane treatment of animals)," the "misguided philosophy" of animal rights, which recognizes that animals, like humans, may be rightholders, "is held only by a small minority in this country." AMP warns that animal rights is "quickly emerging as a popular course of study in our law schools," a "foreboding sign for anyone concerned with health care. These lawyers will be asked to protect these extremists who destroy research facilities and cripple biomedical research with excessive regulation." Such activities will "cost researchers time and money, causing Americans to wait longer for cures and treatments and pay more for their health care."[60] In a 1995 editorial, AMP vice president John M. Clymer reinforced the distinction: "The protection of animal welfare is a moral imperative. The promotion of 'animal rights' extremism is another matter entirely."[61]

Similarly, the administrator of the Alcohol, Drug Abuse, and Mental Health Administration of the Department of Health and Human Services, Frederick K. Goodwin, presents a slide show in which he claims that the animal welfare movement has had "a distinguished history with a primary focus on the prevention of cruelty to animals," prevention that rests upon the notion that "our responsible stewardship of animals involves humane care." Animal rights advocates, on the other hand, subscribe to the view that "humans and animals have equivalent rights" and that "animals have intrinsic rights of their own, a notion that conflicts with the foundation of our entire legal system."[62] In a letter to Representative Dante B. Fascell, Goodwin distinguishes between animal welfarists, who are "reasonable individuals [who] believe that we have a moral obligation to treat the animals in our charge humanely," and "adherents of the animal rights movement," who "believe something quite different" from the welfarists and who "argue that animals are the moral equivalent of humans" and that "we have no right to 'exploit' them for any purpose, even to alleviate human misery." Goodwin characterizes scientists as adhering to the principle of animal welfare because they "have a responsibility to make sure that [animals] are properly fed, watered and housed in decent quarters." Like the AMP, Goodwin labels the animal rights position as "terrorist."[63]

In *Targeted*, Lorenz O. Lutherer and Margaret S. Simon are critical of the animal rights movement, claiming that "according to the philosophy of the animal rights movement, humanity does not have the right to use any animal for any purpose" and that the animal welfare philosophy, on the other hand, is concerned to preserve people's "control over animals."[64] The authors acknowledge that "prominent animal rights groups in the United States claim repeatedly that they are nonviolent," but contend that animal advocacy groups' use of information illegally obtained by groups like the Animal Liberation Front "puts them in the position of actively condoning such acts."[65]

Another academic defender of institutionalized animal exploitation, Ronald M. McLaughlin, claims that "the animal *rights* movement, in addition to holding the position that animals are entitled to the same moral rights as humans, has adopted terrorist tactics." Animal rights activists present an immediate threat to science through the "demoralization of scientists, tremendous financial cost, and erosion of public opinion and political support for animal experimentation in biomedical research and education. The long-term threat is loss of the privilege to use animals and resultant retardation of progress." The author contrasts the rights position with the welfare position, which "generally holds that animals may be used for human benefit, or for the benefit of other animals, provided the animals are treated humanely. Animal welfare is couched in terms of obligations of humans to provide humane care and treatment of animals rather than in terms of moral or legal rights of animals." The author adds that despite any ambiguity concerning the concept of animal rights, one thing is clear: "animal rights *is not* an extension of animal welfare."[66]

Two prominent proponents of the view that animal welfare is legitimate and animal rights is not are the Foundation for Biomedical Research (FBR) and its lobbying arm, the National Association for Biomedical Research (NABR). These groups are heavily supported by commercial animal users and suppliers (such as Merck Research Labs, Merrell Dow, and the Cosmetic, Toiletry, and Fragrance Association), as well as universities and individuals who use animals. In its educational materials, FBR emphasizes the importance of animal welfare and the seriousness with which the research community supposedly regards the welfare of animals used in experiments. For example, one FBR publication states that "many people are unaware of the extensive system of laws, guidelines, regulations and principles that ensure the welfare of laboratory animals in the U.S."[67] FBR and NABR, like AMP, regard animal rights as qualitatively different from animal welfare and support the welfarist view that most people are "concerned, and justifiably so, about the care and treatment of laboratory animals during medical research" and "want assurance that animals are treated humanely, that they do not suffer, and that they are cared for under conditions that ensure that they are as healthy and comfortable as possible." According to FBR, animal welfare requires—and responsible researchers support—the principle of the "three Rs": the reduction of numbers of animals used through proper experimental design; the replacement of animals in experiments, where possible, through alternatives to animal use; and the refinement of experimental procedures to minimize pain and suffering. FBR states that animal welfare is "not a controversial position; there is no constituency for inhumane treatment . . . [responsible research requires that] all research animals receive good care and humane treatment."[68] FBR does not bother to tell the public that the research community that it represents has historically *opposed* the very laws and regulations that FBR describes as adequately protecting the welfare of animals and as obviating the need for animal rights.

The list goes on and on, and indicates clearly that exploiters of animals perceive a distinct difference between animal welfare and animal rights.[69] This is, of course, not to say that these sources accurately or even coherently identify what distinguishes animal welfare from animal rights. For example, many animal exploiters believe that the direct or indirect support of direct action, such as laboratory break-ins, characterizes animal rights theory and differentiates it from animal welfare. There is, of course, nothing inherent in rights theory that supports such a distinguishing criterion. Moreover, many of these exploiters claim that even the most conservative of animal welfare groups are really animal rights organizations. For example, Goodwin claims that the Humane Society of the United States has become "increasingly radicalized" even though it supports animal research and does not advocate vegetarianism.

All of those involved directly in institutionalized animal exploitation but who espouse animal welfare concerns agree, however, that animal rights theory rejects the instrumental view that facilitates human hegemony over nonhumans. Rights theory recognizes that nonhumans, like humans, possess value that is not dependent on their usefulness to others, and maintains that at least some nonhumans have interests that are protected by rights, just as some human interests are protected by rights. Animal welfare theory explicitly denies this, holding in most of its various formulations that *any* "significant" animal interest can be traded away if the benefits for humans justify it. And institutionalized exploiters quite correctly understand that these are two very separate positions. The differences may help to explain why groups like the AMA embrace the concept of animal welfare in various policy statements and political positions. The AMA realizes, as it should, that, as a general matter, the institutionalized exploiter's position is much closer to that of the welfarist. Indeed, the only real differences between the exploiter and the welfarist concern how each defines "necessity." A conservative welfarist who has nothing to do directly with animal experimentation, and a vivisector who really does believe that she ought to treat her animals humanely, are not that far apart—especially relative to the gap between either of these positions and the rights position.

Conclusion

In this chapter, I have argued that what differentiates the modern animal protection movement from its predecessors is the acceptance by the former of the notion of animal rights. The theory of animal rights differs from that of animal welfare, which, though it comes in many different shapes and sizes, always endorses some version of *instrumentalism*, or the treatment of nonhumans exclusively as means to human ends. Scholars who have studied the movement argue that the presence of rights theory distinguishes the modern movement from its welfarist predecessor, and opponents of animal protection argue that advocacy of animal welfare is legitimate, while advocacy of animal rights is not.

CHAPTER Two

The New Welfarists

Rights and Welfare: The View of Animal Advocates

I argue that the defining characteristics of the modern animal movement are the rejection of the instrumentalism of animal welfare and the acceptance of the view that at least some nonhumans possess the basic right not to be considered as human property. These defining characteristics are recognized both by scholars who have analyzed the modern animal protection movement and by those who support institutionalized animal exploitation. Curiously, the only real disagreement about a distinction between animal rights and animal welfare, and about the significance of such a distinction, exists *within* the animal rights movement itself.

Although virtually all modern animal advocates describe their various positions as embodying "rights" views in their fund-raising literature and in the media, many leaders of the movement now explicitly dismiss the importance of rights notions. For example, Don Barnes, education director at the National Anti-Vivisection Society (NAVS), argues that the distinction between animal rights and animal welfare is "artificial" and that it is "elitist" to maintain that the rights position and the welfarist positions are inconsistent.[1]

According to Kim W. Stallwood, editor of the *Animals' Agenda*, there are many different philosophical theories concerning animals, but none of these can be defended as better than any others. Stallwood labels the animal rights position "utopian" and cautions that "some animal rights proponents use particular philosophical theories as yardsticks to measure" fidelity to animal rights ideology. He argues that such efforts are "artificially constructed devices" that are "divisive" of movement unity and are "elitist."[2]

Zoe Weil of the American Anti-Vivisection Society (AAVS) maintains that the philosophical differences between rights and welfare are irrelevant and that only "compassion, concern and respect for animals" matter. According to Weil, "Animal welfare *does* mean something good and positive."[3] The AAVS magazine promotes publications that endorse more "humane" methods of experimentation.[4] Carol Adams, of Feminists for Animal Rights (FAR), claims that rights are patriarchal and that we should go "beyond animal rights" and accept that "sympathy, compassion, and caring are the ground upon which theory about human treatment of animals should be constructed."[5]

Even the more so-called "radical" animal "rights" groups have distanced themselves from animal rights. For example, Ingrid E. Newkirk, director of People for the Ethical Treatment of Animals (PETA), maintains that the "all-or-nothing" position of animal rights is "unrealistic," and argues in favor of animal welfare.[6] According to Alex Pacheco of PETA, as long as people just "care" about animals, it does not matter whether they adopt the animal rights philosophy.[7] PETA's mission statement contains no mention of animal rights.

This rejection of rights theory by supposed rights advocates is becoming increasingly apparent. For example, in 1990, animal advocates held a "march for animal rights" in Washington, D.C. The theme of the march was explicitly to vindicate animal rights, and a highlight of the march was the presentation of the Declaration of the Rights of Animals, which provided that animals "have the right to live free from human exploitation, whether in the name of science or sport, exhibition or service, food or fashion," and the "right to live in harmony with their nature rather than according to human desires." Absent from the 1990 march was the Humane Society of the United States (HSUS), whose chief executive, John Hoyt, criticized the animal rights view as threatening the "kind of respectability that [HSUS] and a number of other organizations have worked hard to achieve in order to distinguish the legitimate animal *protection* movement from the more radical elements."[8]

Animal advocates have planned another march for June 23, 1996. A major sponsor of the 1996 march will be HSUS, along with other groups, such as PETA, which were once considered "more radical." But the original promotional materials for the 1996 march did not mention "rights" at all and, instead, used the expression "animal protection." The march organizers invite animal advocates to join the "largest gathering" in the "history of the *humane* movement." They seek to bring "our message to mainstream audiences around the world" through the "resources of ethical corporations" and "compassionate celebrities and legislators." The tone of the 1996 march is clearly more moderate than that of the

1990 march, and it reflects the deliberate and explicit rejection of animal rights by many animal advocacy groups.

In sum, the dominant view among the organized animal movement is that the distinction between animal welfare and animal rights is, as one leading animal advocate put it, a "distinction without a difference."[9]

New Welfarism Defined

This rejection of rights by animal advocates does not necessarily mean that all of these advocates have simply embraced some version of classical welfarism. Many modern animal advocates see the abolition of animal exploitation as a long-term goal, but they see welfarist reform, which seeks to reduce animal suffering, as setting the course for the interim strategy. For example, Henry Spira, of Animal Rights International (ARI), "sees no contradiction between working for abolition and accepting reform. '[Reform] is basically about strategies, [abolition] is the ultimate goal. . . . The two aren't contradictory.' "[10] Finsen and Finsen have observed, "The ultimate goals of the animal rights movement are clearly different from those of the humane movement," but "many within the movement see the possibility—or even the necessity—of achieving those goals by gradual and reformist means" employed by welfarists.[11] This view posits some sort of causal relationship between welfare and rights such that pursuing welfarist reform will lead eventually to the abolition of all institutionalized animal exploitation.

Many animal advocates see rights theory as seeking the complete and immediate abolition of institutionalized exploitation, and they regard this as unrealistic or "utopian" and as incapable of providing a specific program of change leading to the abolition of animal exploitation. This is what Newkirk means when she characterizes animal rights as involving an "all-or-nothing" approach, and what Stallwood means when he characterizes animal rights as a "utopian" approach. In Spira's words, "If you push for all or nothing, what you get is nothing."[12]

In addition, many animal advocates believe that the only pragmatic way to achieve animal rights is to pursue welfarist reforms as a short-term tactic. For example, Newkirk endorses a rights position and ultimately seeks the abolition of animal exploitation, but she argues that "total victory, like checkmate, cannot be achieved in one move" and that we must endorse the moral orthodoxy of animal welfare as involving necessary "steps in the direction" of animal rights. Newkirk argues that animal welfare facilitates a "springboard into animal rights."[13] Her comments help to elucidate why PETA, a supposedly "radical" organization, joined with the most conservative animal welfare groups, such as HSUS and the Animal Welfare Institute (AWI), in support of the 1985 amendments to the federal Animal Welfare Act. Those amendments explicitly reinforce the moral orthodoxy that exploiting animals is acceptable, and it may be argued quite plausibly that not one animal has been helped as a result of those amendments. So, although PETA espouses an abolitionist *end*, it maintains that at least some welfarist *means* are both a causally efficacious and morally acceptable way of getting to that end.

Similarly, Kenneth Shapiro, president of the board of directors at the *Animals' Agenda*, is also coeditor of the *Journal of Applied Animal Welfare Science*, which "publishes reports and articles on methods of experimentation, husbandry, and care that demonstrably enhance the welfare of farm, laboratory, companion, and wild animals." When asked about the ostensible discrepancy between his occupations, Shapiro denied that there was any discrepancy, arguing that his long-term goal is the abolition of animal exploitation but that his short-term strategy must embrace traditional, reformist, animal welfare. Shapiro regards any difference as one of mere "programmatic implementation" and not of substance.[14]

This position *is* different from traditional animal welfare theory in that the latter explicitly adopts the philosophical position that humans are superior to nonhumans and that the "humane" use of nonhumans by humans is therefore morally acceptable. The classical welfarist seeks to reduce suffering, but has no long-term goal apart from this reduction. Some large number of national animal protection groups still espouse this position, but many do not and, at least in their promotional literature, challenge the instrumentalist position. Regrettably, although these groups challenge prevailing views about animals and state that they seek the abolition of exploitation and not merely its regulation, they often rely on means to the end of abolition that in themselves reinforce moral orthodoxy.

An important and predictable consequence of this coupling of rights ends with welfarist means is that even though "rights" advocates see abolition as a long-term goal, many animal advocates, seeing that both welfarists and "rightists" pursue the same welfarist strategy, have adopted the position that there is *no difference* between animal welfare and animal rights. As long as a person is "compassionate" and "cares" about animals and wants to reduce their suffering, then that is all that is necessary to be an animal advocate. For example, Barnes claims that "the different ideologies arrive at the same conclusion: humans have definite responsibilities to minimize the pain and suffering around them." He states that the distinctions between animal rights and animal welfare are "artificial" and that animal advocacy requires only that "a person [feel] compassion toward other animals and [seek] to aid their plight."[15] Barnes claims that "this whole business that we have to have a philosophical framework and ideology for which we can raise our banners, well, I just don't think that's true, and it's elitist to say so."[16] Similarly, Stallwood states that no action intended to reduce animal suffering should be rejected because it is "considered unworthy of some politically correct theory."[17]

I consider this position—that the means to the long-term goal of animal rights is short-term welfarist reform—the "new welfarism" and its advocates the "new welfarists." New welfarism exhibits five essential characteristics.

First, on some level, the new welfarists reject the instrumentalist notion that nonhumans are solely means to human ends, and they reject the view that the long-term goal of the movement is limited *solely* to ensuring that nonhumans are used "humanely" or not subjected to "unnecessary" suffering. Some new welfarists openly espouse a long-term goal of complete abolition of animal exploitation; others are willing to tolerate continued animal exploitation as long as animal and human interests are given approximately equal weight and animal interests are not devalued because of species bias, or speciesism.

Second, the new welfarists believe that animal rights theory cannot provide a practical agenda for the implementation of animal rights ideology and the achievement of the long-term goal of abolition. That is, they regard the animal rights philosophy as abolitionist and the immediate abolition of any significant institution of animal exploitation unlikely. They infer from this that the animal rights philosophy offers no prescription for incremental or gradual changes in legislative, judicial, or other political contexts.

Third, in light of their view that animal rights theory cannot provide any strategic program short of the unrealistic immediate abolition of all institutionalized animal exploitation, the new welfarists pursue campaigns and strategies that are often identical to those of traditional, conservative welfare groups. For the new welfarists, virtually any measure that is thought to reduce animal suffering is regarded as an animal "rights" measure.

Fourth, new welfarists regard welfarist regulation, which seeks to reform institutions of animal exploitation and make them more "humane" and explicitly reinforces the moral orthodoxy of human hegemony over nonhumans, as both necessary and desirable steps on the road toward animal rights, which can only be achieved as the result of incrementally improved animal welfare, or continued reduction in animal suffering. For example, even those who are committed in both philosophy and lifestyle to vegetarianism support measures that ensure the more "humane" treatment of "livestock" in the belief that more "humane" slaughter measures will lead to vegetarianism sometime in the future. Indeed, some writers, such as Andrew Rowan, make this supposed connection explicit in arguing for an "evonnectionist" position based on "incremental proposals" of animal welfare.[18] Most new welfarists regard reformist means as *causally* related to the end of animal rights or the abolition of animal exploitation. And they argue that animal welfare has, as an empirical matter, improved the treatment of animals and can realistically be expected to lead eventually to the abolition of animal exploitation.

Fifth, the new welfarists see no moral or logical inconsistency in promoting measures that explicitly endorse and reinforce an instrumental view of animals and at the same time articulating a long-term philosophy of animal rights. Instrumentalism denies that animals have any inherent value or that they can themselves be holders of rights—notions that are at the center of animal rights theory. The new welfarists believe that it is both coherent and morally acceptable to disregard the rights of animals *today* (by pursuing welfarist reform that reinforces the property status of animals) in the hope that some other animals will have rights *tomorrow*. As I explained in Chapter One, animal rights theory maintains that animals have certain interests that cannot be sacrificed even if others benefit and even if the animals who are being exploited are treated "humanely."

Just as there is a wide variation among those who adhere to the traditional welfare position, there is also a wide variation among new welfarists. Virtually all new welfarists, however, despite, or perhaps because of, an increasing tendency within the animal advocacy movement to elide the differences between rights and welfare, use the language of rights without hesitation to refer to virtually *any* measure that is thought to reduce animal suffering. Indeed, they identify themselves and their positions with animal "rights." For example, Barnes has long described himself as supportive of "fundamental rights" for animals but claims that the distinction between rights and welfare is "artificial."[19] Stallwood claims that animal rights ideology is "elitist" and "divisive," but the *Animals' Agenda* describes itself as "dedicated to informing people about animal *rights*," and Stallwood often identifies his own position with animal rights. Carol Adams, who seeks to move "beyond animal rights" and who is critical of the concept of rights, is a cofounder and director of Feminists for Animal *Rights*.

An explanation of this peculiar phenomenon is offered by Andrew Rowan, director of the Center for Public Policy and Animals at Tufts University, who rejects the distinction between animal rights and animal welfare as a "false dichotomy" and concludes that "drawing a hard and fast distinction between animal welfare and animal rights is neither accurate or valid." Rowan claims that "it is the political tactics and not the philosophical underpinning" that distinguishes organizations, and that the rights/welfare distinction "causes more obfuscation than clarification." Rowan claims that animal advocates use the language of rights because it "resonates powerfully to the body politic and it appears in the literature of a wide variety of pressure groups."[20] To put the matter differently, many animal advocates use rights language, but this usage is merely rhetorical, and does not, in fact, reflect the philosophy of animal rights as that position was described earlier.

Ironically, some new welfarists have sought to isolate those who argue that rights is more than just a rhetorical notion that may be used to cover any measure that is thought to reduce animal suffering. For example, the *Animals' Agenda* has criticized as "fundamentalist" the position that animal welfare is inconsistent with animals rights.[21] *Agenda* editor Kim Stallwood has called the animal rights position "utopian" and the attempt to distinguish rights from welfare "divisive" because "under this rubric animal welfarists become the enemy."[22] Although Stallwood occasionally still uses rights language in rhetorical, nonideological ways, he now talks about "animal protection" and "animal liberation." Similarly, another movement publication, *Animal People*, has also taken a hostile position toward rights advocates, claiming that those who seek the abolition of exploitation as demanded by rights theory are "fundamentalists" who "will continue to demand impractical absolutes, immediate response, and unlikely abject surrenders."[23]

Some Preliminary Comments on New Welfarism

The remainder of this book illuminates the fundamental assumptions that animate new welfarism. In anticipation of the analysis that follows, I offer three preliminary observations.

First, in order to analyze new welfarism as the ideology of the modern animal movement, it is necessary to evaluate the underlying empirical and theoretical claims of new welfarism. In particular, I discuss at length in later chapters the claim that animal welfare reforms can, as an empirical and theoretical matter, lead to the abolition of animal exploitation. I also examine the claim that animal rights cannot, as a theoretical matter, inform a program of practical and incremental change that is very different from the primary normative prescription of animal welfare to reduce animal suffering. If animal rights theory can provide the normative guidance that the welfarists claim it lacks, or if animal welfare reforms will not or cannot lead to abolition, then important portions of the new-welfarist viewpoint are invalid. Alternatively, doubt cast upon these assumptions of new welfarism should motivate those in the movement to rethink its ideology.

Second, irrespective of the merits of these claims, the relationship between the ends of a social protest movement and the means that it uses to achieve those ends requires some reflection. The new welfarists *assume* that it is morally permissible to use welfarist reforms to achieve the abolition of animal exploitation and that the resultant movement may properly be characterized as a "rights" movement. If "rights" is being used rhetorically, then I suppose that this move could be permitted. But, as I have argued, the defining characteristic of the animal rights movement is, by all accounts, a rejection of the *instrumentalism* that is the very foundation of animal welfare. If that is the case, then it becomes problematic for a movement that aims toward a goal of abolition based on a rejection of the instrumentalism of animal welfare to use welfarist reforms as a means to that end.

It is interesting to note that scholars who have sought to analyze the movement, though they have recognized that those who consider themselves animal rights advocates often promote traditional, reformist measures, have failed to recognize the significance of this posited relationship between ends and means. For example, Jasper and Nelkin argue that animal protection organizations "tend to cluster into three kinds of groups": "welfarist, pragmatist, and fundamentalist." Traditional humane societies are offered as examples of welfarist organizations, which regard animals as "distinct from humans, but as objects entitled to compassion," and which seek as their primary goal to "minimize [animal] suffering and pain." Pragmatists are those who believe that nonhumans are entitled to moral consideration but who also believe that "certain species deserve greater consideration than others and would allow humans to use animals when the benefits deriving from their use outweigh their suffering." According to Jasper and Nelkin, pragmatists "seek to reduce animal use through legal actions, political protest, and negotiation." Fundamentalists are those who demand "the immediate abolition of all exploitation of animals, on the grounds that animals have inherent, inviolable rights." These distinctions, we are told, are "not absolute or rigid. Some activists, for example, believe in full animal rights, but pursue their goals with pragmatic strategies. Many shift their language and tactics depending on the issue or political arena."[24]

What is fascinating about this analysis is that throughout their book Jasper and Nelkin stress that the animal rights movement is historically different from traditional animal welfare because the former rejects the instrumentalism and its incorporation in the law—legal welfarism—that is the very foundation of the property-oriented theory of animal welfare. Indeed, they argue that the modern animal rights movement reflects a rejection of instrumentalism and the rhetoric of "rights" that emerged in the 1970s as part of progressive political thought.[25] The pragmatic position that Jasper and Nelkin describe explicitly acknowledges that the instrumental treatment of nonhumans may in some circumstances be morally justifiable. This pragmatic approach is squarely at odds with what is described as the fundamentalist position, which rejects any instrumental treatment of animals. Nevertheless—and without any argument whatsoever—Jasper and Nelkin assume that fundamentalists, who reject instrumentalism, can use "pragmatic strategies," which explicitly provide for animal exploitation in those cases in which the balance tips in favor of such exploitation. In fact, Jasper and Nelkin argue that as long as a person or organization accepts the rights ideology as a long-term goal, their actual tactics may be reformist: "Those who believe in the rights of animals as sentient beings support modest reforms, but only as a temporary measure, for their ultimate goal is to abolish" the exploitation.[26]

Similarly, Robert Garner ostensibly endorses the view that it is a group's stated goals, not its tactics, that characterize it as challenging the moral orthodoxy, which he defines as the view that animals "have an inferior moral status and the interests of autonomous beings take precedence. Thus, we are entitled to sacrifice the interests of animals to further human interests . . . as part of a cost-benefit analysis."[27] Garner identifies this orthodoxy as the conventional reformist view "held by many traditional animal welfare groups."[28] He acknowledges that "a significant section of the animal protection movement still clings to the traditional welfare ideology." According to Garner, this section includes groups such as AWI, which seeks to " 'reduce the sum total of pain and fear inflicted on animals,' to promote the 'humane treatment of laboratory animals' and to 'reform the cruel treatment of food animals.' "[29] By contrast, the "modern challenge to the dominant welfare ideology" is characterized by an "uncompromising" effort to end "all exploitative uses[s] of animals, whether by individuals or institutions."[30] Nevertheless, Garner assumes that an organization that espouses a challenge to the moral orthodoxy about animals can employ the same reformist tactics that are part of the moral orthodoxy. For example, Garner states that although Advocates for Animals, a British group, advocates the abolition of all vivisection, "it is prepared to countenance a reformist route as a tactic."[31] Similarly, another British group, Compassion in World Farming, seeks to end the use of animals for food altogether, but it, too, is prepared to use the reformist route as a "tactic" and to urge reform of factory farming rather than an end to the use of nonhumans as food.

Garner assumes that the use of reformist means to achieve abolitionist ends is merely a matter of "strategy." In discussing the conflict between nineteenth-century welfarist Stephen Coleridge and antivivisectionist Frances Power Cobbe, Garner claims that the split between the two was "a dispute over strategy as much as objectives."[32] Frances Power Cobbe was adamantly and absolutely opposed to vivisection and did not believe as a moral matter in its "reform." Coleridge believed that reform was appropriate. Those are very different positions, indeed, and should not be dismissed simply as embodying the same objective but using different "tactics" or "strategies." Any attempt to characterize the dispute between Coleridge and Cobbe as one of "strategy," and "strategy" as different from "objective," would be analogous to saying that what divided those who favored the abolition of slavery from those who sought "gradual emancipation" was a matter of "strategy" and not "objective." Both the abolitionists and the those who favored "gradual emancipation" wanted slavery to end, but the latter group believed, for many different reasons, that emancipation could not and should not be effected immediately. They sought to change the system from within, to make slavery more "humane" by reforms such as recognizing the validity of slave marriages to prevent the hardships caused by breaking up slave families. The abolitionists were opposed to such reforms and regarded the institution of slavery and any attempt to regulate or "reform" that institution as morally iniquitous. Those involved would hardly have characterized this as a dispute merely over "strategy" but not over objective, and they certainly would not have felt that any objective / strategy distinction captured the moral importance of their respective positions.

In any event, Garner, like Jasper and Nelkin, fails to see the implications of his analysis. He argues that the modern animal movement rejects the moral orthodoxy that has characterized the traditional animal welfare approach, which includes reformist, rather than abolitionist, measures. He also argues, however, that a considerable segment of the movement still clings to these reformist notions. An organization or individual who claims to challenge the moral orthodoxy by according a higher moral status to animals and advocating the abolition, not merely the reform, of animal exploitation is deemed by Garner "radical" *whether or not the organization or individual adopts reformist "tactics."* So, according to Garner, AWI is a conservative, welfarist, reform-oriented group that represents the moral orthodoxy, while Compassion in World Farming is a radical group that challenges the moral orthodoxy—even though both groups employ the very same reformist "tactics" to reach their respective "goals."

One could argue, of course, that the stated goals of an organization—and not its tactics, strategies, or campaigns—should determine its classification as a "rights" or "radical" organization, but none of the commentators bothers to make any such argument. They simply *assume* that the tactics employed by an organization or individual are irrelevant to any such classification when the stated long-term or short-term goal represents some sort of challenge to the instrumentalist view.

It is, however, quite plausible to maintain that the modern animal protection movement that currently exists in the United States cannot properly be characterized as an animal *rights* movement if what we mean by animal rights is the rejection of the instrumentalist view of animals that characterized the period before the late 1970s. A movement is generally defined by both its ideology and its practical efforts to implement that ideology in the real world. The ideology of the animal rights movement is usually expressed in terms of the long-term liberation of nonhumans from virtually all forms of institutionalized exploitation. On this theoretical level, the animal rights movement is distinguishable from the classical animal welfare position, which holds that the exploitation of animals is morally acceptable as long as the animals are treated "humanely" and are not subjected to "unnecessary" suffering.

On another level, however, many of those who consider themselves rights advocates argue that animal rights (the complete abolition of exploitation) can be achieved incrementally through virtually any measure that is thought to reduce animal suffering, including those measures that merely guarantee animals "humane" treatment or prohibit "unnecessary" suffering. Much of what is described as the animal rights movement has little to do with the theory of animal rights as that term is generally understood *outside* the animal movement. Rather, the animal rights movement has, as a practical matter, adopted a modified version of animal welfare that is more progressive in its long-term goal than classical welfare theory, but nevertheless accepts the notion common to all forms of animal welfare: that it is acceptable to sacrifice the interests of some animals today in the hope that animals tomorrow will fare better. The classical welfarists regard the "better tomorrow" as a more "humane" society. For example, Wayne Pacelle of HSUS argues that the HSUS mission is to "create a humane society that takes into account the interest of animals and eliminates the *gratuitous* harm done to animals by humans."[33] The classical welfarist is concerned with precisely what Pacelle identifies: the prevention of gratuitous harm; the modern animal advocate seeks the abolition of institutionalized animal exploitation as a vague long-term goal but, supposedly out of a concern for "practicality," endorses short-term welfarist reform as both *a* means and the *only* means to reach that long-term goal. This latter position assumes that the interest in reducing animal suffering is primary and that repeatedly vindicating this interest will eliminate the institutionalized exploitation that causes the suffering.

Third, irrespective of the merits of new welfarists' claims concerning the relationship between rights theory and welfare theory, or of the propriety of using means that are ostensibly inconsistent with ends, we can, at the outset, dismiss the claim made by Barnes and other new welfarists that the content of both rights and welfare theories is limited to minimizing pain and suffering. This view simply begs the question by denying that animal rights theory imposes more or different obligations apart from the welfarist admonition to reduce animal suffering. Those who agree with the rights approach explicitly *reject* the notion that human obligations to nonhumans are satisfied by efforts to "minimize suffering." Although it is important to minimize suffering, the goal of the animal rights movement is to secure *justice* for animals by abolishing the institutionalized exploitation that causes that suffering. The nineteenth-century animal welfarist was, like the new welfarists, concerned to "minimize" suffering, but, as the commentators are agreed, the animal rights movement differs from the animal welfare movement precisely in that it rejects the contention that alleviation of suffering alone can satisfy the human obligation to animals. Similarly, the nineteenth-century welfarist, like the new welfarists, maintained that it was "kindness" or something other than a more definite standard that defined our obligations to nonhumans. As Brian Klug argued in 1984—ironically, in the *Animals' Agenda*—animal rights goes beyond the traditional "kindness" ethic of the animal welfare movement and proposes a theory of *justice* for animals. According to Klug, rights theory establishes that animal rights are a matter of "strict justice" for animals, and not mere kindness.[34] The animal rights movement recognizes that although animals surely have an interest in not suffering, they have an even more fundamental interest in *not being part of the institutionalized exploitation that causes this suffering in the first instance and deprives animals of their fundamental right not to be treated exclusively as means to human ends*. For the rights advocate, the goal is to abolish the institutionalized exploitation, not merely to pursue measures that may or may not reduce animal suffering.

Moreover, the position that only suffering or compassion matters in the animal context is significantly different from the position we adopt in the human context and involves a type of moral relativism that we do not employ in the context of human rights. For example, Barnes argues that their criticism of measures or conduct intended to reduce animal suffering represents animal rights advocates' "purer-than-thou" attitude and that it is "elitist" and "judgmental" to criticize animal welfarists.[35] Similarly, Stallwood rejects as inappropriate the characterization of positions as "rights" oriented or "welfare" oriented, and he rejects as "divisive" and "elitist" *any* argument that a particular position is insufficiently protective of the rights or interests of nonhumans. In the context of human rights, these charges would appear to be most peculiar. For example, measures that would require men to rape women more "gently" we would hardly consider acceptable because they would reduce suffering; we insist on a norm that absolutely prohibits the conduct of rape. Our protection of human interests that are subject to claims of right should not depend on whether some group of people feels "compassion" for those whose interests are at stake. It is no more "elitist" to say that animal rights notions require that we *prohibit* eating meat than it is to say that human rights notions require that we prohibit the unjustified taking of human life.[36] To treat the nonhuman context differently from the human context requires a justification beyond the mere assertion that all that matters in the animal context is compassion or the reduction of suffering and that animals are entitled to nothing more. Barnes goes so far as to state explicitly that just because a person continues to eat animal products does not mean that the person should be excluded from the "inner circle of the animal rights elect."[37] But that is like saying that someone who endorses racism should not be excluded from the "inner circle of the civil rights elect" or that someone who endorses sexism should not be excluded from the "inner circle of the women's rights elect." The whole point of a social protest movement is to protest against—and change—institutionalized forms of exploitation.

Whatever other claims that the new welfarist may wish to make concerning the relationship between animal rights and animal welfare, it is clear that the new welfarist cannot coherently claim that there is *no* difference between these different approaches. As I indicated above, the view that these two approaches amount to the same thing can be traced to the simple fact that both new welfarists and classical welfarists are pursuing the same short-term goal: the reduction of suffering. But that means only that the new welfarists have taken a particular position about the *relationship* between animal rights as a long-term goal and welfarist reform as a short-term strategy. It does not mean that the two theories are the same. Indeed, the theories are very, very different.

The rightist and the new welfarist seek the abolition of animal exploitation, but the new welfarist believes that continued welfare reforms will lead to that abolition. Although it remains to be seen whether the rightist can or should provide a theory of practical incremental change that differs from that of the welfarist, the rightist rejects these welfarist reforms because they focus only on one interest that the animal has—the interest in not suffering—and ignores the animal's interest in not being part of the institutionalized exploitation that causes the suffering in the first place. And these theoretical differences often drive animal advocates in different directions when they seek to undertake practical action to ameliorate the plight of animals.

Conclusion

Although scholars and animal exploiters recognize that animal rights and animal welfare are very different approaches to the human / animal relationship, many animal advocates elide the difference. These animal advocates seek to reduce suffering, but they regard this reduction as causally related to their long-term goal of abolishing all institutionalized animal exploitation. They purport to embrace animal rights at least as a long-term matter, but they regard rights theory as "unrealistic" in that it cannot provide any short-term strategy to achieve the long-term goal. Consequently, they urge the pursuit of welfarist reforms as an interim strategy to achieve the abolition of animal exploitation. I call these animal advocates "new welfarists" because they support many of the reforms and approaches of classical animal welfare theory but do so in order to achieve a goal not shared by the traditional welfarists.

Because both new welfarists and more traditional welfarists pursue the same strategy—to reduce animal suffering—albeit with different long-term goals, some animal advocates have collapsed the rights and welfare views, claiming that there is no difference between the theories in that both require only that people act with "compassion" and seek to reduce animal suffering. But that position is not an argument in favor of ignoring the theoretical differences between rights and welfare; indeed, the position merely asserts—and incorrectly—that the central concern of the animal "rights" movement is the "compassionate" treatment of animals and the reduction of suffering, both hallmarks of the classical welfarist approach.

Finally, the suggestion has been made that rights language plays only a "rhetorical" role in the ideology of the animal movement. But for those who take animal rights seriously, rights concepts are more than mere rhetoric, as Rowan suggests. For example, Helen Jones, founder of the International Society for Animal Rights (ISAR) and one of the true pioneers of the animal *rights* movement, stated that her group did not use the term "animal rights" in some rhetorical fashion: "Profound and deliberate thought led to the adoption in 1972 of the term Animal Rights in the name of Society for Animal Rights (SAR)." Jones added that "SAR, now International Society for Animal Rights, was the first organization in the US, and to the best of our knowledge, in the world, to employ the term Animal Rights in its name to reflect the Society's moral and philosophical position."[38] As early as 1981, Jones argued that those who supported welfarist regulation should "have the grace and fairness not to invoke 'animal rights' as their philosophy and program. By doing so, they confuse the issue, the press and the public. Animal rights is too serious to be invoked as a mere slogan."[39]

CHAPTER Three

The Philosophical
and Historical Origins
of New Welfarism

The animal protection movement has for a number of reasons chosen a modified version of animal welfare that purports to challenge the orthodoxy of animal welfare while at the same time claiming that animal rights can be achieved only though reformist measures and, ironically, rejecting the distinction between rights and welfare on a practical level. These reasons are theoretical and practical. As a theoretical matter, the modern animal movement has from the outset been fundamentally confused about the philosophy of animal rights. As a practical matter, the modern animal movement has from the outset seen itself as "radical" in the sense of advocating long-term goals that differed from those of welfarist reformers, but has pursued campaigns that fit comfortably *within* the welfarist paradigm.

Confusion About Theory

As I mentioned in Chapter One, all of the commentators regard philosophical theory as playing a key role in the modern animal movement. The theorists most often mentioned in this regard are Tom Regan and Peter Singer. Much of the present confusion in the animal rights movement is owing to the greater influence that Singer's theory, rather than Regan's, has had on the direction of the movement. I argue that the philosophical origins of new welfarism may be found in Singer's work. It is not my intent to present either a complete description of Singer's theory or a broad consideration of what are regarded as flaws in his view. My intent is only to demonstrate the similarities between Singer's view and new welfarism in order to illuminate the origins of the latter.

Singer maintains that the morally correct choice in a particular situation is that which maximizes or furthers the interests, desires, or preferences of those who are affected. Pleasure and pain matter because they are part of what humans and nonhumans desire or prefer or seek to avoid. In determining the consequences of actions, Singer argues that we must accord equal consideration to equal interests. That is, if I am trying to decide whether to give $5 to John or Mary, and it turns out that John has a greater interest in the money because he is very poor and is starving and will almost certainly die if he is not given the money, and Mary is very rich, then their interests are not equal, and it would most probably maximize utility to give the money to John.[1] If, however, John's interests and Mary's interests—however characterized—are the same, then their interests should weigh equally in any decision because, according to Singer, the principle of equality requires that John's interest in getting the $5 be given the same consideration as Mary's interest. To do otherwise would be to violate the principle of equality by treating similar interests differently. By equal consideration, Singer means that I should not favor Mary over John simply because she is a Caucasian and he an African-American. Similarly, I should not use other criteria such as sex or sexual orientation to decide. Moreover, the principle of equality is a normative principle and not a descriptive one. By this, Singer means that, as a factual matter, people are not equal. They differ in intellectual abilities, physical characteristics, personality, and so forth. Nevertheless, we accord equal moral consideration to equal interests even if, as a factual matter, the people involved are not "equal."

Singer also argues that just as it is morally impermissible to accord differential consideration to equal interests based on race or sex, it is also impermissible to base differential consideration on species. Indeed, to do so would be to engage in speciesism, which is similar to racism and sexism in using morally irrelevant criteria to determine membership in the moral community. For example, if I decide to give the $5 to John *because* he is male, that decision is surely sexist. Similarly, if my dog and I have a roughly equal interest in not being hit, according greater weight to my interests *because* I am human is speciesist. The fact that I am human may mean that my dog and I do not have equal interests in some circumstances. For example, although my dog is very intelligent, she would not benefit from an academic scholarship in the same way that a human being would. Accordingly, the interests involved are not equal, and it would, therefore, not violate the principle of equality to treat our interests differently. But if our interests are roughly equal—and in many cases they will be—then the principle of equality requires that those equal interests receive equal consideration.

Singer's theory does not concern rights, since Singer does not believe that animals *or* humans have rights. Indeed, Singer himself refers to his theory as one of "animal liberation" and states that claims of right are "irrelevant." "The language of rights is a convenient political shorthand. It is even more valuable in the era of thirty-second TVA news clips."[2] In light of Singer's view that only the consequences (understood in terms of the preference satisfaction of those affected) of acts matter, it is easy to understand why he rejects rights. A right is generally regarded as "a moral trump card that cannot be disputed."[3] A right serves as a protection that cannot be sacrificed even if the consequences of doing so would be desirable. Rights, or at least most rights, are not thought to be absolute, but at least some rights provide strong prima facie protection and cannot be compromised without the most compelling reasons. For example, overall social happiness might be increased if I were used without my consent in an experiment whose goal and likely outcome was a cure for cancer. Nevertheless, I have a moral and legal right not to have my interests in my life or liberty traded away in order to secure that admittedly desirable result.

Singer's notion of equal consideration does not mean that animals receive equal treatment, and it does not on either moral or practical grounds preclude a decision to exploit a human or nonhuman. As long as an animal's interests receive equitable consideration (consideration untainted by the speciesism that discounts animal interests simply because they are the interests of a supposed "inferior"), Singer's equality principle is satisfied. But this notion of equality is consistent with exploiting animals if the consequences justify that exploitation and if the decision to exploit is not based on species discrimination. Indeed, Singer acknowledges that he "would never deny that we are justified in using animals for human goals, because as a consequentialist, [he] must also hold that in appropriate circumstances we are justified in using humans to achieve human goals (or the goal of assisting animals)." Singer claims not to be "the kind of moral absolutist who holds that the ends can never justify the means," and he denies arguing that "*no* animal experimentation is ever of use to humans" or that "*all* animal experimentation involves suffering."[4] Garner has noted that Singer does "talk as if the killing of animals for food and their use for experimental purposes should be morally condemned *per se* because the infliction of pain means that they lead miserable lives." Garner adds that "such a view could be taken to mean that [Singer] thinks they have a right not to have pain inflicted on them[,] [but] Singer is clear . . . that he is not an advocate of rights."[5]

Perhaps the clearest difference between Singer's view and the rights position is expressed by Singer himself in the second edition of *Animal Liberation*. Singer argues that many nonhumans—and this class apparently includes food animals—are not capable of "having desires for the future" or a "continuous mental existence."[6] These cognitive characteristics assume "an understanding of what it is to exist over a period of time," and Singer doubts that most animals used for food have such an understanding.[7] This supposed lack of future desire or continuous mental existence is generally irrelevant when the issue involves pain or suffering alone, although I argue later that Singer appears to contradict himself on this point and allows for individual capacities to affect assessments of pain and suffering. Singer believes that these characteristics become relevant, however, when the issue involves killing an animal in a painless or relatively painless manner. Singer expresses "doubts" on the issue, but he concludes that "it is not easy to explain why the loss to the animal killed is not, from an impartial point of view, made good by the creation of a new animal who will lead an equally pleasant life."[8] Singer maintains that it may be morally justifiable to continue "to eat free-range animals (of a species incapable of having desires for the future), who have had a pleasant existence in a social group suited to their behavioral needs, and are then killed quickly and without pain."[9] Singer states that he "can respect conscientious people who take care to eat meat that comes only from such animals."[10]

Clearly, Singer regards most animal experimentation as without merit; he would eliminate factory farming; and he feels that we ought for the most part to be vegetarians because, although it may be morally permissible to eat animals, the practical circumstances surrounding their rearing and killing morally precludes eating them. These views, however, are based on Singer's *empirical* assessments of what the consequences of particular acts are in light of his theory that individual acts ought to further the interests or preferences of those affected. Like all such empirical assessments, the consequences of the acts may be evaluated differently by different people. For example, Singer thinks that the negative consequences for the animals involved in factory farming outweigh its benefits, but, as Regan points out, "the animal industry is big business," and although "it is uncertain exactly how many people are involved in it, directly or indirectly, . . . the number must easily run into the many tens of thousands." Those involved in animal agriculture "have a stake in the animal industry as rudimentary and important as having a job, feeding a family, or laying aside money for their children's education or their own retirement."[11]

Similarly, philosopher R. G. Frey, who is critical of Singer's utilitarianism *and* Regan's rights theory, presents a lengthy list of "practical considerations that must be taken into account" in evaluating Singer's claim that animal agriculture, and especially the practices involved in intensive agriculture, are not justified under Singer's theory of preference utilitarianism. This list includes negative consequences that would befall those directly involved in the raising and killing of animals, such as farmers and slaughterhouse operators; those involved indirectly in the food business, such as food retailers; those involved in the dairy industry; those involved in fast-food restaurants, the pet food industry, the pharmaceutical industry, and the leather goods and wool industries; those involved in agricultural and veterinary research incidental to agriculture; those involved in publishing books about animal agriculture; and those involved in advertising the products of animal agriculture; and so forth.[12] It is clear that Frey is correct that the collapse of factory farming would have a profound impact on the international economy. This is not to say that these negative consequences would necessarily outweigh the animals' interests in not experiencing the pain and suffering incidental to intensive agriculture; it is only to say that if the issue hinges on the aggregation of consequences, *it is not clear* whether it would be morally right under Singer's view to abolish factory farming. What is clear is that, given Singer's view that the rightness or wrongness of action is determined by the consequences it has for the interests of all affected, he simply "cannot say that the interests of those humans involved in [factory farming], those whose quality of life is presently bound up in it, are irrelevant."[13] Once the preference satisfaction of everyone involved in factory farming (humans and nonhumans) is deemed relevant and counted equitably, the result appears to be much more controversial than Singer assumes.

For Regan, on the other hand, a deontologist, right and wrong are not dependent upon the aggregation of consequences across individuals, but instead depend upon compliance with more absolute rules and standards. Regan rejects utilitarianism just as emphatically as Singer rejects moral rules or rights. Regan's rights theory, unlike Singer's theory, calls for the *abolition* of institutionalized animal exploitation *even if* the consequences of that exploitation would justify it under utilitarian theory. In Regan's view, the use of animals for experiments or for food should be absolutely prohibited irrespective of consequences.

It was Regan who developed the rights-based argument; but Singer, not Regan, is regarded as the "founder" of the modern animal rights movement, and Singer's philosophy has permeated the movement to a significantly greater degree than has Regan's rights view.[14] Blum refers to *Animal Liberation* as the "bible of the current animal rights movement."[15] In discussing the emergence of "new animal rights groups," Sperling states that "most activists cited the publication of Singer's *Animal Liberation* as an important event that infused the emerging movement with a cohesive moral and political perspective."[16] Finsen and Finsen, in their discussion of the controversy surrounding the origins of the animal rights movement, state that "many place its beginning with the publication in the mid-1970s of Peter Singer's book *Animal Liberation*" and "date their own awakening to animal rights issues" to that same publication.[17] Finsen and Finsen describe the emergence of the movement in the United States in the 1980s and comment that this interest was "not surprising, since a wave of interest in animal rights issues was sweeping the nation at this time, stimulated most clearly by the publication of Peter Singer's *Animal Liberation* in 1975 and a spate of related works."[18]

According to Jasper and Nelkin, "Almost every animal rights activist either owns or has read Peter Singer's *Animal Liberation*, which since its publication in 1975 has become a bible for the movement."[19] Singer's work also influenced some of those who are credited with being the pioneers of the animal "rights" movement—for example, Henry Spira, described by Merritt Clifton as "the most effective antivivisection activist of our time and perhaps of any time," who, "with a minuscule budget, . . . has accomplished more over the past 17 years toward getting animals out of laboratories than any of the national animal rights groups and antivivisection societies; perhaps more than all of them put together."[20] Spira became involved in the animal issue "after his participation in a New York University continuing education course on 'animal liberation' taught by philosopher Peter Singer." Singer's utilitarian theory "galvanized students who had been interested in our treatment of animals but lacked an ideological frame of reference and spur to action."[21] Spira had read an article of Singer's on animals and had found Singer's argument for animal liberation "direct and powerful."[22]

Similarly, "of the many new organizations devoted to animal rights, People for the Ethical Treatment of Animals (PETA) is one of the most successful."[23] PETA is credited with "spectacular increases" in membership in the animal movement[24] and, with the clandestine Animal Liberation Front (ALF), is considered the group "most widely associated with work for animal rights."[25] PETA was begun after Alex Pacheco, then a college student, visited a slaughterhouse in Canada in 1977. He was disturbed by what he saw, and read Singer's *Animal Liberation*.[26] He became a vegetarian and "soon decided to interrupt his studies. He shipped out on the *Sea Shepherd*, a ship supported by environmentalists to harass illegal whalers. When he returned to the States in 1980, he met [Ingrid] Newkirk. He gave her a copy of *Animal Liberation* and teased her for continuing to eat meat. The same year, they founded PETA."[27] PETA "requires new employees and college students participating in its internship program to read Singer's *Animal Liberation*."[28] No mention is made of Regan's work, and PETA merchandise catalogs no longer even offer Regan's book for sale, although *Animal Liberation*, which is described in the PETA catalog as a book about "animal rights philosophy," is included in a section entitled "animal rights books," together with the advice, "If you only read one animal rights book, it has to be this one."[29]

Singer has, to a considerable degree, encouraged this confusion by referring to his position as an animal rights theory. As Garner has noted, Singer has "not helped matters by agreeing to the assertion of animal rights as 'handy political slogans.'"[30] On the dust jacket of the second edition of *Animal Liberation* are several statements about the book, and the following quote is printed in type about ten times larger than any of the other quotes: "The modern (animal rights) movement may be dated to the 1975 publication of 'Animal Liberation' by Australian philosopher Peter Singer"—which quite deliberately represents *Animal Liberation* as articulating a theory of animal rights. The original quote, taken from a major newsmagazine, simply used "modern movement" without any adjective. Singer, in the book itself, refers to the article's subject as "animal liberation."[31] Nevertheless, when the actual quote was reproduced for the dust jacket, the words "animal rights," rather than "animal liberation," were inserted. In his 1985 anthology, *In Defense of Animals*, Singer is described as "one of the most forceful and best known proponents of animal rights."[32] Moreover, in his 1995 book, *How Are We to Live?* the cover states that Singer is "hailed as the father of the Animal Rights movement."[33] More recently, and in connection with attempts by advocates to secure the release of chimpanzees, Singer claims that "we want chimps to cease to be items of property, and to be seen as persons with rights."[34]

The notion of "rights" is used in at least two different ways. The first use involves a philosophical theory that explicitly rejects instrumentalism, or the notion that it is permissible to treat animals solely as means to human ends. Singer is not using "rights" in this way, since his utilitarian theory is itself instrumentalist in that Singer explicitly recognizes that nonhumans (and humans) may be exploited if the cost-benefit analysis required by his theory weighs in favor of such exploitation.

Singer thereby rejects the very notion upon which the modern animal movement is supposedly based: that animals have moral rights that prohibit their being used as means to human ends. The second use may be called "rhetorical."[35] When Singer uses "rights" with respect to his own theory, he is not rejecting the instrumentalism of animal welfare; rather, he is advocating on behalf of a different type of instrumentalist theory that would allow animal exploitation as long as animal interests are given equitable consideration.

Andrew Rowan observes that "it is ironic" that Singer has been described as the " 'Father of the Animal Rights Movement' for his book, *Animal Liberation,*" because "Singer is a utilitarian and utilitarians argue strongly against the use of rights terminology in philosophy." Although "Singer has acknowledged the issue in his writings," he has "not disavowed the title because he sees the Animal Rights movement as a political and not a philosophical entity."[36] This is somewhat troubling, as Garner has noted, not only because it causes "confusion" within the movement about the distinction between animal rights and animal welfare, but because "the use of this rhetorical device by Singer arouses suspicion that he is an ideologue for animals rather than someone who sees the claims of animals emerging from a more or less neutral and general ethical theory."[37]

There is considerable confusion about the relationship of Singer's theory to instrumentalism in that many commentators do not recognize that Singer's utilitarianism *is* instrumentalist. For example, Jasper and Nelkin regard Singer's theory as rejecting instrumentalism, although they regard Singer (and Spira) as pragmatists, defined as those who argue that animals deserve "moral consideration" but who "would allow humans to use animals when the benefits deriving from their use outweigh their suffering."[38] The problem here is that, according to Jasper and Nelkin, what distinguishes the animal rights movement from the animal welfare movement is the rejection of instrumentalism and the acceptance that "animals have inherent values as ends in themselves,"[39] a notion that Singer expressly rejects.

Singer and New Welfarism

Singer's theory exhibits all five characteristics of new welfarism. Singer's theory, like classical welfarism, requires that we balance the interests of those affected and regards as morally permissible the exploitation of animals in certain circumstances. Nevertheless, Singer's theory does represent a theoretical challenge to the instrumentalism of classical animal welfare in one important sense. Singer argues that the equal interests of humans and nonhumans ought to be accorded equal consideration, and this principle of equality would surely prohibit much animal exploitation *as long as we all agreed with Singer in his necessarily complicated and case-by-case assessment of the consequences of actions.* He would, for example, be opposed to most animal experimentation and the use of animals for food where those animals were not produced under free-range conditions, although, as I argued above, the characterization of consequences is often more controversial than Singer acknowledges. So, Singer shares with the new welfarists their opposition to the traditional welfarist notion that animals are the property of people and are properly viewed exclusively as means to human ends.

But Singer's analysis is very much like traditional welfarism in the sense that traditional animal welfare requires that we balance human interests against animal interests, although traditional welfare then accords virtually no weight to the animal interests, while assigning— through the attribution of rights—considerable weight to the human interests at stake. Singer does not think that *anyone* (human or nonhuman) has moral rights, but he still requires that animal interests and human interests be weighed and that animal interests be treated more seriously than required under classical welfarism. So, the difference between Singer's view and the traditional orthodox theory of welfare is, in large part, a difference in the degree of seriousness assigned animal interests. In light of the fact that humans characterize the competing human / animal interests in the first place, and that it is humans who do the balancing of these humanocentric interests, the acceptance of Singer's approach might do less good for animals than Singer supposes, unless, as I mentioned above, all of those doing the balancing agree with the answers that Singer himself would give to key questions, such as, who has what interests? how are interests to be balanced? and what are the consequences of competing courses of action? As I noted above, reasonable and morally sincere minds can differ widely in responding to these concerns. And as the range of possible responses widens, the conservative interpretation of Singer's theory and more progressive notions of animal welfare meet.

An additional—and for present purposes more relevant—problem is that Singer, unlike most of the new welfarists, does not endorse animal rights *even as a long-term goal of his theory.* Rather, the principle of equality is the long-term goal for Singer. It may, of course, be questioned whether Singer can have even this as his long-term goal; after all, it is possible to conceive of circumstances in which applying the principle of equality would not satisfy Singer's theory of act-utilitarianism. The best result for all affected may require that we *ignore* the principle of equality.[40] For example, if great suffering could be alleviated by capitulating to certain racist or sexist demands that would generate less evil than the good generated by non-capitulation, Singer would be committed to abandoning the principle of utility. In any event, even if the principle of equality is applied in all circumstances—either because they are consistent with the principle of equality or because Singer simply ignores any conflicts—that application does not assure that institutionalized animal exploitation will be abolished. Indeed, as I noted above, Singer's own application of the principle of equality leads him to the conclusion that experimentation with animals (or humans) may be permissible when the consequences so indicate, and that the eating of free-range animals that have been killed "painlessly" is morally justifiable. So, Singer's theory fits the model of new welfarism in the sense that Singer rejects the classical animal welfare view that animals are solely means to human ends. He does not, however, embrace an abolitionist point of view that is espoused by many of the new welfarists as a long-term goal.

Singer's theory also fits the model of new welfarism in that Singer argues that rights theories cannot provide any guidance for practical and incremental implementation of the theory. For example, in discussing the nature of ethics, Singer derides rights theory as "an ideal system which is all very noble in theory but no good in practice."[41] Singer claims that deontological approaches to ethics (e.g., rights theories) have to "rescue" themselves from their inapplicability to moral issues in the world through the introduction of "complexities," such as formulating detailed rules or establishing ranking structures for rules. He argues that utilitarianism starts not with rules but with goals and thus has greater normative specificity because actions are prescribed or proscribed based on "the extent to which they further these goals." Utilitarianism, Singer argues, is "untouched by the complexities" required to make deontological moral theories—including rights theory—applicable in concrete moral situations.[42]

Putting aside for the moment the question whether utilitarianism is really a theory "untouched by [the] complexities" that plague deontological theories, what is interesting is how Singer establishes differential presumptions that must be met by the positions he describes. Either the deontological theory is *presumed* to be incapable of application because it consists of rules that are too vague and that will conflict, or it is *presumed* to contain numerous controversial and complicated moral rules or similarly problematic rules about ranking moral rules. Utilitarianism, on the other hand, is *presumed* to be a theory that more cleanly generates normative guidance without such complexities, since the only relevant moral criterion is supposedly simple and more simply applied: does the action foster the goal that is identified (happiness, pleasure, preference satisfaction, whatever)? According to Singer, "The classical utilitarian regards an action as right if it produces as much or more of an increase in the happiness of all affected by it than any alternative actions, and wrong if it does not."[43]

So, according to Singer, when we encounter a rights theory, we should assume that it is either useless or that it provides normative guidance only through the use of complex and controversial subrules, sub-subrules, and so on. A utilitarian theory, on Singer's view, portends no similar traps. This view is, however, highly questionable in light of the particular difficulties that have been identified with utilitarian moral theory.

As a general matter, Singer's theory, like all utilitarian theories (including classical animal welfare), requires largely normative determinations about the consequences of actions, about the characterization of those consequences in terms of their status as a benefit (and to whom) and as a detriment (and to whom), and about the degree or weight of the particular benefit or detriment. Indeed, Singer's argument for the principle of equality really amounts to no more than a plea to recognize, as a consequence of our actions, that animals suffer in ways that are similar to our own and that this recognition carries certain moral implications. Particular cases, however, will produce great uncertainty and controversy regarding these combined empirical and normative judgments. People who agree with Singer's principle of equality may nevertheless disagree based upon differing assessments of the consequences of particular actions. As I discussed above, one may agree with the principle of equality but may still determine that the economic consequences of abolishing the meat industry, including the loss of jobs and general economic upheaval in light of the importance of that industry, outweigh the benefits to be gained by reducing the suffering of animals used for food. "This is so because, as we saw, utilitarianism, as a consequentialist theory, requires us to measure our actions in terms of a cost-benefit analysis. Now it is far from clear that such an analysis would rule out meat eating."[44]

Singer would apply his utilitarian framework in a way that takes animal interests more seriously than they have thus far been in practice, but Singer's reliance on aggregating consequences across individuals is structurally similar to what is done in classical welfarist theory, which also requires an assessment of consequences. But surely any such assessment—whether under Singer's view or that of classical welfarism—requires a prior *normative* evaluation of the moral importance of animals as well as a determination about the comparable worth of individuals. For example, Singer argues that "a rejection of speciesism does not imply that all lives are of equal worth," because, although a being's cognitive capacities (self-awareness, ability to plan ahead, and so forth) are not relevant to the infliction of pain, "these capacities are relevant to the question of taking life. . . . If we had to choose to save the life of a normal human being or an intellectually disabled human being, we would probably choose to save the life of a normal human being. . . . Normally, this will mean that if we have to choose between the life of a human being and the life of another animal we should choose to save the life of the human."[45] These determinations are certainly controversial and open to dispute even by those who agree in theory with Singer's principle of equality.

But what is most interesting about Singer's argument—that because of its inherent complexity Regan's rights-oriented approach is not amenable to providing any practical guidance—is Singer's failure to appreciate that his own theory does not ensure that short-term efforts to achieve his long-term goal of equality are in accord with the principle of act-utility. Even if one accepts Singer's theory of equal consideration for equal interests as the desired long-term goal, it is clear that in 1996 there is virtually no prospect that any significant portion of society will accept that principle. In order for Singer to achieve this long-term goal, he, like Regan, needs a prescription for day-to-day incremental motion toward that long-term goal.

Singer is an act-utilitarian, and act-utilitarianism requires that moral agents choose from the available options that which will maximize the desired consequences for the largest number of those affected. This would suggest that animal advocates who have the long-term goal of equal consideration or rights choose means that also satisfy the principle of utility, that is, that animal advocates should choose the means that maximize the desired consequences for the largest number. Singer may reply that he cannot subject competing means to such analyses, because, in a situation like the present, when animals are treated as the *property* of humans, all available choices are speciesist.[46] But that would not stop Singer from asking which among competing choices most minimizes animal pain or suffering. For example, if animal advocates have a choice of pursuing legislation that will eliminate all battery cages used for egg production or legislation that will create animal care committees, composed almost exclusively of vivisectors, to review and approve experiments on animals, it would seem to be better, from Singer's viewpoint as an act-utilitarian, to pursue the former because, as long as the chances of getting either law enacted are relatively equal, the egg battery ban will surely minimize suffering more than will a law that merely ensures that vivisectors will review the projects of other vivisectors in order to assure that the vivisection is "humane."

But nowhere does Singer say that animal advocates, when confronted with choosing which incremental measure to use on the road to animal welfare, ought to choose the measure that most minimizes animal suffering or that decreases animal suffering with greater certainty or that satisfies some criterion or criteria. Singer may believe that conventional welfarist reform is necessary for achieving the long-term goal of equal consideration, and that success of the venture does not hinge on subjecting individual means to some principle of utility. Indeed, Singer has stated that it is "inevitable" that animal advocates employ varied means, including conventional welfarist means, to achieve the long-term goal of equal consideration (or rights).[47] And more recently, Singer has stated that he is "prepared to support any measure that reduces the suffering of animals or enables them to meet their needs more fully."[48] These comments suggest that Singer regards welfarist reforms *as a class* to be necessary to achieve the long-term goal of equal consideration for equal interests. But if so, Singer would no longer be an act-utilitarian, because that sort of consequentialism requires that individual acts or individual means to the long-term goal be assessed with respect to the principle of utility. Instead, Singer would be a rule-utilitarian because he would be judging actions by their membership in a *class* of acts that he thinks necessary to achieve the long-term goal. But once Singer gives up any requirement that animal advocates pursue the option that will most minimize suffering (or more certainly minimize suffering given the problems with accurately predicting consequences) and instead supports "any measure that reduces" suffering, then his position, as a practical matter, becomes indistinguishable from that of a classical welfarist.

It is surely understandable that Singer, a utilitarian, is interested first and foremost in reducing or minimizing suffering. But it is perplexing that he apparently sees no need to urge the adoption of an analytical framework that ensures that animal advocacy organizations will pursue measures that, when compared to alternatives, reduce suffering *more*. This is particularly odd in light of Singer's argument that his book *Animal Liberation* is one extended application of act-utilitarianism to specific instances of animal exploitation—something that Singer does in the abstract but that he refuses to do in assessing efforts that are intended by their new welfarist supporters to reduce pain and suffering. Consequently, Singer appears, through his support of reformist approaches, *not* to apply the principle of act-utility to particular efforts to achieve the long-term goal of equality, but to endorse reformist measures as a general matter. This is, of course, not to say that Singer would prefer less radical measures to more radical ones. It is, however, to say that Singer's philosophy, translated into the practical realities of daily animal advocacy, has been interpreted correctly as a mandate to pursue reformist measures with little or no thought to the relative merits of competing reformist measures.

Moreover, Singer seems to share the new welfarists' assumption that some sort of causal relationship pertains between incremental welfarist measures and the achievement of the principle of equality, although he never argues explicitly for this view. For example, he states that a boycott of factory-farmed meat may eventually lead to the elimination of meat products altogether.[49] But it is difficult to understand how this will occur. Singer has already argued that it is morally permissible to eat meat from free-range animals who have been killed painlessly and whose deaths are followed by the births of other animals who will have equally pleasant lives. It is, therefore, difficult to understand how a boycott of factory-farmed meat will lead to anything more than a free-range meat industry.

In addition, reformist measures, such as the elimination of particularly cruel farming practices, actually *reaffirm* the underlying principles that make animal exploitation possible in the first instance. Classical animal welfare is based on instrumentalism, or the notion that animals are means to human ends, and the only difference between these theories is the level of concern to be accorded to animal interests. But *all* forms of animal welfare—even the most generous—assume that nonhumans are, for all intents and purposes, the *slaves* of humans. It is, therefore, somewhat mystifying that Singer thinks continued endorsement of reformist measures, even strong reformist measures, can do anything more than reinforce the status of animals as chattels or slaves of human property owners. In any event, Singer has failed to address this issue and seems content to have animal advocates pursue reformist measures as long as these measures are reasonably thought to reduce suffering, even if other, arguably equally achievable measures, would reduce suffering even more. Unlike at least some of the new welfarists, Singer does not label these reformist measures as animal "rights" measures, except that he uses "rights" rhetorically to describe *any* measure he thinks will reduce animal suffering.

Finally, Singer, like the new welfarists, sees no inconsistency in endorsing reformist measures rather than abolitionist ones, because he does not believe that animals have rights. Therefore, he sees no problem in sacrificing the rights of animals today in the hope that animals tomorrow will have rights. Singer's stated views confirm both that he endorses a view similar to new welfarism and that he fails to apply his own theory to the practice of animal advocacy. At the 1990 march in Washington, Singer stated that the animal movement needed to be "flexible" and that this flexibility would require "different groups, some pursuing short-term goals to stop at least some of the suffering now, and others dedicated to educating people for the long-term goal of animal liberation." Singer, like Garner or Jasper and Nelkin, seems to think that there is no problem in having short-term methods that are very different from long-term goals, and that no argument is needed for this position. In light of Singer's theory that the morally right action requires us to do that which will maximize the preference satisfaction of all affected—human and nonhuman—it is difficult to understand Singer's prescription. For example, certain groups may propose short-term goals that supposedly stop suffering but do not do so as well or as extensively as other methods. May we not criticize ineffectual or less effective strategies as not satisfying Singer's principle of act-utility? Apparently not, for Singer states that "we must co-operate with groups that follow different strategies from our own, and use different methods. We must avoid wasting our energies attacking each other. We must focus on the real enemies, the exploiters of animals."[50]

Regrettably, when animal "rights" advocates are pursuing welfarist short-term goals, it is sometimes difficult to tell exactly who the animal "exploiters" are. Singer "sees the movement as a political and not as a philosophical entity." But a political "entity" needs some sort of ideology or philosophy. Singer is certainly not denying this. He has a philosophy that animates his political action, and that philosophy is a form of welfarism. He argues that the animal movement ought to seek to minimize animal suffering, although he offers absolutely no guidance in determining what, as an empirical matter, will reduce suffering to any significant degree or, given that Singer is a utilitarian, which of the available suffering-minimizing choices will reduce suffering *the most*. Instead, he urges only that we try to minimize suffering, and he cautions that we ought not to criticize efforts that have as their declared purpose the reduction of suffering. Singer admits that his theory is not a rights theory, but for "political" reasons he calls it a rights theory nonetheless.

But then, some might argue that such is the nature of politics.

Confusion About Practice

In Chapter One, I noted that modern animal advocates are more confrontational than their predecessors and that the character of activism on behalf of animals changed dramatically in the late 1970s and through the 1980s. Although this activism seemed qualitatively different from its welfarist predecessor, upon closer examination it is clear that from the outset the modern animal rights movement has never really embraced the rejection of instrumentalism that is supposed to characterize the movement. Instead, these advocates have seen animal rights as a long-term goal to be reached by the same type of welfarist reform that has characterized past efforts.

For example, Henry Spira's early efforts represented an aggressive, *abolitionist* approach, but Spira very early on adopted what Jasper and Nelkin call the "pragmatic" view, which they connect with Singer's philosophy and Spira's activism.[51] Spira concluded that his abolitionist efforts up until 1979, although highly successful, were "largely symbolic, involving a few thousand animals."[52] He became willing to *reform* institutionalized cruelty. Spira adopted a more welfarist approach in undertaking a more ambitious project—the use of animals in cosmetics and product testing. He targeted the Draize test, which is intended to ascertain the irritancy of a substance and involves applying the substance to be tested to the unanesthetized eyes or genitalia of animals, usually rabbits. Spira chose the Draize test as a target in part because even experimenters generally in favor of animal use were critical of the test and believed that alternatives to it were feasible, and because the purpose of the test—to produce additional cosmetics and consumer products—was clearly trivial. After researching the issue, Spira approached Revlon and requested that it fund research into alternatives to the Draize test. Revlon politely did nothing, and Spira organized a coalition of over four hundred organizations, including traditional welfarist groups such as the Humane Society of the United States (HSUS) and the American Society for the Prevention of Cruelty to Animals (ASPCA), as well as antivivisection organizations, to end the tests.[53] In May 1980, Spira's coalition organized a demonstration outside Revlon's New York office, and in the fall of 1980, the coalition organized demonstrations against Revlon in Britain, Canada, and Australia. By December 1980, Revlon capitulated to the Spira coalition and provided a $750,000 grant to Rockefeller University for the purpose of developing alternatives. According to Spira, the Revlon campaign "transformed the search for alternatives from some kind of flaky antivivisectionist issue to something that received large-scale support from a multi-billion dollar corporation and was linked with one of the most respected medical institutions in the country."[54] Spira then approached other companies willing to cooperate with his coalition. For example, Avon Products, Inc., contributed funds to establish a center for alternatives research at Johns Hopkins University.

Spira then directed his coalition toward another testing target—the LD50 test. This test, which is intended to determine the acute toxicity of substances, involves force-feeding animals—usually rabbits, dogs, rats, or mice—the substance to be tested, until the lethal dose (hence "LD") for 50 percent of the animals is ascertained. Spira chose this target in part because at least some segments of the chemical, drug, and cosmetics industries had already indicated dissatisfaction with the test, which is expensive and involves inherently inexact extrapolations in order to assess chronic effects on human beings. This time Spira's aim was not to get industry to fund alternatives studies at universities; he believed that "the real expertise for reduction and replacement might reside in the corporations themselves."[55] Spira approached Procter & Gamble, Inc., and indicated that he wanted the company to develop a model internal program to reduce the numbers of animals used in toxicity testing, to find alternatives for those tests, and to publicize the results of their efforts, thereby persuading other companies to follow. Procter & Gamble agreed, and by 1984, according to Spira, it had reduced its own animal use, and other companies had followed as well.[56]

It is important to understand how Spira's efforts with respect to product testing differed from his earlier efforts to stop the experiments at the Museum of Natural History or his efforts to secure the repeal of the pound seizure law in New York. In the latter, Spira sought to abolish the objectionable practice altogether; in the former, he pursued the admittedly reformist, welfarist strategy of refinement, reduction, and replacement. This did not mean that Spira had changed his philosophy; indeed, Spira remained committed throughout to the long-term abolition of animal exploitation, but he became willing to use animal welfare to achieve animal rights.

Spira employed the long-term-rights/short-term-welfare approach in other contexts as well. Later in the 1980s, Spira, who had combined his various coalitions into Animal Rights International (ARI), turned his attention to farm animals and charged chicken producer Frank Perdue with abusing his chickens and misrepresenting the conditions in which they were raised and slaughtered. Specifically, Spira pointed to over-crowded conditions that caused cannibalism, disease, and stress in the chickens, as well as the debeaking of chicks with a hot knife. Although Spira recognized that "animal rights and eating animals don't mesh,"[57] he sought to "reduce pain and suffering" by instituting certain reforms in the meat industry. It was clear, however, that Spira had not changed his long-term goal of eliminating all animal exploitation. Spira remained steadfastly committed to the long-term abolition—and not merely re-form—of the institutionalized exploitation of animals for food and clothing and in experiments. In the face of criticism that he had "sold out" on the issue of vegetarianism, Spira replied, "My dream is that people will come to view eating an animal as cannibalism."[58]

Despite Spira's long-term commitment to abolition, his short-term welfarist strategy was criticized by animal advocates who believed that it was inappropriate to pursue what was essentially a welfarist strategy. Spira's biggest critic has been PETA, which claimed to seek the immedi-ate abolition of all animal testing. PETA claimed that Spira's strategy of gradual reduction of testing was inadequate and conflicted with the animal rights position. PETA formed its own Compassion Campaign, which eclipsed Spira's efforts so much that most people who have be-come active in the animal movement since 1988 do not even know who Spira is, and they do not realize that he, rather than PETA, pioneered efforts against animal testing. PETA called for a boycott of companies that still tested on animals. In addition, PETA used undercover inves-tigations, direct action, and shareholder initiatives against companies that did animal tests. According to PETA, the amounts allocated by various companies for alternatives testing was inadequate; the reduc-tion in numbers claimed by Spira was overestimated; and certain com-panies with which Spira was working, most notably Procter & Gamble, had actually *increased* the numbers of animals used in testing. Moreover, PETA opposed Spira's efforts to get Perdue to make poultry raising and slaughtering more "humane." A 1989 *New York Times* article stated that although Spira's long-term goals are "not . . . less revolutionary than those of the most radical animal-rights advocates . . . [Spira] has shown no qualms about infuriating many animal-rights groups by praising companies that continue to test products on animals as long as he be-lieves that they are working to develop alternatives."[59] In particular, PETA's Newkirk stated that "[Spira] is hobnobbing in the halls with our enemy. Six or seven years ago, we had a lot in common. Everything he did then was putting gravel down for other people to pave roads, which is crucial. But I think Henry was deceived by the industry response. [He] was unable to cut himself loose from the mire of becoming an industry mediator."[60] According to Peter Singer, Spira's efforts had meant that "millions of animals . . . escaped acute pain and suffering because of the work already done on alternatives."[61] Newkirk was unimpressed: "The search for alternatives is a quite transparent ploy to maintain the status quo."[62]

PETA, however, despite its flair for attention-grabbing media events and its generally confrontational tactics, was and is no more (though no less) radical on a substantive basis than Spira, and has always accepted the view that although the long-term strategy is abolition, the short term may require reformist compromise. Both Spira and PETA espouse a radical rights ideology, but seek to effect change within the system. This inevitably requires the acceptance of reformist measures, which are then seen by these "radicals" as necessary stepping stones to the abolition of exploitation. So, although PETA and Spira have long-term goals that Jasper and Nelkin label "fundamentalist," they both adopt tactics that are "pragmatic."

The criminal prosecution of Taub was undoubtedly important, but the case itself had nothing to do with animal rights per se. Taub was prosecuted for violating the Maryland anticruelty law, and nothing more. As others have observed, Taub was not prosecuted for crippling monkeys; he was charged with failing to provide proper veterinary care to the animals. The anticruelty case "centered solely on his treatment and care of his monkeys rather than on the merits of his research."[63] In short, the case had nothing to do with *what* Taub was doing, but everything to do with *how* he was doing it. The Taub case involved a prosecution for a misdemeanor under an anticruelty statute. The case did not and *could not* make new law. Admittedly, most prosecutors would have deferred to Taub's "scientific expertise" and would not have prosecuted him even for the husbandry violations with which he was charged. The *fact* of the prosecution was, therefore, highly unusual in and of itself but not in and of itself enough to effect any systemic change. PETA portrayed the prosecution as the beginning of a movement challenge to vivisection, a movement that would use anticruelty law to challenge vivisection *as a practice*; but that portrayal fails to mention that the prosecution *never challenged* Taub's right to perform that *type* of experiment and maintained only that Taub could not inflict pain and suffering that went beyond what was necessary to exploit the animals in the way that

Taub had chosen. The prosecutor did not maintain that it violated the law per se to perform somatosensory deafferentation experiments with live animals or even just with macaques, which would have been a rather shattering development from a legal point of view.

Rather, the authorities were concerned with how Taub was performing the experiments and whether he was providing the required level of care. And this level of care, which limited how the prosecution could interpret "cruelty," was the minimum needed to ensure that the animals were good research subjects. In a sense, the authorities were prosecuting Taub for being "careless" or "wasteful" of his animal property. Had Taub done the *exact* same experiments in the *exact* same way, except that he provided adequate and minimal veterinary care and a sanitary environment, the Taub case would never have gotten past the desk of the local police sergeant for one simple but important reason: the experiments, however horrible, were not illegal. What was illegal was that Taub's lab was untidy and he was not providing adequate veterinary care to the animals. But there was nothing illegal about crippling the monkeys or applying "negative stimuli," such as a flame from a cigarette lighter, to unanesthetized animals. There was no question in the Taub case of what "humane" treatment meant as an abstract matter; the issue was not whether Taub was inflicting unspeakable pain and distress on these animals in the course of deafferentation experiments. The only question was whether Taub was doing anything to them that was not justified by the experiments themselves, anything that went beyond the use, including deafferentation, legitimated by the experiments' protocol. Apart from the clandestine infiltration that produced the prosecution, and the admittedly unusual decision by the state of Maryland to prosecute a research scientist, the Taub case was an ordinary anticruelty case, all of which assume that animals are our property and that they may be exploited as long as we do not impose wholly gratuitous, socially useless suffering or pain on them. The question was only whether Taub's treatment of the animals fell below the level required to get reliable data from research animals. In light of the status of the animals as property, that low level of treatment is the *only* conduct that anticruelty statutes can address.

This is not to deny that PETA used the Taub case effectively to press its long-term goal of abolishing, rather than regulating, animal experimentation.[64] But it was clear that although PETA endorsed the long-term goal of abolition, it also acknowledged that short-term welfarist reform could, in Newkirk's words, act as a "springboard into animal rights." Nothing about the short-term Taub campaign as a *political* matter distinguished it from the concerns of the more traditional welfarists. In other words, animal advocates did not use the Taub matter to press for any legislative demands that transcended the *precise type of demands that were then being made by welfarists* before the Taub matter arose. Animal advocates did not use Taub to make legislative demands that would involve the abolition of certain types of experiments, such as the ones Taub was conducting. Rather, PETA and other animal advocates used the case to focus attention on the abuse of animals used in research—an issue that had been highlighted in the 1970s by welfarist groups such as AWI—and to argue for *reform* of the oversight system. For example, at the hearings on the Taub case, Pacheco indicated that PETA had three short-term goals: (1) providing more information to the public about the use of animals in experiments; (2) eliminating statutory exemptions from anticruelty laws for research scientists using animals; and (3) reforming the system of oversight of animal experimentation through elimination of the peer review system as the primary means of criticizing the use of animals in science. Pacheco made it clear that although he was "opposed to live-animal experimentation," he strongly supported "any measures that will help alleviate or eliminate suffering."[65] He then stated that he supported moderate legislation that was pending before the committee. Blum notes that "Pacheco didn't bother to find out if Taub, if pressed, would have improved conditions. . . . [H]e thought whistleblowing might have a more dramatic effect." Pacheco stated, "I was trying to clean up the whole system. If I'd gone to [Taub], at best I might have cleaned up one lab and gotten myself fired."[66] This statement makes clear that PETA regarded the Taub case as an opportunity to make changes in the mechanism that regulated animal experimentation, and not as a forum for aggressively urging its immediate abolition or the abolition of any aspects of the practice of vivisection. PETA's long-term goal (abolition) differed significantly from AWI's long-term goal (the creation of an effective system to regulate animal experimentation), but they shared the short-term goal of reforming the system. Indeed, nothing about PETA's political use of the Taub material for short-term reform precluded avowed animal welfarists' condemning what occurred with the Silver Spring monkeys or criticizing the federal oversight of grant recipients like Taub. In testimony before Congress, groups that supported animal use joined with PETA in criticizing Taub. For example, AWI's Christine Stevens was highly critical of the federal oversight mechanism that had failed to monitor the animal use in Taub's laboratory.[67] The Fund for Animals also testified, and its representative made clear that although the Fund was "not opposed to all animal research," there were "problems that USDA has in their inspection system."[68]

Most striking, however, was the support offered to PETA by HSUS, arguably the most conservative bastion of animal welfare. The HSUS representative, Michael W. Fox, one of the veterinary experts Pacheco had taken through Taub's lab, not only criticized Taub's treatment of his monkeys in the congressional hearings, he also provided one of the affidavits that was used to obtain the warrant to raid Taub's lab in the first place. Nevertheless, HSUS was not then, is not now, and never has been opposed to all use of animals in experiments. At the same congressional hearings at which Fox showed slides of the Silver Spring monkeys and criticized both Taub and the federal regulators responsible for oversight of animal use, he spoke in favor of legislation, then pending before Congress, that instituted animal care committees and required pain relief during experimentation unless withholding relief was scientifically "necessary," and urged its adoption because it would not jeopardize "legitimate and necessary animal research" and would "strike an acceptable balance between the needs of scientific research and the concerns of the mainstream animal welfare movement."[69] Fox argued on the basis not only of ethical concerns but of a "scientific imperative because animals that are not optimally cared for will jeopardize scientific progress."[70] Andrew Rowan, another moderate animal welfarist, also decried Taub's treatment of his animals.

Indeed, the Taub case indicated clearly that from the outset of the modern animal protection movement in the United States even "radical" groups have sought what political theorists call "insider" status; that is, animal advocates have sought to influence the legal and political processes as participants *within* established political and legal institutions. As Robert Garner has correctly pointed out, however, insider status is "largely dependent upon a group being perceived as moderate and respectable."[71] Garner claims correctly that most animal organizations, with the exception of clandestine groups like the Animal Liberation Front, want and seek the insider status that Garner argues persuasively can only be had by those willing to compromise or forgo the radical message of animal rights.[72]

The essentially conservative nature of the Taub case has not gone unnoticed by at least some commentators. For example, in *Monkey Wars*, science writer Deborah Blum observes that "for all of its impact . . . it's important to keep Silver Spring in context. It was a turning point, beyond a doubt, but it was hardly the birth of animal welfare movements in this county."[73] As Blum points out, "Pacheco's techniques at Silver

Spring had been tried earlier," and "PETA was not the first group of activists to gain information by masquerade."[74] She argues that "PETA had really only accelerated things"[75] and that conservative welfarists such as Stevens and Shirley McGreal of the International Primate Protection League had long been concerned about animal abuse in laboratories. McGreal had even agreed to join as the lead plaintiff in PETA's subsequent effort to get custody of the Silver Spring monkeys after Taub's conviction was reversed.

If there is an enduring legacy of the Taub case, it is not the awakening of the United States or the world to the horrors of vivisection as a general matter; it is, instead, the 1985 amendments to the federal Animal Welfare Act. During the 1981 hearings, Congress had before it several bills, one of which sought to create animal care committees to monitor animal experiments as well as to ensure that animals used in experiments receive adequate anesthesia or analgesia unless scientific "necessity" dictates otherwise. This legislation was supported by all of the welfarist organizations that condemned Taub—and it was supported by PETA as well. The bill was modified, but its essential provisions remained intact, and it was passed in 1985 as an amendment to the federal Animal Welfare Act. As I discuss later, the Animal Welfare Act is a law that does not give any rights to animals, that is not enforced, and that is used primarily by the biomedical establishment as a public relations device to assure an otherwise uniformed public that the use of animals in American laboratories is carefully monitored.

Interestingly, Rowan argues that "the distinction between Spira on one hand and Ingrid Newkirk of PETA on the other is not a matter of basic philosophy—both espouse a strong animal 'rights' position that holds that animals should not be used as tools for scientific investigation, meat production or pleasure." Rather, Spira and Newkirk simply "use different tactics when seeking to persuade society to move toward their world view." Spira tries to negotiate with animal exploiters and, when unsuccessful, may use tactics such as product boycotts. When he succeeds, Spira allows the exploiter to present the animal welfare initiative in the best possible light and not as a concession to Spira. "As a result," Rowan tells us, "Spira has built a reputation as an opponent whose word can be trusted."[76]

PETA's tactics, on the other hand, are different, according to Rowan. Unlike Spira, who tries to negotiate and is cautious not to be confrontational, PETA uses confrontational rhetoric and portrays the exploiter as "morally suspect or as downright immoral." And PETA "acts as a spokesperson for the relatively small number of animal activists who engage in acts of vandalism, property destruction and theft of incriminating materials." But these are, Rowan contends, matters of "political tactics" and not matters of "basic philosophy." And this leads Rowan to conclude that the distinction between animal rights and animal welfare is "neither accurate nor valid."[77]

Rowan is correct to observe that Spira and Newkirk are agreed on "basic philosophy" concerning the rights/welfare question. PETA maintains that abolition is the ultimate goal but that animal welfare reforms are "sometimes necessary" and are "steps in the right direction." Similarly, Spira claims that though reform "is basically about strategies, [abolition] is the ultimate goal." According to Spira, "the two aren't mutually contradictory." Spira notes that in social movements progress is made incrementally, through continual reform. "If you push for all or nothing, what you get is nothing."[78] And not only do Spira and Newkirk agree on "basic philosophy," they have also represented as much in explicitly endorsing the notion that welfarist reform is, on a moral level, acceptable and is, on a practical level, *the only way* of achieving the ultimate long-term goal of animal rights.

Finally, as I mentioned in Chapter One, commentators have agreed that two practical aspects of the modern animal movement differentiate it from its welfarist predecessors. The first aspect was the involvement in the movement of clandestine organizations such as the ALF, which some commentators have pointed to as expressing the position that "animals have inherent, inviolable rights."[79] The most notable of ALF actions involved the removal of videotapes from the University of Pennsylvania head-injury laboratory. Despite the "radical" action used to procure the tapes, the campaign that followed had a very reformist tone. Again, animal advocates did not for the most part use the purloined tapes to mount a campaign against vivisection *per se* (although some advocates undoubtedly held and promoted that view); rather, they focused attention on violations of federal laws and regulations (for the most part technicalities) and attacked the scientific methodology as flawed. Just as in the Taub case, supposedly "radical" groups like PETA joined forces with avowedly conservative groups such as HSUS and AWI. For example, AWI's Stevens criticized the laboratory for its filthy conditions and violations of the federal Animal Welfare Act and NIH regulations. Stevens supported PETA's efforts to close the laboratory, and even supported PETA's request to NIH that it include a neutral third party to view the videotapes that had been removed from the Penn laboratory. But Stevens cautioned that the ALF "seeks to discredit all animal experimentation. I want to emphasize this point to distinguish the ALF philosophy from that of groups . . . which seek reform, not abolition."[80] Again, PETA and other more progressive advocates argued that though their long-term goal was the abolition of all or most experimentation, the problems with the particular experiments at Penn involved violations of federal and state animal welfare laws and regulations, poorly conducted science, and a waste of taxpayer funds. All of these concerns pointed in the direction of "moderate and respectable" short-term changes in federal oversight, but not toward any fundamental changes concerning the acceptability of the practices involved.[81]

The other aspect of the modern animal movement that supposedly differentiates it from its welfarist predecessor is the rejection of the corporate animal charity in favor of grassroots organization. The commentators are correct to connect radicalism on an ideological level with grassroots organization, but they fail to note that the grassroots approach was short-lived. The animal advocates of the late 1970s and early 1980s had little use for the centralized approach, but the character of the American movement changed dramatically in the second half of the 1980s, when the animal rights movement became more centrally focused on a handful of national organizations. This change was facilitated by PETA, which began as a grassroots group but soon relinquished control to PETA "headquarters," with all policies and campaigns determined by Newkirk and Pacheco. As Lawrence Finsen and Susan Finsen have noted, PETA initially "sponsored chapters around the country, and many were highly visible in their regions."[82] Indeed, PETA chapters were often involved in action that was every bit as visible and controversial as that supported by Newkirk and Pacheco.[83] But by the mid-1980s, "PETA had decided to close its chapters." Finsen and Finsen note in connection with PETA's decision to close its chapters in favor of top-down, more centralized organization that "of particular concern to PETA's leadership was the problem of control of what the organization does when offices are scattered throughout the country, staffed mainly by volunteers who are not answerable in the end to an employer."[84] Of course, that is precisely what grassroots organization is—there is little or no elite hierarchy.

In an interview with Finsen and Finsen, Pacheco stated that the chapters were closed because grassroots activists often fail to understand that "the world is run on politics, decisions are financial. That's the world that needs to be addressed. We're in the business, figuratively speaking, of selling compassion." On Pacheco's view, ideology is unimportant; it is not necessary that people adopt the philosophy of animal rights: "They just have to care."[85] The problem is that no one—including those who use animals in experiments and those who exploit them in other ways—would deny *caring* about animals or that it is a moral imperative to treat them *humanely*. This notion of the movement as a "business" is reflected in the increased commercialization of the movement; for example, PETA's monthly magazine featured Alex Pacheco modeling nonanimal clothing accessories designed for everything from "Monday morning 'power'" meetings to Saturday night "nightclub" outings. There is never mention of any philosophical ideas or ideologies, let alone discussion. There is no serious discussion of grassroots campaigns or advice on how local activists can really effect meaningful, institutional reforms. Instead, activists are encouraged, for example, to throw fund-raising parties for PETA: "Hey! Fundraising can be a blast," says the article.[86]

In any event, PETA's closure of its chapters was significant not only because it ended several dynamic groups that had made significant contributions to educational and other efforts in their local areas, but because it allowed the large national welfare groups ostensibly to embrace animal rights rhetoric without making any significant changes in the essentially welfarist orientation of the organizations. By 1988, approximately two-thirds of the money collected for animal causes went to national groups; in 1995, that figure had risen to "roughly three quarters."[87] And Animal Rights Mobilization, which acts as a clearing house for grassroots groups, reports that, since 1993, 25 percent of the 365 "action alerts" it sends out to grassroots groups have been returned and that groups are being "squeezed out financially" by large, national groups.[88] The New Jersey Animal Rights Alliance (NJARA), which began life as PETA's New Jersey chapter but was then closed by PETA, reports that approximately $400,000 in animal dollars is contributed by New Jersey residents to national organizations that not only do little to assist the grassroots but in some cases actively frustrate NJARA's campaigns in New Jersey.[89] As Finsen and Finsen have noted, the vision of the movement oriented toward the grassroots "seems somewhat contrary to the vision of PETA, which has become more centralized, more 'businesslike' over the years."[90] Although PETA closed its local grassroots chapters, it has, in more recent years, engaged in an international expansion, and now has corporate offices in Canada, Great Britain, Italy, the Netherlands, and Germany. The leaders of the large, national organizations meet annually at an event called the Summit for the Animals, but this event has been particularly noteworthy for not producing agreement on any sort of political agenda, and many grassroots animal advocates do not acknowledge any summit authority to set movement policy.

This is not to say that PETA and other national organizations do not cooperate with local organizations. Indeed, a number of national groups have one or more "outreach" people whose primary job is to interact with local groups. Almost all of the large animal advocacy organizations provide some sort of financial support to local activist efforts, as well as literature and professional expertise, though this support is usually nominal at best. Worse, whatever support or cooperation is lent often comes with a "price": the appropriation by the national organization of any case on which the local group may be working. For example, in one case in which I was involved, a local organization defined a campaign and did all of the preparatory work without any help from the national organizations. When the local group approached a national group for help in publicizing the matter, the latter obliged, holding a press conference at which the national group made no mention of the local group. Sometimes, the corporate imperatives of national groups have a negative impact on local efforts. For example, in another case, a local group collected over thirty thousand signatures to hold a referendum on a deer hunt. They needed several thousand names more, and they asked a national animal advocacy organization for the names of its members in that particular area. The national group refused, claiming that it was doing a fund-raising appeal in that area and for that reason could not release member names.

Perhaps most revealing of the change in character of the movement, from the standpoint of the connection Garner draws between radicalism and grassroots organization, is the negative attitude that national groups now openly display toward grassroots activism. Until recently, it was considered politic on the part of national leaders to nod favorably in the direction of grassroots efforts, and it has been rare to find national leaders explicitly attacking the concept of grassroots activism per se. This changed in 1995, when Don Barnes of the National Anti-Vivisection Society (NAVS) argued in an essay in the *Animals' Agenda* that it was "foolish and divisive" to counsel animal advocates to give financial support to local efforts instead of national groups.[91] He published a similar essay in the *NAVS Bulletin*. Barnes condemned as "grassroots elitism" the criticism of national groups by local activists. Barnes's solution was that everyone should join a national organization. He stated that "if you agree with the philosophy, tactics, and strategies of a national group, join it and support it. If you do not agree with the philosophy, tactics, and strategies of a national group, join anyway and work to make changes within the organization."[92] This is, of course, a prescription for the death of grassroots activism, and Barnes's essay provides further support for the notion that at least some movement leaders have profoundly reactionary views about ideology and the relationship between theory and practice.

Finally, all of the commentators have argued that the rejection of instrumentalism represented by the animal rights position is historically and ideologically related to other progressive social movements that have rejected the instrumental treatment of other humans, namely, people of color and women.[93] Unfortunately, the animal rights movement has for the most part never, as a matter of theory or practice, acknowledged the relationship between the animal rights movement and other progressive social causes. This is in part because the champions of welfarist reform, who are embraced by the rights advocates as well, have tended to be political conservatives. For example, the undisputed champion of American animal welfare is Kansas senator Robert Dole, who has either sponsored or played a major role in virtually every piece of welfarist reform initiated since the 1960s.[94]

Moreover, in recent years, the promotion of animal causes has increasingly relied on sexist and racist imagery. For example, the fur campaign has from the outset been tainted by sexism. The trapping or ranching of animals for fur is certainly barbaric and immoral, but fur is no more or less morally obnoxious than leather or wool. The primary difference is that furs are worn by women, and wool and leather, although also worn by women, are worn by virtually all men. Fur became an early target of the animal rights movement, and from the outset the imagery was, not unexpectedly, sexist. An early poster shows a pair of women's legs (no torso, no head, just legs) clothed in black stockings and spiked high heels. The woman is dragging a fur coat, which is trailing blood. The caption reads, "It takes up to 40 dumb animals to make a fur coat. But only one to wear it." And in the nineties, PETA has promoted its "I'd rather go naked than wear fur" ads, featuring billboards with naked models, as well as demonstrations in which women appear naked.[95] In one particularly notable example, a PETA staff person "stripped" on Howard Stern's radio station in order to make her point about fur, and Stern described each phase of the event in considerable detail. Unfortunately, some animal advocates have harassed women wearing furs. The fur industry is certainly indefensible according to any moral standard (other than an extreme form of ethical egoism), but using sexist imagery or assaults on women to make that point is extremely problematic not only because it is violent but because men wearing their expensive wool suits need not worry about animal rights advocates harassing them.

And these are not the only aspects of sexism in the movement. In 1994, Patty Davis, daughter of former president Ronald Reagan, appeared naked in a *Playboy* spread and donated half of her $100,000 fee to PETA, which cohosted a party in New York City with *Playboy*. PETA issued a press release announcing that Davis "turns her other cheek in an eye-opening spread" and that "revealed in *Playboy* alongside her body is Davis' animal rights activism." This "activism" is then described: the contribution of half her fee for the *Playboy* pictorial to PETA, "her favorite charity," and her vegetarian diet, to which she attributes her "well-toned physique." The release also states that Davis was photographed naked with one of the dogs who live with *Playboy* publisher Hugh Hefner, and that the photo would be used in a PETA antifur campaign.

In August 1995, PETA announced a new campaign to encourage organ donation and to discourage the use of nonhumans in xenografts, or cross-species transplants.[96] Instead of joining efforts with an organ donation program, PETA chose to join again with *Playboy* and adopted a campaign featuring Hefner's spouse, Kimberley, a *Playboy* model, with a slogan reading, "Some People Need You Inside Them." Newspaper reports of the campaign state that although the campaign is not subtle, "PETA makes no apologies. Boasts spokesman Dan Matthews: 'Just because we are softhearted doesn't mean we can't be soft-core.' "[97] Many in the movement defend these antics, claiming that "if it helps animals, it's acceptable." This is, of course, the essence of instrumental thinking and is no different from (or better than) the claim that animal exploitation can be morally justified by claiming that "if it helps (or amuses or enriches) humans, it's acceptable." Two news reports of the PETA organ donation campaign asked, "Marketers use sex to sell cars, liquor—why not organ donation?" And on the level of a rejection of instrumentalism, this is precisely the problem: PETA is seen as a "marketer" that "sells" animal rights and does so using the very same oppressive and exploitative images and slogans that are used in the society at large. Indeed, PETA's Alex Pacheco has stated that "the only way to get through to America is to do it the same way the politicians and business people do it ... by being politically savvy and business savvy, using all the modern techniques of selling a concept and selling a philosophy." According to Pacheco, animal rights advocates are "in the business, figuratively speaking, of selling compassion."[98] The merits of the matter are, for present purposes, beside the point, which is only that these campaigns, and the philosophy that the animal movement should use "soft-core" sexism to "sell" the concept of compassion, are a far cry from a rejection of instrumentalism and an embrace of the rights of women and other disempowered groups, tactics that are supposed to distinguish the animal rights movement from its animal welfare predecessors.

There has thus far been little criticism of such sexism on the part of the national organizations, in part because *any* criticism is usually met with a response that the critic is "disloyal" or is not acting with "the best interests" of animals in mind. An exception is Feminists for Animal Rights (FAR), which did condemn the ads in their newsletter. Newkirk was removed from the FAR board of advisers.[99]

Other disempowered groups have also been made the object of exploitation in the supposed hope of reducing animal exploitation. For example, in 1994, *Animals' Agenda*, which states as its mission "informing people about animal rights and cruelty-free living," featured a story about how violence to children and other humans is connected with violence against animals.[100] The cover of the issue had a face that was half that of an African-American child and half that of a cat. The cover evoked criticism from African-Americans, and there was even a demonstration organized by African-Americans against the use of the ad on billboards in the Washington, D.C., area.[101] According to Shelton Walden, an African-American radio announcer in New York City who criticized the *Agenda* cover on the air, "The face, which was half human and half cat, not only tended to reinforce the idea that African-Americans are closer to being animals, but, more important, it reinforced the notion that it is African-Americans who are abusing both their children and their animals. It was simply insensitive and unnecessary. And it demonstrated that lurking right below the surface are some pretty traditional and reactionary attitudes."[102]

Conclusion

The origins of new welfarism may be found at both the level of theory and that of practice. On the theoretical level, the animal "rights" movement has been dominated by Peter Singer's theory, which explicitly denies that animals have rights. Singer's theory resonates with all of the key features of new welfarism. On the practical level, the seeds of new welfarism were present in the American movement from the outset. Advocates such as Henry Spira and Ingrid Newkirk, although viewed as representing very different positions, shared the same basic philosophy. They both have maintained from the outset that the abolition of institutionalized animal exploitation is the long-term goal but that it is morally acceptable and practically necessary to seek welfarist reform in the short term. Interestingly, both Spira and PETA deliberately accept Singer's utilitarian philosophy and equally deliberately reject Regan's rights theory. Singer and Spira are close allies, and Spira has acknowledged Singer as his primary intellectual influence and as the person who brought him into the movement.

CHAPTER Four

The Results of
New Welfarism
The "Animal Confusion" Movement

People concerned about nonhumans face a situation in which animals are daily exploited in the most horrendous ways, and those who object to this exploitation are powerless to do anything about it. The magnitude of animal exploitation can be overwhelming, and the resultant frustration can easily produce a mindset that says something like, "Animals are suffering, theoretical differences are irrelevant, and we have to put aside individual differences and work for the common goal." To put the matter another way, many animal advocates argue that intramovement differences are irrelevant and that, despite our differences, we must stand together against the "real" opponents—the exploiters of animals. For example, according to Peter Singer, "we must co-operate with groups that follow different strategies from our own, and use different methods. We must avoid wasting our energies attacking each other. We must focus on the real enemies, the exploiters of animals."[1]

In this chapter, I argue that new welfarism has created tremendous confusion within the animal movement, and I examine this confusion in three contexts. First, I focus on the use of animals in experiments and argue that new welfarism makes it difficult to distinguish animal advocates from animal exploiters. Second, I examine some campaigns of the modern animal rights movement in order to demonstrate that these campaigns do not promote animal rights and are instead virtually indistinguishable from animal welfare reforms of the past. Third, I discuss several instances in which a failure to distinguish rights from welfare has led to disastrous consequences for animals.

Intramovement Confusion: Who Is an Exploiter?

Once we abandon animal rights idealism in favor of a standard that requires only that we "care" or feel "compassion" toward other animals, it becomes impossible any longer to differentiate animal rights theory from welfarist notions that are accepted by virtually everyone— *including animal exploiters.* In a 1995 article in *Vegetarian Times,* investigative journalist Jack Rosenberger provided a list of organizations that purport to be animal *welfare* organizations but really promote the "interests of meat companies, trappers, hunters, furriers, and vivisectors."[2] For example, the American Animal Welfare Federation is, according to its stated position, constituted "to promote the humane use and general welfare of animals, and to educate the public about the vital distinction between animal welfare and animal rights."[3] According to a spokesperson for the organization, funding is provided by the fur, meat, and pet industries, hunting interests, and "other pro-animal-use individuals and organizations."[4] Ted Nugent, rock star and zealous defender of bow hunting, is a member of the group's board of directors. Rosenberger's list includes five other groups that ostensibly promote animal welfare but are really nothing more than trade groups for animal exploiters. Moreover, everyone—from governmental agencies such as the National Institutes of Health and the U.S. Department of Agriculture to the quasi-governmental research organizations such as the Institute for Laboratory Animal Resources and associations such as the American Meat Institute—embraces the principle of animal welfare: that animals ought to be treated "humanely" and that no "unnecessary" suffering ought to be inflicted on them.

The response of many animal advocates to this posture is not, as one might expect, to distance themselves from animal welfare. Ironically, many animal advocates interpret exploiters' embrace of animal welfare as an attempt to drive a wedge between animal rights advocates and animal welfare advocates rather than to identify their differences. Any attempt to distinguish rights from welfare is perceived to be "divisive," to threaten destruction of the movement by violating the imperative that animal advocates must all "stick together." In an attempt to avoid this disintegration, the animal protection movement no longer endorses a philosophical concept of animal rights; instead, it endorses the principle that as long as we "care" or have "compassion" for animals, then we are all walking the same road. We should, so the common wisdom goes, focus on the common "enemy": the animal "exploiter." The problem is that in some cases there may be very little difference between the position of the animal advocate and the animal exploiter. And if any difference is one of degree (more or less), how does this effect our notion that the animal rights movement is, as commentators have argued and as most animal advocates believe, *qualitatively* different from the animal welfare views that have dominated thinking about these issues since the mid-nineteenth century?

In order to illustrate the problem, consider the following seven items in light of their probable origins and where they should be placed on the exploiter–welfare-rights "scale":

1. An article entitled "Meeting the Needs of Captive Mice and their Caretakers," written by an experimenter who has had "forty years of using mice," advocates a new caging system that better meets the needs of the mice and researchers. The author argues that her caging system ensures proper confinement of laboratory animals, maximizes their "productivity," and is designed to be "adaptable to accessories concerned with research." The author reports that she has successfully "bred a number of delicate mutants as well as several strains of wild mice" in her new cage.[5]

2. In an article entitled "Arguments for Single-Caging of Rhesus Macaques: Are They Justified?" the author, a veterinarian, argues that "common arguments in justification of the traditional single-caging of rhesus macaques are often based on subjective assumptions rather than on scientific facts." The author argues that single-housing should not be allowed unless "absolutely essential" and that criteria are needed to ascertain when single housing is justified. There is no condemnation of vivisection per se or even of single-caging per se, although the author recognizes that the animals are social and should not be deprived of contact with others unless there is a good justification.[6]

3. An article entitled "Synopsis: Recognition and Alleviation of Pain and Distress in Laboratory Animals" maintains that its views are based on the assumption that "animals deserve to be free from preventable pain and stress" and that "people who use animals in research have an ethical responsibility to treat them humanely."[7]

4. A rule states that "proper use of animals, including the avoidance or minimization of discomfort, distress and pain when consistent with sound scientific practices, is imperative." The rule establishes a presumption that "procedures that cause pain and distress in human beings may cause pain or distress in other animals."[8]

5. An article entitled "Promoting Psychological Well-Being in a Biomedical Research Facility" argues against any structural change in standards and in

favor of promoting increased awareness on the part of laboratory personnel. The authors, including the director of the New England Regional Primate Center Animal Research Review Committee, maintain that "the animals are our partners in the research endeavor." The authors seek ways to "enrich" the lives of primates used in invasive experiments.[9]

6. In an article entitled "A Minimum Stress Procedure for Repeated Measurements of Nociceptive Thresholds and Analgesia," the author, a researcher who uses animals in addiction studies, indicates that such studies often require the researcher to inflict pain on animals in order to measure the effect of various drugs; this is often done by placing part of the animal's body (e.g., a rat's tail) on a hotplate. Based on an experiment he conducted with approximately seventy rats, he proposes that lower degrees of heat could be used.[10]

7. An article entitled "A New Invasiveness Scale: Its Role in Reducing Animal Distress," written by two psychologists, proposes a six-step pain scale. The lower end of the scale, level 2, which represents "laboratory experiments and field studies involving mild pain/distress and no long-term harm," includes "frequent blood sampling," "intramuscular injection, skin scraping," "negative reinforcement" such as "mild electric shock" and "brief cold water immersion," "food deprivations" that do not result in more than a 10% weight loss, "water deprivation slightly exceeding particular species' requirements (e.g., deprivation in rats of less than 18 hours)," and "procedures involving anesthetized animals with mild post-operative pain/distress and no long-term harm."[11]

All seven of these positions embody the instrumentalist view—that animals may be used as means to human ends as long as certain "safeguards" are employed—supposedly rejected by the animal rights movement. Some of the sources of these positions are, not unexpectedly, prominent supporters of institutionalized animal exploitation.

The article described at (3) is contained in the news bulletin of the Institute for Laboratory Animal Resources (ILAR), organized under the National Research Council, which advises the government on scientific issues and is administered by the National Academy of Sciences, the National Academy of Engineering, and the National Institute of Medicine. ILAR is a quasi-governmental "think tank" that addresses various issues involving animal use in experiments and develops guidelines for animal use. I strongly suspect that Singer would regard ILAR and similar organizations as in the "exploiter" camp.

The regulatory rule described at (4), which, standing alone, looks as though it could have been written by a progressive animal welfarist, is contained in the Public Health Service Policy and Government Principles

Regarding the Care and Use of Laboratory Animals, which is one source of federal regulation of animal experimentation. The rule is contained in a booklet, produced by the National Institutes of Health (NIH), that also contains the NIH *Guide for the Care and Use of Laboratory Animals.* Again, I would guess that Singer and other like-minded animal advocates would regard the National Institutes of Health and the Public Health Service as paradigmatic examples of animal "exploiters."

The article described at (2) was written by a veterinarian affiliated with the Animal Welfare Institute (AWI), which is perhaps the most important and effective of the traditional animal welfare organizations. The article described is contained in an issue of the *Animal Welfare Information Center Newsletter* (or *AWIC Newsletter*), which is published by the U.S. Department of Agriculture. The article takes a straightforward animal welfare approach; it argues that rhesus macaques are social animals and that their welfare demands social housing, a demand that should be satisfied unless contrary treatment is "absolutely essential" for scientific reasons. I would guess that Singer does not view AWI as on the "exploiter" side.

The source of the articles at (1), (5), and (6), however, may be more surprising. They are printed in a journal entitled *Humane Innovations and Alternatives* (called *Humane Innovations and Alternatives in Animal Experimentation* before 1991), which is published by Psychologists for the Ethical Treatment of Animals (PSYeta). The journal contains numerous articles on eliminating "unnecessary" suffering in experimentation and animal husbandry and on encouraging the "humane" treatment of animals. PSYeta, "while recognizing the benefits of research, . . . hold[s] that the rights and the interests of the non-human animals involved are substantial and must be respected."[12] PSYeta is "dedicated to the promotion of animal welfare" and attempts "to balance the value of experimentation and other animal use against the suffering of animals."[13] PSYeta promotes group living arrangements for calves,[14] and praises as "an effective and talented hero" an agricultural scientist, Temple Grandin, a "respected consultant to the meat industry" who develops supposedly more "humane" ways to slaughter cows and pigs.[15] The PSYeta journal has received funding (for which it felt "deeply honored") from the U.S. Department of Agriculture.[16] The executive director of PSYeta is Kenneth Shapiro, a prominent member of the animal protection community and president of the board of directors of the *Animals' Agenda.* As of 1995, Shapiro also serves as coeditor of the *Journal of Applied Animal Welfare Science,* which "publishes reports and articles on methods of experimentation, husbandry and care that demonstrably enhance the welfare of farm, laboratory, companion and wild animals."[17] The articles described in (1), (5), and (6) are indistinguishable from many found in the *ILAR News* or the U.S. Department of Agriculture's *AWIC Newsletter*.

More disturbing is that the article described at (7), which I mentioned in the Introduction, advocates the use of a "pain scale." This article was written by Shapiro and another psychologist, Peter B. Field. The Shapiro/Field scale carries a powerful normative message: that an animal "rights" position is consistent with classification of activities such as "mild electric shock" and surgical procedures involving "mild post-operative pain/distress and no long-term harm" on some sort of scale, and moreover on the "low" end of that scale. The Shapiro/Field scale represents a set of normative judgments about the activities that are described at the various levels of the scale. Shapiro and Field argue that their scale may be used by institutional animal care committees, which may "find their task made easier by the use of a simple, reliable quantitative measure of animal distress."[18] Studies of reported pain assessments by institutions have shown, however, that even when there is no intent to misrepresent, experimenters often dramatically underestimate pain and distress caused to animals, and that even when the same procedures are involved, there is little consistency among judgments concerning pain and distress.[19] Moreover, even governmental agencies involved in regulating animal use in experiments have stated that objective assessments of pain are impossible.[20]

Although these problems are inherent in any attempt to assess and rate pain and distress, the Shapiro/Field categories are particularly elastic. For example, one of the "mild" pain or distress categories involves surgical procedures on an anesthetized animal that cause only minor pain or distress in the postoperative phase. But *most* experimenters using animals in surgical contexts would probably place their activities in this "low-end" category of "mild" pain or distress, just as most experimenters indicate on their government reporting forms that they have not used animals in painful experiments without the benefit of anesthesia or analgesia—which has been documented by the Animal Welfare Institute to be wrong in many cases.[21]

Putting aside the conceptual difficulties in assessing animal distress according to a "pain scale," there is certainly something peculiar about animal rights advocates' use of a "pain scale" to determine what experiments involving animals are "permissible" or warrant less moral scrutiny, and about these advocates' simultaneous insistence that this scale and their implicit normative judgments are consistent with a coherent notion of animal rights. Indeed, one can easily imagine a scenario in which the experimenters themselves could use the invention of some animal rights advocates to rebut the charges of other animal rights advocates: relying on their adoption of an animal-rights-approved "pain scale" and their self-placement at one of its lower rungs, researchers wielding this animal rights "preapproval" could thus parry animal rights objections to their experiments. Remarkably, Shapiro and Field explicitly envision such use: they suggest that institutions could use of the Shapiro/Field pain scale to collect information about the invasiveness of the institution's experiments. "Overall statistics could eventually be available showing the average invasiveness of research at the institution. Such statistics would not necessarily point fingers of blame—in fact, they could rebut charges of undue invasiveness, although on the other hand they might also pave the way for needed changes."[22]

There is no doubt that Shapiro sincerely sees both himself and PSYeta as oriented toward animal rights. When challenged about the apparent inconsistencies in promoting animal rights while advocating for "humane" experimentation and animal husbandry, Shapiro replied that as a "philosophical" matter he opposed animal exploitation "largely from a rights point of view" and that his endorsement of animal welfare was a matter only of "programmatic implementation."[23] I am certain of Shapiro's sincerity, but I am equally certain that his statement represents a textbook example of new welfarism: Shapiro maintains that the only thing separating the rights view from the welfare view is *tactic* and that choice of tactic is not really open to question, because the tactic of using welfarist reforms—and that tactic alone—will lead to movement recognition of the long-term goal of animal rights, the complete abolition of animal exploitation. As long as abolition is the long-term goal, Shapiro deems acceptable the short-term advocacy of animal welfare measures that are indistinguishable from the welfarism defended by institutional animal exploiters and by groups that explicitly reject the rights perspective.

Singer would surely reject any suggestion that Shapiro's views are on the "exploiter" side of the scale. After all, Shapiro is the president of the board of directors of Animal Rights Network, which publishes the *Animals' Agenda*, and Singer is on the *Agenda* board of advisers. Shapiro has served as coordinator for the Summit for the Animals, a yearly gathering of leaders of large national animal advocacy organizations.[24] It is, however, difficult to distinguish Shapiro's position from that of any animal welfarist or, indeed, of an experimenter who is sincerely concerned to prevent all "unnecessary" pain and suffering. Similarly, it is difficult to distinguish the positions taken in the articles about rodent-caging systems, nociceptive thresholds, and the "enrichment" of primate housing—all of which have been published in the journal of an organization that explicitly endorses animal rights—from those of traditional animal welfarists or, again, from the position that is adopted more warmly by a growing number of animal exploiters. This is a most serious difficulty and has never been addressed either by Singer or by any other adherent of new welfarism.

Consider another animal advocate, one who not only is identified as an animal rights advocate but is thought to be one of the most influential of this century—Henry Spira, head of Animal Rights International (ARI). Spira, despite his unquestionable commitment to animals, often takes positions that are uncomfortably similar to those taken by the most odious exploiters and their defenders. For example, the Foundation for Biomedical Research (FBR) and its lobbying arm, the National Association for Biomedical Research (NABR), are funded by industries that breed and exploit animals in experiments, as well as by universities that depend heavily on grant funds for animal experimentation.[25]

Despite its hard-line opposition to animal rights, FBR literature admits that "most people support the humane use of animals in biomedical research," that they "are also concerned, and justifiably so, about the care and treatment of laboratory animals during medical research," and that "no one enjoys research with animals." According to FBR, researchers must use animals in experiments to ensure human health, but these animals must be treated humanely because "only those animals that are cared for properly will be good research subjects." Moreover, researchers recognize "their special obligation to safeguard the welfare of laboratory animals," and "they take this position for ethical and scientific reasons. *It is not a controversial position; there is no constituency for inhumane treatment.*"[26] FBR states that the " 'three R's' concept . . . first presented in . . . 1959 . . . is now generally accepted by both scientists and the animal welfare community."[27] The "three Rs" concern the reduction of the numbers of animals used, the refinement of existing procedures to minimize pain and discomfort, and replacement of animals with nonanimal models where feasible. The concept of the "three Rs" is unquestionably an animal welfare concept in that it purports to regard the exploitation of nonhumans as morally legitimate but subject to some limitation the extent of which is determined and applied by the scientific community.

In a 1993 interview—in the *Foundation for Biomedical Research Newsletter*—Spira, asked whether he opposed "all forms of animal research," replied that the moral ideal of animal rights means that "nobody has a right to harm another, period, whether it's one human to another human or a human to an animal," but added that "we're living in the real world, and I think in the real world what one is looking for is not the unattainable ultimate but what's practical or doable." Spira added that "what's practical and doable is the concept of the Three R's. I don't believe that there's anyone who can rationally or reasonably make a dent in the Three R's. That's something that is unassailable, I believe." Spira argued, "For now, let's reduce pain and suffering."[28]

Spira's position represents a paradigmatic example of new welfarism. He accepts that the long-term goal is the abolition of animal use, but he argues that the short-term goal can accommodate animal exploitation subject to whatever limitations are imposed by the "three Rs." It is difficult, if not impossible, to distinguish this position from that of FBR. FBR readily admits that "no one enjoys research with animals" and that experimenters look forward to a time when animal use will no longer be necessary. So, like Spira, FBR claims to have abolition of animal use as its long-term goal. And Spira and FBR agree on the short-term goal as well: implementation of the "three Rs."

This leaves the area of disagreement between Spira and FBR quite narrow, restricted *solely* to the implementation of the "three Rs." As the issue has been framed by Spira, both animal advocates and animal exploiters argue in favor of the "three Rs" as the "doable" and "practical" solution to the controversy over the use of animals in experiments; they disagree only in their assessments of the current success of that solution's implementation. Spira, an animal rights advocate, seeks immediate implementation of the "three Rs"; FBR and NABR agree that the "three Rs" constitute a moral mandate that binds those who use animals in experiments, but they believe that the principle of the "three Rs" is being implemented as scientists find more and more alternatives and "adjuncts" to animal use. So, Spira and FBR/NABR essentially disagree over the timetable for implementation of the "three Rs."

In this area, however, Spira's position is not at all distinguishable from that of the traditional welfarists, who, unlike Spira, do not endorse the concept of animal rights. Consider, for example, the welfarist position of AWI's Christine Stevens: she has been a leader in calling for the use of alternatives and for procedures that reduce animal pain and distress. Indeed, the concept of the "three Rs" dates back to 1959 and was quickly adopted by the animal welfare movement as well as many in the research community.[29]

New Welfarism and Recent Campaigns

Another consequence of the central tenet of new welfarism—that animal welfare leads to animal rights—is that animal *rights* advocates often end up supporting laws that *reinforce* the property status of animals and that represent positions indistinguishable from the classical welfarist reforms proposed over the last one hundred years. Such support should, of course, not seem surprising in light of the confusion, discussed above, that is rampant among certain animal advocates. A review of several campaigns illustrates how new welfarism is much more like classical animal welfare and much less like the abolitionist theory of animal rights.

The Federal Animal Welfare Act

Although Great Britain in 1876 passed the first statute regulating the activities of those who used animals in experiments, numerous American legislative efforts to regulate the use of animals in experiments were unsuccessful until 1966, when Congress passed the Laboratory Animal Welfare Act, which, when amended in 1970, became known as the federal Animal Welfare Act (AWA).[30] The AWA was also amended in 1975, 1985, and 1990. I want to focus on the 1985 amendments—which constituted the most extensive revision of the AWA, occurred within the period of the modern animal "rights" movement, and were supported by many animal rights advocates—but it is necessary to discuss the AWA in some detail so that the more recent amendments are understood in context.[31]

The original, 1966 law was not so much an attempt to regulate animal experiments as a response to public concern over the theft of domestic animals—cats and dogs—for sale to laboratories. Senator Robert Dole, an instrumental force behind the legislation, characterized the 1966 act quite accurately as "the dognapping bill of 1966."[32] It was clear, as Congressman Robert Poage had noted, that a "substantial percentage of cats and dogs sold to hospitals and research laboratories are family pets which have been stolen."[33] The stated purpose of the house bill was not to protect animals from particular harms but rather "to protect the owners of dogs and cats from theft of such pets and to prevent the sale and use of stolen dogs and cats for purposes of research and experimentation."[34] The act as passed added to this concern for pet theft the purpose "to insure that certain animals for use in research facilities are provided humane care and treatment," but there can be no dispute that the purpose of the original act was to protect the *property* of people.

Thus, the act explicitly reinforced the status of animals under the law as the chattels, or personal property, of their owners. But then, the year was 1966 and *no one* was talking about animal rights at that time. The property paradigm was really the *only* rubric under which such issues could have been discussed at all.

The 1966 act was targeted primarily at animal dealers, who were suspected of trafficking in stolen animals. Dealers were required to be licensed, and certain record-keeping and identification requirements were imposed. The act also required the regulation of certain animal auctions. Interestingly, the most recent revision of the AWA—the Pet Protection Act—returns full circle to this focus on the protection of property, of animals as property of people.[35]

The 1966 act did impose certain administrative and record-keeping requirements on research facilities as well as animal dealers, but the provision of the 1966 act fought for so strenuously by many animal advocates of time, such as Christine Stevens of AWI, was a directive to the secretary of agriculture to "promulgate standards to govern the humane handling, care, treatment, and transportation of animals by dealers and research facilities." These standards were to provide "minimum requirements with respect to the housing, feeding, watering, sanitation, ventilation, shelter from extremes of weather and temperature, separation by species, and adequate veterinary care." The act very carefully qualified this requirement, however, stating that the secretary was not empowered to "prescribe standards for the handling, care, treatment, or inspection of animals during actual research or experimentation by a research facility" and was not authorized to propose any "rules, regulations, or orders for the handling, care, treatment, or inspection of animals during actual research or experimentation as determined by such research facility."[36]

In 1970, Congress, which recognized a "continuing commitment . . . to the ethic of kindness to dumb animals," reaffirmed that "small helpless creatures deserve the care and protection of a strong and enlightened public."[37] The 1970 act expanded the definition of covered animals from dogs, cats, nonhuman primate mammals, guinea pigs, hamsters, and rabbits to include "such other warm-blooded animal, as the Secretary may determine is being used, or is intended for use, for research, testing, experimentation, or exhibition purposes, or as a pet."[38]

There were other changes provided for in the 1970 act, but the most important for present purposes was a requirement that the "adequate veterinary care" required by the 1966 act include "the appropriate use of anesthetic, analgesic, or tranquilizing drugs, when such use would be proper in the opinion of the attending veterinarian of such research facility." Again, the amendment made clear that there was no authority whatsoever to regulate the "design, outlines, guidelines, or performance of actual research or experimentation by a research facility as determined by such research facility."[39] Those who supported the legislation made it clear that they did not oppose animal experimentation per se, and that they did not want to affect the content or conduct of research.[40]

What is most important for the present discussion is that the AWA, although originally passed in 1966, was not amended in any significant way until 1985—at what was arguably the height of the emerging animal rights movement. Animal advocates had succeeded in getting the State of Maryland to prosecute Edward Taub, a research scientist, for mistreatment of animals that he used in neurological experiments. In 1984, the Animal Liberation Front had illegally removed videotapes showing federally funded researchers at the University of Pennsylvania behaving in ways that shocked some of the most strident defenders of animal experiments. Congress had heard testimony concerning the Taub and Penn cases. Henry Spira had succeeded in closing a laboratory at the Museum of Natural History that was conducting gruesome experiments on cats. Animal advocacy groups were springing up around the country, and the idea of animal rights was stirring controversy and widespread discussion. As Spira noted in his testimony before Congress: "Animal rights is in the air."[41] In 1982, Congress considered legislation that would have created "merit review" of projects involving animals. The scientific community and its government representatives, NIH and USDA, opposed the legislation, but it was clear that the 1980s would see some significant piece of animal legislation.

Advocates such as Helen Jones of the International Society for Animal Rights (ISAR) and Alice Herrington of Friends of Animals (FoA) understood the time was ripe for legislative initiatives that would abolish some forms of research, not merely regulate them through further refinement of the notion of "humane" treatment. Jones had always argued that the regulation of experimentation was unacceptable, and she urged strong efforts to educate the public, combined with legislation that would abolish particular forms of animal experimentation. Herrington proposed, among other things, a complete ban on experiments that cause pain in animals without complete and effective pain relief, although Herrington opposed the AWA altogether.[42] At about the same time, Herrington formed the Medical Research Modernization Committee, which was "funded by, but philosophically independent of, Friends of Animals, Inc." The purpose of the committee was to establish that at least some types of experiments involving live animals were scientifically unsound. Herrington then planned to push for legislation that would block the use of federal funds for the targeted experiments, thus effectively ensuring their cessation. The committee identified experiments involving behavior modification, drug addiction, and trauma as inquiries that had provided few, if any, benefits to humans other than those who received the grant funds.[43]

In addition, FoA and another antivivisection group, United Action for Animals (UAA), succeeded in having introduced in Congress a bill that would seek to develop alternatives to the use of animals in research.[44] The bill provided not only for the development of alternatives but for the development of a National Center for Alternatives Research and for the dissemination of information concerning alternatives. The bill was opposed by virtually every institutional user of animals because it was thought to require a reallocation of some funds (although this would have been a rather insignificant amount) from actual animal experiments to the development of alternatives to animal use and to support of the federal oversight mechanism; the bill was ultimately defeated.[45]

Despite the momentum that the movement had achieved by 1985, the legislative result was disappointing, to say the least. Congress refused to move from the position—adopted in 1966—that Congress would not do anything to interfere with the actual content or conduct of research, and would only regulate issues of animal husbandry. As I argue later, once regulation affects only or primarily issues of husbandry, and once it is accepted that those who use the animals get to determine questions of scientific necessity, then the law will, as a practical matter, regulate (and prohibit) only those uses of animals that involve the *gratuitous* infliction of suffering and death. Nevertheless, the animal rights movement rallied around the 1985 AWA amendments and refused to support the more progressive measures urged by FoA or ISAR, and even refused to support the alternatives bill sponsored by UAA and FoA.

Many animal advocates recognized that the 1985 amendments were problematic: the amendments were "written with a great deal of input from the scientific community and, for the most part, [were] viewed as just another paper curtain." Nevertheless, the animal advocacy community was urged to support the amendments: "The word of the wise in the animal rights movement is: don't drop the ball now; work to get currently-pending legislation passed. But next time, get it together and get it right."[46] Supporters of the amendments (halfhearted as some of their support was) claimed that the law contained at least four significant steps forward for animals used in experiments.

First, supporters argued that Congress, for the first time in the history of the AWA, had finally *required* that pain relief be provided during actual experimentation.[47] This assertion was inaccurate. The 1985 amendments directed the regulation of animal treatment *during* experiments, but Congress had already in 1970 required facilities to report annually that they were using professionally acceptable standards of veterinary care *during* actual experimentation. But the law was as clear in 1985 as it was in 1970: even though the law ostensibly requires anesthesia or analgesia during actual experimentation, government cannot regulate the design, outlines, or guidelines of actual experimentation and is prohibited from interfering with the performance of actual research or experimentation as determined by the research facility.[48] Although the experimenter must justify withholding pain relief to the institutional animal care committee, the ultimate decision whether to provide pain relief is left to the vivisector, who is permitted to withhold pain relief "when scientifically necessary" and for "the necessary period of time"; and the animal care committee is explicitly not empowered to make decisions about actual research.

Second, supporters of the amendments also claimed as a huge step forward for animals used in experiments the requirement that each research facility, including federal facilities, have an animal care committee. In theory, the animal care committee was to be an entity analogous to the institutional review boards required under federal law to assess the propriety of using human subjects in research. The analogy is, of course, inapposite: animals cannot give the informed consent that is required of human subjects.[49]

The individual experimenter must, at least in theory, justify to the animal care committee the withholding of pain relief and must provide to the committee written assurances that alternatives to animal use have been considered and the experiment is not duplicative. Nevertheless, the ultimate determination whether to use animals or whether to provide pain relief during that use still rests with the individual experimenter. And the law is clear that the experimenter is permitted to withhold pain relief "when scientifically necessary" and for "the necessary period of time." That is, once the investigator justifies the position that infliction of pain is required by the experiment, the animal care committee must abide by that decision and has no authority to interfere. Just as the statute prohibits the secretary of agriculture from regulating in any way the "design, outlines, or guidelines of actual research or experimentation by a research facility as determined by such research facility," so too is the federally created animal care committee disabled from such interference. Indeed, in response to concerns from the scientific community that animal care committees would regulate scientific methodology or design, the USDA stated explicitly that the authority of the animal care committee is "limited to the animal care and use part of a proposal to determine how the research will treat or affect an animal and its condition, and the circumstances under which the animal will be maintained. It does not extend to evaluating the design, outlines, guidelines, and scientific merit of proposed research."[50] In short, the animal care committees impose upon experimenters no substantive constraints that were not already imposed by the research facilities in which they conducted their experiments.

This last point requires particular scrutiny. As I mentioned above, the 1985 law requires that the animal care committee evaluate animal use at the facility not by reference to any absolute standard but by reference to, and in complete deference to, the "needs of the research facility." If the facility engages in particularly objectionable research, such as the use of animals in painful psychological experiments, then that "need" of the institution must be used to measure "humane" treatment and "necessary" pain. Moreover, the animal care committees are composed almost completely, if not exclusively, of those who engage in vivisection or who believe that it is morally justifiable. As a practical matter, such people are not likely to interfere with the judgment of a colleague at the same facility concerning a determination about the "necessity" of a painful procedure.

Moreover, Congress explicitly permitted researchers to depart from *any* of the law's requirements as long as the departure was approved by the committee. Again, once the experimenter provides that justification, the committee is without power to interfere in any way with the design, outline, or guidelines of experimentation. The committee is, under the statute itself and under the USDA regulations that purport to implement the statute, prevented completely from making any ethical judgment about the experiment and cannot evaluate the scientific merit or design of the experiment. The committee can suspend or disapprove an experiment should it determine that the infliction of pain on animals is "unnecessary," but the committee is prohibited from making such a determination in the context of an ethical merit review and can only determine that the infliction of pain is gratuitous.

Finally, a 1995 audit performed by the Office of the Inspector General of the USDA found that USDA was not effectively monitoring the operation of the animal care committees. In particular, the audit found that out of twenty-six facilities evaluated, twelve of the committees had failed to observe the legal and regulatory requirements, with the result that "there is insufficient assurance that the committees minimized pain and discomfort to research animals and prevent unnecessary experimentation."[51]

Third, animal advocates supported the legislation because it purported to limit "survival" surgery, or the use of a single animal for multiple surgeries from which the animal is permitted to recover. The 1985 amendments provided that experimenters may not use an animal for "more than one major operative experiment from which it is allowed to recover." But the legislation added that multiple survival surgeries would be permitted when "scientifically necessary" or condoned by the secretary.[52] In essence, Congress enacted a rule with a loophole large enough to negate it entirely.

Fourth, animal advocates supported the 1985 amendments because they required that the secretary promulgate minimum standards to govern the "humane handling, care, and treatment of animals" and "for exercise of dogs . . . and for a physical environment adequate to promote the psychological well-being of primates."[53] It took USDA six years to promulgate these regulations because the scientific community objected to the original standards that were proposed, and the final regulations reflected precisely what the research community wanted—continued unfettered discretion to set the standards for the care and use of dogs and nonhuman primates used in experiments.

In short, despite the fact that vivisection was clearly the most visible issue discussed within and without the emerging animal rights movement in the 1980s, the 1985 amendments to the Animal Welfare Act did nothing more than their predecessors or, indeed, *any* piece of welfarist legislation: they prohibited "unnecessary" cruelty but left the determination of what is "necessary" to the research community itself. Indeed, the 1876 Cruelty to Animals Act in Britain imposed more rigorous requirements on researchers, and these were tightened even more in 1986, leaving the American legislation significantly less rigorous than its British counterpart. The 1985 amendments provided for the establishment of an information service at the National Agricultural Library to provide, in conjunction with the National Library of Medicine, information on unintended duplication of experiments and on methods of experimentation that will reduce animal suffering, but gone completely was federal support for alternatives to animal use.

Moreover, the 1985 amendments not only failed to provide any real protection for animals; they arguably made it more difficult for the public to obtain information about animal use in federally funded experiments. A provision of the law imposes substantial criminal penalties on any animal care committee member who releases "any confidential information of the research facility," including information pertaining to the "trade secrets, processes, operations, style of work, or apparatus" or "the identity, confidential statistical data, amount or source of any income, profits, losses, or expenditures of the research facility."[54] It is clear from other provisions that Congress was referring to proprietary information, such as trade secrets and patentable inventions, but research facilities have relied on this provision in both refusing to provide information to the public about experiments and in chilling the free speech rights of committee members who may wish to discuss publicly issues concerning experimentation at the particular facility.[55]

Despite the fact that the 1985 amendments represented nothing but complete capitulation to the desire of the research community to continue doing business as usual, "groups that supported the amendments included NAVS [the National Anti-Vivisection Society], PETA, the Humane Society and most other animal-rights and animal-welfare organizations."[56] HSUS vice-president Wayne Pacelle defended movement support of the amendments: "If animal suffering was relieved even to a small extent then a good purpose was served. If 60 animals are going to suffer, and we can stop 30 of them from suffering, by God we're going to do it. We're not just going to stand by and do nothing if we can't get all 60."[57] There is, of course, no empirical evidence that the 1985 amendments did *anything* to decrease animal suffering. Indeed, USDA annual enforcement reports indicate that the supposedly fundamental shift to a largely local supervision scheme represented by the animal care committee has not had much effect on the total number of animals used or on the numbers of animals used in painful experiments without the benefit of pain relief. For example, in 1991, USDA's Animal and Plant Health Inspection Service (APHIS) reported that, of the number of covered animals reported—1,842,420—6 percent, or 108,866, were used in procedures that caused pain or distress and for which no relief was provided.[58] In 1992, USDA/APHIS reported that, of the 2,134,182 animals used, 6 percent, or 120,208, were used in procedures that involved pain or distress and where no pain relief was provided.[59] In 1993, USDA/ APHIS reported that, of the 2,369,439 animals used, approximately 7 percent, or 160,480, animals were used in painful procedures but not provided with pain relief.[60] In 1994, USDA / APHIS reported that, of the total number of covered animals used, 1,624,649, roughly 11 percent, or 179,187 animals, were used in procedures that cause pain or distress but where no pain relief was provided.[61] These numbers indicate that, at least as far as the USDA numbers are concerned, animal use is certainly not showing any significant decreasing trend and the percentage of animals used in painful experiments without anesthesia is also not decreasing, and may be increasing.[62] Moreover, these figures must be understood in light of serious concerns about USDA reporting procedures, which allow research facilities to decide for themselves whether an experiment should be classified as one causing pain and for which pain relief is appropriate.[63]

In sum, then, the central tenet of new welfarism—that there is a causal relationship between animal welfare reforms and the achievement of the long-term goal of animal rights or the abolition of the use of animals in experiments—leads animal advocates to support laws like the AWA, which do nothing but reinforce the extant instrumentalist paradigm. Moreover, although animal exploiters often lobby against any regulation because in their view the law has no business regulating science, the experimenters endorse the AWA and similar laws as representing *their* perspective on the "appropriate" or "legitimate" use of animals in biomedical experiments. Indeed, the Foundation for Biomedical Research applauds laws like the AWA and claims that "professional and scientific societies have developed their own guidelines, which reinforce and expand on legal and regulatory requirements."[64] Again, it becomes difficult to identify precisely who the "exploiters" are when virtually everyone agrees on the same standards.[65]

The "Humane" Slaughter of Animals

The animal advocacy movement in the 1980s concentrated heavily on the use of animals in biomedical experiments, but the most significant use of animals numerically occurs in the food industry, where, in the United States alone, some eight billion animals are slaughtered for food every year. The staggering number of animals involved is overshadowed only by the heinous conditions and practices of intensive agriculture that are involved in virtually every phase of the tragic lives of these animals. In 1958, Congress passed the Humane Slaughter Act, which requires that animals be slaughtered "humanely," using "a single blow or gunshot or an electrical, chemical or other means that is rapid and effective, before being shackled, hoisted, thrown, cast, or cut," or severing the carotid arteries in accordance with the ritual requirements of certain religions. The law applied to slaughterhouses that sold meat to the federal government or its agencies, and Congress thought that the several states would enact their own laws to ensure the humane slaughter of all animals used for food purposes.

Witness after witness testified in the 1958 hearings to the horrible condition of slaughterhouses but, not surprisingly, did not conclude that the process of mass slaughter could *never* be made "humane"; rather, witnesses suggested that there were ways—such as the use of stunning devices—that could somehow make the process morally acceptable. Indeed, one witness talked about the success of a "stunning tool . . . now in regular use," which had "been tested on calves, lambs, and hogs. . . . Contact of this trigger rod with the animal's head discharges the cartridge, which we know as the powerload, forcing this out and striking the animal's head." The stunning tool was "originally proposed by Mr. John C. Macfarlane, of the Massachusetts Society for the Prevention of Cruelty to Animals, who is a member of the joint committee of the American Meat Institute and the American Humane Association," and "was developed by the Remington Arms Co. working in conjunction with the joint committee of the American Meat Institute and the American Humane Association."[66] Christine Stevens of the Animal Welfare Institute testified that although hammer blows to the heads of animals, if "properly inflicted," would "certainly be humane," she favored stunning or anesthesia.[67]

It should, of course, come as no surprise that the humane community in 1958 would have supported this legislation or that humane organizations at that time would actually have been involved in collaborative efforts with arms manufacturers and the meat industry to find "better" ways to destroy life. Stevens was probably correct in saying that in 1958 no member of the humane community would have thought that anesthesia and stunning were not "humane." After all, in 1958, just about everyone in the humane movement ate meat and did not question the morality of doing so. The problem was not *that* animals were being used for food; the problem was *how* the animals were slaughtered. And no one argued that improving the slaughtering conditions would lead eventually to the cessation of animal agriculture, or even to better slaughtering methods. Indeed, in response to questions about whether improvements in slaughtering would be a continuing issue, Stevens made clear that with stunning or anesthesia "all animals can be slaughtered humanely, and I would like to assure the committee that no animal protective worker could possibly take issue with the humaneness of these methods. They are humane." When asked about her position *should* more humane methods be developed, Stevens replied that "once you have a standard as humane as carbon dioxide and instant stunning really properly done, that standard would remain no matter what you discovered later," and that "no honest person could ever deny the humaneness of effective anesthesia or instant stunning, and the assertion that a packer might adopt one method only to have found it inhumane later and have to change it, falls into the realm of unfounded or irrational fears."[68] Stevens represented the classical welfarist position: it is perfectly acceptable for us to eat animals as long as we kill them "humanely."

Ironically, despite the intervening emergence of an animal rights movement that supposedly challenges the instrumentalist view of animals, the positions have not really changed. In 1978, Congress amended the Humane Slaughter Act to extend its provisions to all federally inspected slaughterhouses and not just those that sold meat to the federal government. Moreover, the amendment applied to foreign slaughterhouses that exported meat to the United States. Interestingly, Representative George Brown of California and Senator Robert Dole from Kansas, the two lawmakers who sponsored the 1985 amendments to the federal Animal Welfare Act, also sponsored the slaughter legislation. Just as in 1958, the humane community enthusiastically supported its provisions. For example, Robert F. Welborn, a member of the board of directors of HSUS, stated that he was "a farmer by avocation" and had "been involved with farm livestock most of my life." Welborn, in 1995 still a member of the HSUS board, stated that HSUS "members have committed our organization to work for the adoption and enforcement of legislation that will insure that meat that is purchased in this country comes from animals that have been slaughtered humanely."[69] John C. Macfarlane, who had originally proposed the stunning device that was at the center of the 1958 hearings and who had served as president of the Livestock Conservation Institute, also testified in support of the legislation, as did a representative of the American Meat Institute. At the time of the 1978 hearings, Macfarlane was a member of the board of directors of the Livestock Conservation Institute as well as the livestock handling consultant of the American Humane Association. Emily Gleockler, a representative of the Humane Information Services, whose founder, Frederick Thomsen, was a prominent supporter of welfarist legislation, stated that the bill was not only supported by the humane community, but it was embraced by the meat packers themselves, who "found humane slaughter practices more efficient in labor utilization and resulting in lower costs"; and Gleockler also stated that the bill would "not impose any significant burden on the government which enforces it, on the livestock industry, the meat-packing industry, or consumers."[70] Ann Cottrell Free, representing the Rachel Carson Trust for the Living Environment and the Albert Schweitzer Fellowship, stated that the bill "would carry out the ethic to which Miss Carson and Dr. Schweitzer so heartily subscribed."[71] Other enthusiastic supporters included the National Association for Humane Legislation, the Massachusetts Society for the Prevention of Cruelty to Animals, the Animal Protection Institute, and the International Society for the Protection of Animals. Christine Stevens again played a major role in supporting the legislation, arguing that, in addition to moral reasons, "it has been very well proved that humane slaughter in the long run saves money for packing plants" and helps to prevent "labor difficulties."[72] Indeed, there was little, if any, opposition to the legislation from either the humane community or the meat industry.

The 1978 amendments came before Congress at the dawn of the new era of animal rights, which supposedly rejected the instrumentalism of animal welfare. In a sense, then, the amendments may be explained as part of the prerights welfare period. This interpretation would suggest that later animal advocacy efforts in the area of animal agriculture would reflect the animal *rights* perspective. But just as the organized animal rights movement supported legislation that merely regulated animal experimentation, so too, for the most part, they supported agricultural legislation that seeks only to "fine tune" the slaughtering process. Three examples are particularly relevant.

First, in 1994, animal advocates, again led by Animal Rights International and Henry Spira, threatened to propose a resolution to shareholders of McDonald's. The resolution required that " 'animals should be housed, fed, and transported in a practical manner least restrictive of their physical and behavioral needs,' that 'animals should be afforded individual veterinary care when needed,' and that 'methods should be designed to produce a quick and humane death.' "[73] Spira withdrew the resolution when McDonald's agreed to issue a statement of "humane principles" to meat and poultry slaughterhouses that supply McDonald's restaurants. The statement provides that "McDonald's believes the humane treatment of animals, from the time of their birth and throughout their lives, is a moral responsibility. The Company fully respects the independence of its suppliers and requires them to adhere to pertinent laws, regulations, and industry guidelines concerning the humane treatment of animals such as those recommended by the American Meat Institute."[74] Animal advocates who purport to endorse animal rights, prominent animal rights advocates among them, applauded McDonald's endorsement of the meat industry guidelines, which had been drafted by animal agriculture scientist Temple Grandin, who is held in high regard by some animal advocates.[75] Grandin claims that although federal laws dictate "strict animal handling and slaughtering standards for packing plants" and although the "meat packing industry takes these standards very seriously," there is room for improvement because "healthy animals, properly handled, keep the meat industry running safely, efficiently and profitably."[76] Grandin's guidelines include design suggestions to assure efficient animal movement through the slaughterhouse, recommendations for "improving meat quality and animal welfare" (e.g.: "Electric prods should be used sparingly to move livestock"), and information on trucking and unloading animals—all to ensure animal welfare and maximum efficient use of the animals. Grandin's guidelines contain drawings to illustrate the proper place to apply electric stunners to animal heads, as well as a discussion of a "humane" restraining device, designed by the American Society for the Prevention of Cruelty to Animals (ASPCA), for ritual slaughter. In another publication, Grandin states that "handlers can often control animals more efficiently if they exert dominance over an animal." Grandin recommends that the handler shove a pig against a fence with a board pushed against the pig's neck.[77] Grandin has made it clear that she does not consider herself as holding a rights view. She maintains that, "properly performed, 'slaughter is more humane than nature.' " She says that she wants to "reform the meat industry[, whereas the] activists want to shut it down." Grandin rejects the activists' approach, claiming to "have a radical dislike of radicals."[78]

In a 1994 article, Grandin argues that "newborn calves should not be sold at auction until they are old enough to walk, their haircoat and navel are dry, and they have received colostrum to help them fight disease." She urges that farmers "cull cows before they become infirm."[79] The editorial notes that follow the article state that Grandin "is a respected consultant to the meat industry. In fact, 30 percent of the cattle and pigs in the United States pass through facilities and equipment designed" by Grandin. The notes state that Grandin "received the Livestock Conservation Institutes Award for Meritorious Service in 1983, and the Innovator's Award for Technology from the meat industry in 1981." The editorial praises Grandin as a "talented hero . . . with a mission." The editorial—and Grandin's article—appear in a publication of Psychologists for the Ethical Treatment of Animals, which purports to recognize and respect the "rights and interests of nonhuman animals" and whose executive director, Kenneth Shapiro, is president of the *Animals' Agenda*, a self-described animal rights magazine on whose advisory board Singer serves as a member. Grandin has been praised by other animal "rights" activists, such as Henry Spira, and is the subject of glowing praise from *Animal People*, a "movement" newspaper. Apparently, Grandin is part of the "diversity" Singer believes animal advocates should welcome, because Grandin is pursuing one of his "short term goals to stop suffering now." Apparently, Grandin is not one of the people Singer would classify as an "exploiter of animals." It is, of course, difficult to understand how such a view differs at all from classical animal welfare theory.

Second, although more poultry are slaughtered for food than cows or pigs, poultry are excluded from coverage under the Humane Slaughter Act.[80] Animal advocates have been trying to have the law amended. Again, the rightists and the welfarists and the exploiters are, for the most part, on the same side.

A primary force behind these efforts is Karen Davis and her group, United Poultry Concerns. Davis, a longtime animal rights advocate, is herself a vegan[81] and takes a hard-line animal rights approach to the general issue of killing animals for food: "The slaughter of the innocent is intrinsically wrong. There is no such thing as humane slaughter; that is 'humane slaughter' is an oxymoron."[82] Nevertheless, Davis takes a position characteristic of new welfarism and argues that even though "humane slaughter is an oxymoron," she feels that "as long as we're slaughtering them, . . . they are at least entitled to the consistent coverage with cattle and sheep."[83] Although Christine Stevens is neither a vegetarian nor an animal rights advocate, she too supports the legislation, arguing that she believes that "chopping off the head of a chicken" causes "death without prolonged pain, fear and suffering" and that "we just wish that all the commercial slaughter houses were doing the same thing." Like Davis, Stevens supports stunning the animals with an electric charge sufficient to render the animals insensitive to pain: "It is possible to do electric stunning correctly, and it would be undoubtedly done right if a law is passed."[84] According to Davis, most chickens are supposedly stunned before being decapitated and plunged into scalding water to remove feathers, and the level of electricity commonly employed immobilizes the chickens but does not render them insensitive to pain. The birds are "in a condition where they cannot move or express their pain and their other feelings, but they are conscious."[85]

Again, the position of the parties Singer would label as "exploiters" or as the "real enemy" is very similar to that of Davis or Stevens. For

example, a representative of the American Meat Institute (AMI) testified that "AMI supports humane slaughter of all animals" and that
"humane slaughter has been employed in poultry plants on a voluntary
basis for the past 30 years." AMI expressed concern over the bill, but
the concern was not over whether poultry ought to be "humanely"
slaughtered. Instead, AMI questioned whether the methods proposed
by Davis and Stevens, which would require rendering the birds insensitive to pain immediately before or after the birds are shackled, would be
"humane": "Many years of industry experience has clearly shown that
attempting to render a bird insensible immediately after being shackled
does not achieve the desired result of humane slaughter," because the
birds are agitated after being shackled (in an upside-down position)
and should be allowed to "relax" before stunning or other methods
are applied. The AMI representative stated that although the industry
questioned whether legislation was necessary at all, "if legislation is
deemed necessary, it should certainly be one that represents the most
humane methods available."[86]

Third, an injured food animal is often referred to as a "downer," and
these nonambulatory animals are often left for days without food, water, shelter, or veterinary care to suffer and die. Farm Sanctuary, an
animal advocacy group that operates sanctuaries in New York and California to care for rescued food animals, has taken a leading role in
publicizing this problem. Their efforts have resulted in the introduction
of legislation at the federal level and its passage at the state level. The
proposed federal legislation, the Downed Animal Protection Act, as it
exists as of this writing, would prohibit auctions and stockyards from
selling these animals to slaughterhouses and would require stockyards,
market agencies, and dealers to euthanize these animals. As I argue
later, such legislation, which seeks to *prohibit*, not merely to regulate,
some aspect of exploitation, arguably represents an incremental approach that is more consistent with rights theory than incremental approaches that prohibit nothing and merely require that animals be
treated "humanely."

It is disturbing, however, that Farm Sanctuary has on the state level
agreed to regulation of the "downer" problem that does not even contain the prohibition provided for in the federal bill. Farm Sanctuary
originally sought passage in California of a "downer" law that would
have required the euthanasia of all nonambulatory animals. Under
pressure from the meat industry, Farm Sanctuary agreed to amendments that eliminated any requirement that nonambulatory animals be
euthanized. Instead, the law requires only that the animal be eutha-

nized "or removed." Although stockyards are prohibited from selling the animals, the owner of the livestock, or other parties who are not regulated under the law, such as feedlots and ranches, may sell these nonambulatory animals to USDA slaughterhouses. These amendments defeated the primary purpose of *any* sensible downed-animal legislation—to eliminate the market for these animals and to require their immediate euthanasia. The Humane Farming Association (HFA), a generally welfare-oriented reform group, opposed these amendments and claimed in testimony before the California state senate that Farm Sanctuary had formed an alliance with the meat industry, which joined with Farm Sanctuary and lobbied in favor of the bill that was passed.[87] Indeed, in opposing the federal downed-animal legislation, a meat industry spokesperson, representing the Farm Animal Welfare Coalition, stated that "interestingly, in the case of California's new law, Farm Sanctuary actively negotiated a bill that is vastly different and far less rigid than" the proposed federal legislation, and that "the California law can be described as codifying industry practice and philosophy."[88] When HFA attempted to inform readers of the *Animals' Agenda* about Farm Sanctuary's negotiations with the meat industry, *Agenda* refused to print anything about the matter, although *Agenda* had printed an article praising the California legislation for its supposedly humane aspects and, quite astonishingly, because it protected "consumers from tainted meat." At the time, Farm Sanctuary director Gene Bauston was a member of the board of directors of the Animal Rights Network, which publishes *Agenda*.[89] Again, animal advocates found themselves applauded by what Singer would clearly call an "exploiter"—the Farm Animal Welfare Coalition—which, incidentally, represents itself as protecting the *welfare* but not the *rights* of animals.

What is clear is that these campaigns—the support of the 1985 amendments to the federal Animal Welfare Act and various initiatives to assure "humane" slaughter—are functionally indistinguishable from earlier welfarist campaigns.

New Welfarism and Animal Sanctuaries

I have argued throughout this book that what distinguishes animal rights theory from animal welfare theory is that the latter is concerned primarily with the suffering of animals, while the former is concerned more with the treatment of animals as ends in themselves and not as means to human ends. This focus on pain and suffering to the exclusion of other interests is manifested in the position adopted by new welfarists, who claim that animal interests are vouchsafed as long as a person "has compassion toward animals and seeks to aid their plight," because the rights and welfare "ideologies arrive at the same conclusion: humans have definite responsibilities to minimize the pain and suffering around them."[90] The problem is that this is *not* the case. As I have shown, animal rights theory is characterized by a rejection of the instrumental status of animals exclusively as means to human ends. As I discuss in greater detail later, rights theory goes beyond a focus on animal pain and suffering and requires that we treat animals consistently with a particular conception of *justice*, that we not think, for example, that it is acceptable to kill animals for no reason, even if we have given them a better life—or a better death—than they had. Moreover, to use "compassion toward other animals" as the single criterion for identifying an animal rights advocate is, to say the least, disturbing.

In this section, I discuss two instances in which these new welfarist views have led to disastrous consequences for animals. Both incidents involve animal sanctuaries, which, ironically, play a role of some significance in the animal rights movement. That is, animal rights advocates take the position that the killing of healthy animals solely for the convenience of humans is morally similar to killing unwanted groups of people for reasons of social convenience. This notion is reflected in the scholarly literature written about the movement. For example, as sociologists Jasper and Nelkin argue in their 1992 study, animal shelters, founded on a notion of "compassion" rather than animal "rights," kill "from twelve to twenty million animals a year."[91] The ideal—often not achieved—of the animal shelter is to provide a "painless death" to unwanted animals.[92] Indeed, traditional animal welfare groups feel strongly about the role of "humane" societies in providing "painless deaths" to animals. For example, both HSUS and ASPCA are actually *opposed* to animal shelters that do not kill unwanted animals, because of fears of overcrowding and other problems that they believe are incidental to such shelters.[93]

Although there can be no doubt that those who work in shelters are deeply distressed about such killings, it is also clear that such killings are problematic for animal rights theory. As Tom Regan has argued, "It is no more true to say that healthy dogs and cats are euthanized when they are 'put to sleep' to make room for other cats and dogs at animal shelters than it would be true to say that healthy derelicts would be euthanized if they were 'put to sleep' to make room for other derelicts at human shelters."[94] Regan's point is that these killings *are* killings and cannot be considered "euthanasia" unless one accepts the proposition that although animals have rights, they can be killed for human convenience. Jasper and Nelkin observe that "animal rights groups have tried to resolve this dilemma by building, not animal shelters, but 'sanctuaries,' as protective refuges. Instead of painless death, [sanctuaries] provide the means for animals to live out their 'natural' lives."[95] In two recent cases, however, new welfarists who operate sanctuaries demonstrated that they do not take seriously the principle that the fundamental interests of animals cannot be traded away for human convenience. These examples demonstrate clearly that it is wrong to say, as does Don Barnes, that the rights and welfare "ideologies arrive at the same conclusion."

The Black Beauty Ranch

In 1979, Cleveland Amory, founder of Fund for Animals (FFA), established the Black Beauty Ranch to hold burros rescued from the Grand Canyon. The ranch took its name from Anna Sewell's classic novel *Black Beauty*, Amory's favorite book when he was a boy. Above the ranch gates is a sign that has the final lines of the book: "My troubles are over. I have found a home." By the late 1980s, the ranch was home to over six hundred animals, including horses, monkeys, raccoons, and the signing chimpanzee, Nim, and had become the celebrated animal sanctuary of the animal rights movement. In 1990, in a controversial and provocative article in the *Village Voice*, investigative journalist Jack Rosenberger revealed that the manager of the Black Beauty Ranch, Billy Jack Saxon, "in tandem with his duties as manager of the animal sanctuary, raised hogs and cattle for slaughter. Not only did he use the Fund's personnel and equipment to transport animals to local auction barns and slaughterhouses, but soon after assuming stewardship of the ranch, he interbred domestic Yorkshire boars with the Fund's wild hogs and sold the offspring to be slaughtered for human consumption."[96]

Amory acknowledged that he had known Saxon was involved in raising animals for slaughter but had hired him anyway, stating that "unfortunately no one believes that a man who raises animals for slaughter can care about animals."[97] When the Black Beauty Ranch opened, the Fund placed an advertisement in a local newspaper announcing a " 'free Texas-Style Bar-B-Q Bash at the Black Beauty Ranch,' which included steaks, hamburgers, and plenty of baby back ribs."[98] In any event, Amory fired Saxon shortly before the *Village Voice* story came out, although Saxon was paid as a "consultant" to the ranch for months afterward.

Rosenberger's story was disturbing not only because Saxon was using an animal rights sanctuary to facilitate his meat business but because Rosenberger alleged a very deliberate cover-up of the matter by the movement. Rosenberger documented that in response to an *Animals' Agenda* article that had "compared Saxon to the 'fabled Dr. Doolittle' and described him as 'a gentle down-home Texan,' " a neighbor of Saxon's had written to *Agenda* and alleged, among other things, that some of Saxon's animals were seriously mistreated.[99] *Agenda* did not print the letter, or reveal that it had been accompanied by a videotape showing animal abuse by Saxon at the Black Beauty Ranch. At the time, Fund executive director Wayne Pacelle was a member of the *Agenda* board of directors, and Amory was a member of the *Agenda* advisory board.[100]

Jasper and Nelkin state that "Amory came under increasing fire in 1989 and 1990 from more radical activists angry that the manager of the Black Beauty Ranch also raised and sold livestock," but these radicals "kept their criticism private." The purported reason for the silence was to "avoid hurting the credibility of the movement."[101] The matter had been made public in Rosenberger's 1990 article, and Saxon's neighbor had written to *Agenda* in 1989, but there was no detailed coverage of the matter within the movement until 1991, when the *Animals' Voice* printed an article by editors Vanessa Kelling and Laura Moretti that was as disturbing as Rosenberger's. According to Kelling and Moretti, they learned in 1990 that Saxon had 175 cows that he wanted to sell for slaughter. They decided that immediate public disclosure of the matter might jeopardize the credibility of the Fund and Amory, and instead tried to negotiate with Amory and Pacelle to save the 175 cows. When these negotiations were unsuccessful, they reported that Pacelle requested they not report the story and that prominent animal advocates, including Tom Regan, urged the *Animals' Voice* "*not* to print anything that might damage" Amory or the Fund.[102] The 175 cows were slaughtered.[103]

Aspects of the Black Beauty Ranch matter certainly suggest a simple cover-up. After all, the primary movement publication of that time, the *Animals' Agenda*, did not report the matter, and its failure to do so may have been related in large part to the fact that Amory was a member of the *Agenda* board of advisers and that Fund executive director Wayne Pacelle was a member of the *Agenda* board of directors. When the *Animals' Voice* finally reported the matter in 1991, its editors claimed that movement leaders had tried to pressure the *Animals' Voice* not to write about the scandal. But the Black Beauty Ranch scandal, and the failure of any intramovement dialogue to develop about the scandal, suggest something about the nature of new welfarism.

When Amory defended his hiring of Saxon, contending that "a man who raises animals for slaughter can care about animals," he was articulating a core tenet of new welfarism: as long as a person cares about animals, the ends to which those animals are put, including raising them for slaughter, are irrelevant. Indeed, Amory fits almost exactly Ingrid Newkirk's description of the welfarist who has "embraced animal rights" but still has "bull roasts." Amory's group, Fund for Animals, popularized the expression "Animals Have Rights, Too"—a position that Amory did not perceive to conflict with his having a "Texas Style Bar-B-Q Bash." According to Wayne Pacelle, who used to be national director of Fund for Animals and became a vice-president at HSUS, the distinction between animal rights and animal welfare is a "distinction without a difference."[104] For the animals abused at the Black Beauty Ranch, and for the animals sent to slaughter by Billy Jack Saxon, the distinction was far more meaningful than Pacelle's comment suggests.

PETA and the Aspen Hill Sanctuary

In 1991, it was disclosed that PETA had killed healthy rabbits and roosters at its sanctuary, Aspen Hill, located in Silver Spring, Maryland.[105] Although fund-raising literature for Aspen Hill claimed that animals at Aspen Hill would receive a "permanent home" there, the rabbits and roosters, which had been "rescued" from abusive situations, were killed by lethal injection, as animals are now killed in animal shelters that are supposed to be distinguished from animal sanctuaries.

When questioned about this matter, PETA's Ingrid Newkirk stated that PETA has "never been opposed to the humane killing of animals." Newkirk defended the killings as "euthanasia": "'Euthanasia means mercy killing,' she said. 'What we are opposed to is unnecessary slaughter of animals for frivolous reasons."[106] The Aspen Hill killings were supposedly necessary because, according to PETA spokespersons, PETA "just [didn't] have the money" to build facilities for the animals.[107] Newkirk stated that PETA would "not overcrowd our animals. . . . We really didn't have anything else to do."[108] This contention is difficult to understand not only in light of PETA's supposedly radical animal rights philosophy but in consideration of PETA's budget, which, at the time of the Aspen Hill killings, was in excess of $6 million per year. Moreover, popular media regularly feature PETA employees traveling around the globe to accompany rock stars who promote animal rights or to stage antifur demonstrations in Rome, Japan, and countless other places. Presumably, these activities involve considerable financial expenditures.

It should be noted that Newkirk also argued that these animals were not really at the sanctuary permanently, but were only in an "interim situation" that did not make their killing inconsistent with PETA's statements about Aspen Hill in its fund-raising literature.[109] Again, it is difficult to know what to make of such a contention. Assuming that the animals are rightholders and that they have a right to live their out their natural lives—a right that PETA seemed to recognize explicitly in its literature promoting Aspen Hill—then it is irrelevant that the rabbits were in an "interim" situation, whatever that means. Animals are either rightholders or they are not. If they are, then it is incoherent to say that humans can still deprive them of their most fundamental interests because of human convenience. No one doubts that PETA could have afforded to accommodate the animals; the point is that PETA made a decision to spend funds for other purposes, most of which have no direct impact on animals anyway. But then, how does Aspen Hill differ from the shelter whose purpose is to provide a humane death? And how is it any different from the dog owner who has her dog "put to sleep" because the dog is no longer convenient to the owner's lifestyle? PETA may have believed that funds spent on its educational campaigns would help more animals, but so does the person who says, "I will kill some animals today in the hope that I will obtain greater benefits for even more animals at some point in the future." It is precisely this sort of trade-off that characterizes the reasoning behind most institutionalized animal exploitation.

Reports suggested that some of the rabbits needed veterinary attention. But even if so, that would not have meant either that they needed to be killed or that the need for minor veterinary care morally justified their killing. And there was also never a suggestion that the decision to kill the roosters involved any concern about their ill health.[110] I am in no way claiming to question PETA's motivation in this matter, but it is difficult, if not impossible, to square any coherent notion of animal rights with the killing of healthy animals, especially at a sanctuary that, as Jasper and Nelkin observe, is supposed to represent a "rights" improvement over the welfarist's notion that we are obligated only to provide a "humane" death.

Again, the Aspen Hill matter resonates with the view that all that matters to animal advocacy is "compassion" for animals and that the "different ideologies arrive at the same conclusion." That view is simply not true. PETA surely has "compassion" for animals and seeks to improve their plight. But that does not end the matter. It is now necessary to decide what to do with *these* particular rabbits and roosters. To the extent that the decision made is to kill animals that do not absolutely require to be killed for reasons that would similarly justify the euthanasia of *any* moral agent, the different ideologies do not lead to the same conclusion. Indeed, that is why Jasper and Nelkin argue that the sanctuary approach is the "rights" alternative to the welfarist view that the purpose of shelters is to provide a "humane death."

I do not doubt that the roosters and rabbits at Aspen Hill were killed "humanely," in the sense that their death was inflicted with an absolute minimum of pain and suffering. I am absolutely certain that the killings were performed with "compassion." But that does not make the killings right. The animals had interests other than the simple the right to be free of pain and suffering. If that were the only interest that animals had, then it would be acceptable to eat animals who were raised and killed "humanely." And, as I pointed out earlier, that is precisely the position that Peter Singer takes in *Animal Liberation*. But the rights advocate believes that although animals certainly have an interest in avoiding pain and suffering, they have other interests as well, such as not being treated as means to ends within a system of institutionalized exploitation that causes the pain and suffering in the first instance. For the animal rights advocate, "happy" slavery *is still slavery*. This is not to say that the rights position is correct on this ground alone; it is only to establish that the two views, despite the claims of the new welfarists, lead to very different results.

Again, there was virtually no intramovement coverage of the Aspen Hill issue. In its "news shorts" section the *Animals' Agenda* had a single paragraph on the incident in which *Agenda* reported that the "PETA chairman pointed out that the group has never opposed euthanasia as a last-resort alternative to letting animals suffer." The *Agenda* "news short" did not discuss the fact that there was no indication of any need to kill any of these animals apart from the need created by PETA's decision not to spend the funds necessary to obviate the killings. And PETA continues to be identified by some with the very concept of animal rights. In my view, this is less an indication of attempts to cover up inappropriate or even outrageous behavior than it is more seriously a failure by some advocates to see the problem. This failure is understandable; in a movement that valorizes "compassion" above all other virtues, it should come as no surprise that the actions of "compassionate" people are excused even when those actions fly in the face of any coherent understanding of animal rights theory. But the confusion is compounded in light of wholly incorrect assertions that the "different ideologies arrive at the same conclusion." Animal rights theory would *not* lead to the same conclusion, and in this case, the difference certainly did make a difference—at least as far as the rabbits and roosters who were killed were concerned.

Conclusion

Many in the movement endorse "diversity" and urge that anyone who "cares" for animals, or who has "compassion" for animals, is really "walking along the same road" with those whose long-term goal is the abolition of animal exploitation. This desire to embrace "diversity" in the movement leads to positions that are difficult to understand and that make it difficult to formulate criteria for distinguishing who is the "exploiter" and who is not. For many new welfarists, the only criterion for belonging to the animal movement is having "compassion toward other animals" and a desire to "aid their plight." Any other criteria are considered to be exclusionary or "elitist."

If, however, the only difference between those whom Singer refers to as "exploiters" and at least some leaders of the animal rights movement is that the latter "feel compassion," then truly *this* is a "distinction without a difference" and is useless in helping to understand how the modern movement differs from its historical predecessors or from those whom it purports to oppose.

New welfarism rests on two notions: (1) that animal welfare ameliorates the plight of animals and can lead to the abolition of animal exploitation through incremental welfarist reform, and (2) that animal rights theory *cannot* provide a theory of incremental reform leading to abolition. I believe that both notions are mistaken.

CHAPTER Five

The Empirical and Structural Defects of Animal Welfare Theory

An underlying assumption of new welfarism is that welfarist reform will somehow lead incrementally to the abolition of institutionalized animal exploitation. As Finsen and Finsen point out, many animal advocates "see the possibility—or even the necessity"—of achieving their long-term goals, which are "conceptually distinct from the notion of welfare," through the very "gradual and reformist" means used by the animal welfarists.[1] New welfarists maintain that although the abolition of animal exploitation is the desired long-term goal, it is acceptable and necessary to pursue short-term welfarist reform as a means to that end.

Advocates of animal rights are not interested in *regulating* animal exploitation, but in *abolishing* it. The primary concern for the rights advocate is not kindness; after all, we do not make respect for the interests of minorities or women dependent upon some "kindly" disposition toward those people. Respect is instead a question of *justice*; if animals are rightholders, then those interests that are protected by right cannot be traded away simply because their "sacrifice" will benefit humans. Animal rights advocates reject the supposed superiority of humans over animals and challenge institutionalized animal exploitation as violative of relevant animal interests, irrespective of the "humaneness" with which the exploitation is supposedly conducted. For animal rights advocates, the status of animals as the *property* of humans facilitates treating animals only as means to human ends; the rights advocate seeks a status for animals that is closer to the notion of *personhood*.

The abolition of institutionalized animal exploitation sought by rights advocates can be achieved immediately or may be achieved as a result of a more lengthy process of incremental change. The immediate abolition of all institutionalized exploitation is, of course, unrealistic.

The abolition of slavery in America occurred relatively quickly, but the American economy was far less dependent on slavery than it presently is on institutionalized animal exploitation, which, when all relevant activities and support industries are included, is the largest sector of the national economy. Moreover, unlike the situation in 1865, when the largest section of the population was not involved in the targeted behavior—slave ownership—an overwhelming majority of people participate in institutionalized animal exploitation directly and indirectly, and they have indicated no receptivity to stopping that behavior anytime soon.

The eradication of animal exploitation will occur, if at all, through incremental change, but there has been a tendency of animal rights groups, especially in the United States, to assume for the most part that *all incremental measures are created equally.* These animal advocates regard *any* incremental measure that is thought to minimize suffering as a morally permissible step on the road to animal rights. Moreover, in light of their view that the only alternative to incremental change is an "all-or-nothing" demand for immediate abolition, these undifferentiated incremental means are seen as the *only* practical way of achieving the long-term goal. There has been no recognition that the rights advocate can pursue incremental changes, but should pursue only those incremental measures that differ significantly from the types of measures considered permissible within the welfarism paradigm.

For the most part, this is an assumption on the part of new welfarists, who have so far not offered any argument in favor of their position. Political theorist Robert Garner has presented the most sophisticated defense of this position to date—and I discuss it later—but Garner is a political scientist and academic, who is, after the fact, attempting to understand the workings of a social movement. It is difficult to know whether the new welfarists would accept his argument, but they themselves provide little theoretical justification for their views. They just assume that any measure that is thought to minimize pain is desirable and that any such measure is a step in the direction of animal rights.

Nowhere is this more apparent than in the views of Singer. As I discussed earlier, Singer sees as the long-term goal a time when the equal interests of all sentient beings are given equal consideration, which may or may not result in complete abolition but will probably require the abolition of much animal exploitation.[2] Nevertheless, Singer assumes that end can be reached by employing very conventional, welfarist reforms, and he thinks that animal advocates have an obligation to support these conventional reformist tactics. Singer, however, never explains why he believes that welfare reforms, as a *class* of actions, will lead somehow to the long-term goal. I mentioned earlier that Singer seems to think, for example, that more and more animal advocates boycotting meat and other animal products produced under factory-farm conditions will eventually lead "restaurants and food manufacturers to eliminate animal products altogether."[3] But given Singer's other view—that it may be permissible to eat animals that are not raised intensively, that are killed painlessly, and that are replaced by an equally "happy" animal—the elimination of intensive agriculture would, in all likelihood, not result in the elimination of animal agriculture, but only in its transformation.

Nevertheless, Singer does seem to believe that welfarist reform as a *class* of conduct (i.e., Singer does not evaluate particular incremental measures) will have some sort of moral effect on society that will lead to greater and greater sensitivity and to better and better reforms, although he never explains how this will occur.[4] Unfortunately, he stands on rather shaky ground. Anticruelty laws have existed in the United States since before there were states to be united; in 1641 the Massachusetts Bay Colony prohibited animal cruelty. As of the last check, it would stretch things considerably to argue that these statutes have helped make people more considerate of each other. And it would stretch things equally as far to say that these reforms have moved society further in the direction of abolishing animal suffering and exploitation. After all, more animals are used now by human beings than ever before, and though the pain and suffering to which animals are exposed now may be different from that which they suffered in the nineteenth century, most of us would still not want to be a nonhuman in *either* time period. Things are hideously bad for animals, and a little more or a little less pain really does not matter when the choice is between the slaughterhouses of nineteenth century London and the factory farms of modern-day America.

Most new welfarists seem to perceive no real inconsistency between the long-term goals of animal rights or equal consideration for equal interests and the short-term strategy of endorsing or aggressively supporting welfarist reforms. And most just assume that welfare will somehow "lead" to rights, that welfare is just some "milder" form of rights. This position involves four separate but related inquiries. The first inquiry is whether, as an empirical matter, there is anything to indicate that animal welfare works to ameliorate the plight of animals. The second inquiry is whether, as a structural matter, animal welfare *can* lead in the direction of abolition. The third inquiry is whether welfarist reforms can meaningfully be said to create any "rights" for animals. And the fourth inquiry involves the relationship between what I call the micro and macro aspects of moral reasoning.

Animal Welfare: Has It Worked?

If the central tenet of new welfarism is correct, and if, as a matter of fact, animal welfare is causally related to animal rights and indeed is necessary to achievement of the long-term goal, then we should be able to verify, one way or the other, whether animal welfare is, in fact, working. After all, we have had animal welfare solidly entrenched in political and legal doctrine for several hundred years, and hardly anyone disagrees with the notion that we ought to treat animals "humanely" and should not subject them to "unnecessary" suffering. The first anti-cruelty law was enacted in 1641, and there are welfare-oriented laws at both the federal and state level that require that the slaughter of animals for food be performed in a "humane" way, and there are hundreds of federal laws and regulations that purport to regulate the use of animals in experiments. Despite these laws, and despite the ubiquitous acceptance of the welfarist requirement of "humane" treatment, however, the measurable progress of the animal movement has been minimal.

In a recent study of the American animal rights movement, Lawrence Finsen and Susan Finsen discuss the issues and campaigns that are the subject of most activity by animal advocates, and they conclude that progress has not been significant in terms of either the extent of animal exploitation or the effect that animal advocates have had on the character of animal exploitation. Finsen and Finsen note that "the extent of animal usage has increased tremendously in this century" and that intensive agriculture involves practices that would, in the past, have been regarded as cruel but are now considered as normal and accepted by the government, agricultural researchers, and the exploiting industries.[5] Moreover, they argue that the effect of campaigns on institutionalized exploiters has been minimal.

Robert Garner, who discusses both the British and American movements but concentrates on the former, which is universally acknowledged as more radical than the American movement, argues that although animal advocates have experienced some successes, "much of the animal welfare agenda has been obstructed and it is difficult to think of legislation improving the welfare of animals that has seriously damaged the interests of animal users."[6] For example, Garner notes that there are many laws that pertain to farm animals, and "in theory, given the regulations surrounding the slaughtering process, the suffering of farm animals in the last moments of their lives should be minimal." Nevertheless, "there have been many disturbing reports . . . that these regulations are regularly broken"; "in general, problems occur because animal welfare often takes second place to cost-cutting."[7] He concludes that "the animal protection movement has made relatively little progress in influencing decision makers."[8]

This is not to say that animal advocates—be they rightists or welfarists—have not raised public consciousness about the issue of the social treatment of animals. On the contrary, there has been a marked increase in awareness about the subject, but there can also be no doubt that this increased awareness has not yet translated into significant decreases in animal exploitation. For example, with respect to the use of animals for food—and particularly the intensive farming of animals, or animal agriculture, a practice that developed well *after* animal welfare had become deeply entrenched in moral thought—Finsen and Finsen note that while there has been "some progress" made in Europe,[9] "there has been no meaningful improvement in the welfare of farm animals, at either the state or national level," in the United States.[10] Finsen and Finsen note that "there is evidence that Americans are reducing their consumption of meat, although the role of ethical considerations in these decisions is not altogether clear."[11] They do note, however, that it appears as though many people for ethical reasons no longer eat veal. Similarly, Finsen and Finsen caution that any improvement in the plight of animals used in experiments is unlikely because "vivisection has become a deeply entrenched feature of modern biomedical science, supported by powerful economic and political forces."[12]

With respect to animal experimentation, there have been many laws and regulations enacted, but there is nothing in the law that *prohibits* any type of experiment, however much pain or suffering is caused to animals. Indeed, there are still psychological affection-deprivation studies, as well as trauma experiments that involve the burning of unanesthetized animals, despite the opposition to vivisection that these types of experiments fueled in the 1970s. As I discussed earlier, the federal Animal Welfare Act (AWA) does little beyond regulating issues of animal husbandry and explicitly provides no restriction of what can be done to animals or how it can be done. Garner, who is explicitly sympathetic toward welfarist reforms, observes correctly that the aim of the federal act "is not primarily to regulate the kind of procedures adopted but only the supply and care of animals destined for research institutions (purchase, transportation, housing, and handling)."[13]

Moreover, the *types* of animal experiments are, if anything, getting more objectionable despite the "humane" ethic that should be pushing in the opposite direction. Not only do millions of animals continue to be used in laboratories, but genetic engineering and cross-species transplants present new and arguably worse threats to animals in terms of pain and suffering. As critics of biotechnology such as Jeremy Rifkin have argued, animals used in invasive experiments may experience pain and suffering for some period of time, which is usually shorter than the duration of the animal's entire life, whereas genetically engineered animals experience intense pain and suffering from the moment they first become conscious and until the time at which they die.[14] Even the "successes" of the American movement have been less important than supposed. The government ended funding for Taub's experiments, but Taub has been rehabilitated within the scientific community and has received a number of awards. The head-injury experiments at the University of Pennsylvania were stopped in 1985 after the government found that the animals had not been provided with adequate veterinary care. Federal dollars began to flow to the Penn lab again in 1993, after Gennarelli announced that he would use pigs instead of baboons in his experiments.

In addition, there have always been serious criticisms of the enforcement of the laws and regulations concerning laboratory animals, and in particular of the enforcement of the federal Animal Welfare Act by the U.S. Department of Agriculture (USDA), which enforces the AWA through its Animal and Plant Health Inspection Service (APHIS). Ironically, the most effective critiques of USDA / APHIS enforcement of the AWA have come from the government itself. In 1985, the General Accounting Office (GAO) issued a report that found, among other things, that training and written guidance for USDA inspectors was insufficient, that the frequency of lab inspections was inadequate, that APHIS did not follow up on serious deficiencies in a satisfactory manner, and that inspection quality and reporting was uneven and inconsistent.[15] A 1986 study by the Office of Technology Assessment was also critical of USDA / APHIS enforcement of the AWA.[16] In 1995, the USDA Office of the Inspector General issued a report finding, among other things, that "APHIS does not have the authority, under current legislation, to effectively enforce the requirements of the [AWA]," that research facilities were obtaining animals from shelters without observing the requisite waiting period, that "APHIS could make more effective use of its existing enforcement powers," and that APHIS was failing to monitor animal care committees properly, with the result that "there is insufficient assurance that the committees minimized pain and discomfort to research animals."[17] Conservative welfarist groups, such as the Animal Welfare Institute (AWI)[18] and the Humane Society of the United States,[19] have also criticized USDA/APHIS enforcement of the AWA as inadequate in many respects.

Moreover, not only have welfarist reforms not moved society closer to the abolition of violence toward animals, but animal exploiters often point to welfarist reforms to defend their activities and to seek public support for their continuation. Nowhere is this more apparent than in the area of animal use in experiments. Groups like the Foundation for Biomedical Research produce educational materials in which they assure the public that laws such as the federal Animal Welfare Act provide for "proper care of laboratory animals" and set standards for "veterinary care and use of anesthetics or analgesics."[20]

There has been some success in the area of product testing, but "the campaign to end animal testing of even the most frivolous products has not been won by animal advocates yet, despite the gains made."[21] Moreover, the connection between decreases in animal use in product testing and the efforts of animal advocates is unclear because the industries involved were themselves at least somewhat critical of animal tests before animal advocates focused on the area.[22] These efforts are generally undertaken to influence consumers to use their purchasing power to avoid products that contain animal products or that have been tested on animals. Such efforts are undoubtedly important, but there are structural limits to this form of advocacy. As Garner correctly points out with respect to all products involving animal exploitation, "Consumers are not usually given enough information on which to make an effective choice. Animal protection groups can, of course, seek to provide this information but have limited resources particularly when compared to the wealth of business concerns using animals." Garner also notes that "some companies are making misleading claims by, for instance, marketing as 'cruelty-free' products where the ingredients, as opposed to the finished product, have been tested on animals."[23] Animal groups have sought to focus pressure on companies that test (rather than try to persuade consumers not to purchase those items), but "there are doubts . . . whether the consumer strategy has *any* long-term worth without a parallel campaign for legislative change."[24]

In the area of furs, Finsen and Finsen state that the "anti-fur cam-

paign is one campaign in which activists can claim to have made progress," but they acknowledge that "knowing with any degree of assurance to what extent a variety of potential causal factors was operative in
the fur slump is enormously difficult." Moreover, they observe that "at
the same time that the [fur] market is very bad, the fur industry in the
United States is also undergoing some changes that may have profound
implications for the anti-fur movement."[25] Finsen and Finsen cite the
widespread opening of foreign markets for fur, especially in Japan, and,
"even more ominous," the increase in imported fur coats and the emergence of vertically integrated companies, such as Jindo, a South Korean
company that manages all phases of the fur operation from ranching to
retail selling.[26] In addition, the price decrease resulting from cheaper
furs made abroad, as well as excess supply in the United States, may
create greater demand as prices inevitably drop.

Most Americans do not hunt and are opposed to recreational hunting, but the movement has failed to make any significant dent in this
activity, and much of the public is still deluded by erroneous claims that
hunting is necessary to thin herds "humanely," and is unaware that
federal and state agencies manipulate habitats "in order to maintain the
'maximum sustainable yield' for the hunters."[27] Not only have animal
advocates failed to make any significant inroads against hunting, but
hunters have succeeded in getting Congress and many state legislatures
to enact "hunter harassment" laws that have been upheld as constitutional and that have the practical effect of chilling the speech of anti-
hunting animal advocates. Finally, animals continue to be used for
pigeon shoots, rooster pulls, pig wrestling, mule diving, donkey basket-
ball, captive-animal shoots, and motion pictures.[28]

Indeed, if anything, animal exploitation is, as a general matter,
worse—in terms of both the numbers of animals exploited and the ways
in which they are exploited—than ever before. Again, it would be wrong
to maintain that the movement has not helped to raise consciousness
about the plight of animals, but even those educational efforts have
been tainted to some degree by the unwillingness of animal advocates
to draw the line between rights and welfare. For example, although
many animal rights organizations claim to embrace the complete abolition of animal exploitation as a long-term goal, they often couch this
message in more "conservative" terms in order to make their message
more acceptable to the public. The problem with this approach is that it
allows animal exploiters to respond that animal advocates are not honest or that they have some "secret" agenda, which is arguably harmful
to the overall credibility of the movement.[29]

In addition, the argument in favor of animal rights is often ignored or presented as secondary to arguments that animal experimentation is unsound from a scientific point of view or that the eating of animal products is bad for human health or for the environment. Although many of these arguments are important, they sometimes are allowed—and sometimes are intended—to become more prominent than the ethical argument. These arguments shift the moral focus from issues of justice for a disempowered group to the self-interest of the empowered group and open the debate to various empirical considerations, such as how dangerous meat eating really is or whether vivisection is really "scientific fraud."[30] There is considerable disagreement within the movement about the importance of these nonmoral arguments, and even commentators from outside the movement disagree about their relative importance. For example, Garner claims that "the animal protection movement has achieved most in recent years when it has sought to challenge the importance (and sometimes the very existence) of the benefits it is claimed humans derive from making animals suffer rather than from the ethically-based denial that humans have a right to benefit from such suffering."[31] Other commentators are more skeptical of these arguments, since opposition to animal exploitation, according to these commentators, is based on factual considerations that may allow for animal exploitation, depending on those considerations. For example, many animal advocates gloss over the moral arguments in favor of vegetarianism and argue that eating meat is bad for human health. Although that may be (and in all probability is) true, the focus of much genetic engineering is the production of food animals that are "safer" to eat. If agricultural vivisectors someday succeed in producing an animal whose meat is as safe to eat as are vegetables raised with commercial pesticides, then the arguments against meat eating will lose a certain amount of force. Moreover, risk taking is a feature of human life. Many people smoke cigarettes even though everyone is now aware that the habit is very dangerous. Most people eat saturated fats and all sorts of food that they know carry a greater risk of heart disease and other maladies than a "health" diet. Focus on health matters assumes that people place a great deal of weight on such things, and, as an empirical matter, that is simply untrue.

The Failure of Animal Welfare: Blame Animal Rights

Certain new welfarists have implicitly recognized that the results of animal welfare have been disappointing, but have blamed animal rights advocates for these results. For example, Henry Spira, who defends using reformist, welfarist measures to achieve the long-term goal of abolishing animal exploitation, argues that "self-righteous antivivisection societies had been hollering 'Abolition! All or Nothing!' But that didn't help the laboratory animals, since while the antivivisection groups had been hollering, the numbers of animals used in United States laboratories had zoomed from a few thousand to over 70 million. That was a pitiful track record, and it seemed a good idea to rethink strategies which have a century-long record of failure."[32] Similarly, Andrew Rowan criticizes those who oppose animal experimentation, claiming that "their *error* is clearly demonstrated by the fact that, in the hundred years during which antivivisection groups have campaigned against animal research, animal research has grown from very modest beginnings into a multibillion dollar exercise, utilizing tens of millions of animals annually."[33]

For a number of reasons, it strains credulity to attribute the dramatic rise in the numbers of animals used in experiments to the antivivisection movement. As most scholars agree, the antivivisection movement—both in the United States and Great Britain—had been rather dormant in the twentieth century until the modern animal "rights" period.[34] Moreover, to the extent that there was any animal protection movement in the United States before 1980, that movement—the American animal welfare movement—"has always been strongly proscience and largely concerned with encouraging humane treatment of animals, particularly of pets, in a variety of nonscientific settings."[35] Indeed, during the period of time that Rowan acknowledges experienced a tremendous increase in animal use, most of the large, traditional, animal welfare organizations *supported* animal experimentation and only sought its regulation, not its abolition. The historical evidence strongly supports an inference *opposite* the one that Spira and Rowan draw: it is acceptance of the welfarist paradigm, as well as support by welfarists of regulationist legislation, not the policies of antivivisectionists, that has been coincidental with the dramatic rise in animal use.

Animal Welfare: A Nonsuccess Story
Not only do some new welfarists sometimes make rather surprising (and unsupported) charges that animal rights advocates are to blame for the failures of the movement, they also make equally surprising claims that there are success stories for which animal welfare reforms are responsible. For example, just as Rowan mistakenly concludes that antivivisectionist sentiment somehow caused an *increase* in animal use, he also—and just as mistakenly—argues that animal welfare policies have

somehow caused a *decrease* in laboratory animal use since 1967. A recent study performed by Rowan and two coauthors concludes that "it appears as though animal use (or at least the use of the six species primarily counted by the USDA) has declined by almost 50% since 1967."[36] Rowan concludes that this decrease demonstrates that those who support animal welfare have had a positive impact on animal exploitation—and, accordingly, have validated their approach—in contrast to the disastrous results (increase in animal use) supposedly caused by the antivivisectionists.[37] Rowan's study and the causal inferences that he draws are, however, seriously deficient for at least two reasons.

First, the methodology of Rowan's study is seriously flawed. Rowan relies largely on figures reported by the Institute for Laboratory Animal Resources (ILAR), a quasi-governmental organization that vehemently supports animal use. Rowan claims that ILAR "reported a 40% decrease in the number of animals used in the U.S. in the ten years between 1968 and 1978, based on the 1968 and 1978 national surveys conducted by ILAR." Rowan admits that it is "not clear how much confidence can be placed in the [ILAR] methodology or results,"[38] because, in addition to general data-collection problems resulting from reporting inadequacies and inconsistencies, there were inconsistencies among various ILAR reports and an "unexplained discrepancy" between ILAR figures and USDA figures.[39] Indeed, in congressional testimony in 1981, Rowan stated that although ILAR surveys had been used to support the notion that animal use was declining, the ILAR figures were, according to Rowan, "just not credible given all the other conflicting information."[40] Curiously, Rowan relies on these same figures as part of his study, but he does not explain what in the intervening years changed his view about the credibility of ILAR figures. In addition, Rowan's reliance on the ILAR figures is problematic because they include supposed decreases in the numbers of rats and mice used, although current federal law does not require that the use of these animals be reported and reliable data collection is therefore virtually impossible.[41] Nevertheless—and quite remarkably—Rowan concludes that "despite these problems," animal use "has declined by almost 50% since 1967."[42]

Second, even if animal use in laboratories has declined, Rowan offers no support whatsoever for the contention that this decrease is, in any way, attributable to efforts by animal welfarists, just as he and Spira can show no evidence that the increase in animal use in laboratories is attributable to the actions of antivivisectionists. Indeed, in an earlier work, Rowan argued that laboratory animal use increased from 1965 to 1970, but "then steadied in the 1970's when users began to increase their demand for higher quality animals."[43] That is, animal use is determined by myriad variables, and most of these variables have little, if anything, to do with the advocacy of animal welfare *or* animal rights groups. There are many possible explanations for declining use of animals in laboratories, if, as Rowan argues, that use has, in fact, declined. To attribute any decline to the efforts of animal welfarists in light of the extant empirical data would be purely speculative and without the solid foundation required of scholarly analysis.

Moreover, although USDA reporting requirements are anything but accurate, the government's own recent data indicate that animal use in experiments is not decreasing in the way that Rowan asserts, and it also appears that the 1985 amendments to the Animal Welfare Act have not had a significant impact on the number of animals used in painful experiments. This is important because a central tenet of new welfarism is that welfarist reforms are acceptable as a short-term tactic insofar as they lessen animal suffering. As I mentioned earlier, recent numbers reported by the USDA indicate that the overall number of animals used has not decreased and that the number of animals used in painful ex- periments without the benefit of anesthesia or analgesia has also not decreased.

In an interesting twist on this discussion, Rowan and his coauthors reissued their 1994 study in 1995, although nothing in the 1995 version indicated that there had been an earlier version.[44] The 1995 version of the study discusses the problems with the ILAR data and then con- cludes that, "despite these problems, it appears as though animal use (or at least the use of the six species primarily counted by the USDA) has declined by at least 23% and maybe as much as 40%."[45] When questioned about this discrepancy, Rowan replied that "when [his 1994] analysis occasioned so much comment and reaction, [he] went back and had a second look at the data and changed the percentage figures to be more precise."[46] In addition, in the 1995 version of the Tufts study, Rowan tries to explain why there has been an *increase* in animal use in the 1990s, according to USDA statistics. As I mentioned earlier, the USDA does not require that rats and mice be reported, because they are not defined as "animals" under the federal Animal Welfare Act. Rowan argues that as of 1990, "if any institution voluntarily reports rat and mouse numbers (as more and more are doing), these data are tabulated in the 'other' category [i.e., category other than the six covered species]. As a result, animal use has apparently 'increased' in the 1990s."[47] The problem with Rowan's explanation is that it is explicitly contradicted by the USDA reports. Both the 1991 and 1992 reports state clearly that the total number of animals reported "excludes birds, rats, and mice, and farm animals used in agricultural research." Rowan has since admitted that he was incorrect in asserting that voluntarily reported rats and mice are included in the "other" category.[48]

It should be noted that *Animal People*, which had run several stories defending Rowan's original claim of a 50 percent reduction, refused to print anything about Rowan's revised assessment (from 50 percent to 23 percent and maybe 40 percent) or his error concerning the "other" category. *Animal People* editor Merritt Clifton claimed that the matter was one of "semantics and not of fact."[49]

In any event, there is little empirical evidence that animal welfare either decreases suffering or leads to anything but more animal welfare.

The Structural Defects of Animal Welfare

I have noted throughout this book that the new welfarists themselves have offered very little in the way of argument for their contention that there is no inconsistency between animal rights and animal welfare or for their contention that animal welfare is causally related to animal rights. Moreover, commentators have observed that the movement's long-term goals often differ from its short-term positions, but these same commentators then characterize the movement, or individual groups within the movement, based on long-term goals alone and seem unconcerned about their inconsistency. There is, however, one scholar who has tried to analyze the adoption by animal rights groups of short-term strategies that represent welfarist reforms. In *Animals, Politics, and Morality*, political theorist Robert Garner presents what I regard as the most sophisticated analysis of the movement to date. It should be noted that although Garner is a British political theorist and writes mostly about British animal advocates, he makes extensive reference to "other countries and particularly the United States where developments have been remarkably similar."[50] Moreover, Garner has allied himself closely with American welfarist groups such as the American Humane Association and *Animals' Agenda*.

Garner himself recognizes that welfarist reform has not worked and, in a startling acknowledgment, states that despite years and years of domination by animal welfare groups with insider status, "it is difficult to think of legislation improving the welfare of animals that has seriously damaged the interests of the animal users."[51] Garner maintains that welfarist reform is the only "realistic" or "practical" way of improving matters for nonhumans. After he surveys the views of Regan and Singer, he seems to favor Regan's views, claiming that he regards orthodox animal welfarism as "seriously flawed" in certain respects; he states that he "is more convinced by the protection afforded to humans and animals by rights than [he is] by utilitarianism, with the difficulties of measurement and its unpredictable results." Nevertheless, Garner ends up endorsing a version of animal welfare as the result of his concern for "practical politics" and his belief that animal welfare, although it may have problems, has played a "key role" in protecting nonhumans and that "there is still a great deal of scope for reform" within the more traditional animal welfare context.[52] Garner does discuss—albeit extremely briefly—the view advanced by myself and others that an animal rights approach can accommodate incremental changes, but he disputes whether abolitionist means to abolitionist ends can produce a coherent alternative to the new welfarist approach of using welfarist means to achieve a supposedly abolitionist end. Garner is skeptical that animal rights advocates may, like animal welfare advocates, seek incremental changes, though these incremental steps may have a different character than the incremental measures of animal welfare. Again, Garner's assumption of the *need* for animal welfare overshadows his attempts to present any sort of developed argument on the subject.

Underlying Garner's notion that welfarist incremental measures are the only "practical" solution to the problem is Garner's view that the orthodox welfare theory is adaptable in that its *legal* requirements of "humane" treatment and its prohibition against "unnecessary" suffering develop alongside evolving *moral* notions about animal care. This assumption is central to Garner's analysis and represents the only really sustained (but ultimately unsuccessful) attempt to show that there is some causal relationship between animal welfare reforms in the short term and achievement of animal rights in the long term.

Animal Welfare: The Scope of Reform

In order to understand Garner's arguments—and the serious flaws in his analysis—it is necessary to understand what Garner means when he talks about the animal advocacy position reflected in "moral orthodoxy."[53] Moral orthodoxy is the view that animals, although capable of experiencing pain and pleasure, are not, like human animals, autonomous beings. As a result, "we are entitled to sacrifice the interests of animals to further human interests."[54] According to Garner, it is not just "any human interest" that justifies this sacrifice of animal interest. Indeed, Garner claims that "the painful death of any amount of animals in order to provide entertainment for humans" is not "seriously defended" by anyone. Instead, the position of traditional animal welfare is that the human interest at stake must be "significant."[55] The focus of traditional animal welfare, Garner notes correctly, is on determining whether any particular infliction of suffering, pain, distress, and the like, is "necessary."

The thrust of Garner's argument is that there is considerable scope for reform within the parameters of moral orthodoxy, or welfarism, because the notion of "necessary suffering" is inherently flexible and radicals are provided thereby with an opportunity "to extend the range of activities which humans regard as unnecessary."[56] For example, in discussing British efforts in the mid-1980s to secure better regulation of the use of animals in experiments, Garner argues that some of the "radical" British animal advocacy organizations disagreed with the welfarists and sought legislation that would have prohibited, and not merely regulated, "certain areas of research, such as cosmetics and weapons testing."[57] Garner concedes that these abolitionist demands were "reasonable," but he claims that these demands were simply unrealistic because "in the present climate no parliament will prohibit research on animals for medical purposes."[58] Instead, in 1986, Britain enacted a law that forbade imposition of "unnecessary suffering," and despite its failure to prohibit any particular procedures, Garner claims that such legislation offers "great potential" for reformers who may use the "necessity" standard to their advantage by challenging "the conventional wisdom both that animal experimentation is valuable and that we are entitled to inflict suffering for that end." Garner concludes his discussion by noting that "the key point is that, although the [1986 Scientific Procedures Act] does not prohibit any particular type of research on animals, it does not protect any either. Indeed, it offers the prospect of abolition of animal experimentation *without any further legislation.*"[59] The "concept of unnecessary suffering is sufficiently flexible for there to be a great deal that could be done, and is beginning to be done, to improve the lot of animals."[60]

Garner argues that in the areas of product testing, furs, animal fighting, and so forth, social consensus has changed and is changing more, and that reformers can hope to achieve greater gains for animals by focusing on the "necessity" of animal use. The "flexibility" provided by animal welfare theory enhances "the chances of persuading the public and decision makers of the need for reform" but comes at the cost of working "within a value system which holds that the exploitation of animals is justified providing that substantial human benefits can be established."[61] Finally, Garner claims that the "animal protection movement has achieved most in recent years when it has sought to challenge the importance (and sometimes the very existence) of the benefits it is claimed humans derive from making animals suffer rather than from the ethically-based denial that humans have a right to benefit from such suffering."[62]

Garner's argument, albeit interesting and certainly the only attempt that I have seen thus far to employ rational discourse and argument in support of the central tenets of new welfarism, is invalid because it assumes as a structural matter that the notion of "necessity" is sufficiently flexible not only to accommodate progressive welfarist reforms but to lead to gradual prohibitions sought by more radical rights advocates. In order to see Garner's error, it is necessary to return to his description of the moral orthodoxy he claims characterizes traditional animal welfare. According to Garner, no one defends the view that animals' interests can be sacrificed for trivial human interests; the prevalent view is that animals' interests can be sacrificed only for "significant" human interests. Indeed, Garner describes the position of traditional animal welfare as allowing for the sacrifice of animal interests when and where such "significant" human interests are identified.

Garner understandably relies on the notion that just about everyone in most societies would agree that humans ought not to exploit nonhumans for trivial reasons. Paradoxically, however, despite the almost ubiquitous recognition that it is morally wrong to inflict "unnecessary" pain on animals, we still have circuses, bow hunting, pigeon shoots, rooster pulls, animal fights, pig wrestling, mule diving, and the like. These practices cause many animals tremendous pain and suffering, and none serves a purpose beyond the mere entertainment of humans, and yet all are legal and permitted under the very laws that new welfarists argue will help us "springboard into animal rights." So, although, in one sense, Garner is correct to say that no one defends the sacrifice of animals for "trivial" purposes, human interests that are nevertheless "trivial" under any coherent interpretation of the concept override the competing animal interests in virtually every instance.

Indeed, the whole notion of what constitutes a "trivial" or "significant" interest in the first instance is very much a normative notion. Garner would not regard the use of animals for food as falling into the category of acts that inflict pain on animals "in order to provide entertainment for humans." But, as Garner concedes, evidence is mounting that meat is not only unnecessary for the human diet but may even be harmful to human health. Consequently, the eating of meat arguably constitutes a use of animals for human "entertainment" that does not differ from the human use of recreational drugs—an area in which animal advocates have argued against the use of animals precisely because such drug use constitutes the sort of gratuitous conduct that cannot serve to justify the imposition of suffering on animals. In any event, and however the notion of triviality is understood, it would be absurd to deny that the law (both in the United States and Great Britain) allows animal interests to be sacrificed for completely trivial human purposes. So, from the outset, Garner defends the moral flexibility of an apocryphal regulatory structure bearing no resemblance to the actual workings of animal welfare laws.

The Importance of the Property Status of Animals

Animal welfare laws require that we *balance* the interests of humans and nonhumans in order to determine whether particular treatment is "humane" or whether suffering is "necessary." This balancing structure, however, serves to obscure an important normative consideration that renders meaningless any such attempt to balance human and animal interests. Under the law, animals are *things*; they are regarded as *property*. The legal systems of most Western nations contain two primary types of entities: *persons* and *property*. Most legal scholars claim that legal relations can exist only between persons and that property cannot have rights. The class of "persons" is not limited to human beings; corporations and other nonnatural entities are regarded under the law as "persons" for purposes of owning property and carrying out various activities.

Humans are entitled under laws of property to convey or to sell their animals, consume or kill them, use them as collateral, obtain their natural dividends, and exclude others from interfering with the owners' exercise of dominion or control over them. This is, of course, not to say that the law cannot and does not restrict the use of animal property; indeed, the law regulates the use of virtually *all* types of property, including animal property. Whether those restrictions have the actual or the intended result of providing protection for animals is another question. In any event, as far as the law is concerned, animals as property are, as a matter of law, regarded only as means to the ends of persons.

When humans seek to exploit animals for food, science, entertainment, clothing, or any other purpose, there is an obvious conflict between the interests of the animals and the interests of the humans who seek to exploit those animals. The law, which embodies a welfarist approach, requires that we balance the human and animal interests in order to determine which interest is more important. But this supposed balancing process prescribed by animal welfare theory is defective because it requires that we balance completely dissimilar normative entities. Human interests are protected by rights in general and by the right to own property in particular. Animals have no legal rights and are regarded as the property of humans. As far as the law is concerned, such a conflict is identical to that between a person and her shoe. The winner of the dispute is predetermined by the way in which the conflicting parties are characterized under the law.

When we balance animal interests against human interests, the animal interest never prevails, precisely because of this "hybrid" system that requires that we juxtapose the interests of a rightholder with that of a nonrightholder who, in addition to being a nonrightholder, is also the object of the rightholder's exercise of her property rights. As property, animals are *chattels*, just as slaves once were. And just as in the case of human slaves, virtually *any* interest possessed by animals can be "sacrificed" or traded away as long as the human benefit is sufficient. There are plenty of laws that prohibit "unnecessary" suffering or require that we treat animals "humanely," but humans are nevertheless allowed to use animals not only for experiments or as food, but for dog trials, racing, cock fights, ritual sacrifice, carriage rides in the middle of a congested city, or as "exhibits" in zoos. All of these uses of animals are "unnecessary." Indeed, as I noted above, few health care professionals still maintain that animal products are "necessary" for a healthy diet, and an increasing number of such professionals claim that the consumption by humans of animal products presents serious health risks. Nevertheless, animal agriculture, which accounts for the largest institutionalized use of animals, and these and other activities, which account for fewer animals but nevertheless result in the imposition on animals of hideous pain and suffering, are permitted under the very laws that prohibit the infliction of "unnecessary" suffering on animals and require their "humane" treatment.

Different social systems may accord greater or lesser importance to property rights, but there can be little doubt that property rights in the Anglo-American context have generally been regarded not merely as "positive" rights, or rights that may be said to exist only by virtue of their being enacted in some prescribed and accepted manner, but as "natural" rights, or moral rights that exist whether or not they are recognized by some legal system. The status of property rights as natural rights was articulated by the primary architect of Anglo-American property theory, English philosopher John Locke.[63] Locke argued that people had property rights in their bodies and in their labor, and that they could acquire property by "joining" their labor with an object in nature that was, by virtue of divine creation, held by humankind in common unless and until it became the property of a particular person. So, for example, even though all of the "objects" in the woods are owned in common by all humans, if I go into the woods and take a piece of wood, and if I "join" my labor to that wood by, say, carving it into a piece of furniture or even by cutting the piece of wood from a tree, then I have, through using my labor, made that piece of wood my "property." For Locke, "the sole ground of *original* [and] exclusive property rights" was the labor of the person. And because the rights secured were natural, or moral, rights, and not merely rights created by positive law, the state could not make property rights "subject to whatever constraints society deems proper."[64]

Locke simply assumed that animals, unlike humans, did not have a property interest in their bodies, and, indeed, he regarded them as *objects* that people could transform into property. All animals in nature are owned in common by all humans; when, however, a particular person hunts and kills a particular hare, the person has "thereby removed [the hare] from the state of nature, wherein she was common, and hath begun a property." "Thus this law of reason makes the [d]eer that *Indian's* who hath killed it; [it is] allowed to be his goods who hath bestowed his labour upon it, though before, it was the common right of every one."[65] Although Locke recognized that animals possessed a complex psychology, he maintained that "the inferior ranks of Creatures" were made by god for the use of humans.[66]

Locke's theory had an important impact on the law of property. One of the most highly regarded English judges, William Blackstone, stated that "there is nothing which so generally strikes the imagination, and engages the affections of mankind, as the right of property; or that sole and despotic domination which one man claims and exercises over the external things of the world, in total exclusion of the right of any other individual in the universe."[67] Blackstone, citing the passage in Genesis (1:20–28) in which man is given "dominion over the fish of the sea, and over the birds of the air, and over the cattle, and over all the earth, and over every creeping thing that creeps upon the earth," considered that "by holy writ, the all-bountiful Creator gave to man 'dominion'" over all animals.[68] Blackstone relied on Locke's theory of property as a natural right and formulated a broad notion of property that would not tolerate the "least violation" of the right.[69]

The importance of property rights has not diminished over time and is particularly strong in our legal system, which prohibits state interference with life, liberty, or property—establishing property rights on the same level as arguably more fundamental rights in life and liberty. Indeed, the so-called revolution that began with the 1994 congressional elections is based largely on the notion that "liberal" social policies have impermissibly assumed that it is appropriate to make partial redistribution of wealth through taxation and social welfare programs. The critique of government is increasingly centered on laws and regulations that are claimed to infringe on property rights, such as environmental regulations, which are claimed to deprive landowners of the economic value of their real property, or gun laws, which are claimed to deprive gun owners of their rights to use property the ownership of which is claimed to be protected by the constitution. The status of animals as property has also not diminished. Indeed, that status is so secure that even when humans do not want to consider animals merely as property and instead view at least some animals, such as dogs and cats, as members of their families, the law refuses to recognize that status. If a veterinarian negligently kills someone's dog or cat, most courts will limit recovery to the fair market value of the dog or cat, as though the animal were inanimate personal property.[70]

Legal standards that concern the "humane" treatment of animals or the prevention of "unnecessary" pain assume that the human hegemony over animals is legitimate, in the first instance, and that the only issue is *how* this power is to be exercised. The law assumes that animals are "things" and that "things" exist primarily to satisfy the needs and wants of persons. The only question is whether, and under what circumstances, the law will interfere with property use in light of the importance of property as a social institution and in light of the belief, which is very strong at least in most Western legal systems, that the owners of property should be left alone, to the furthest extent possible, to determine the uses to which their property is put. As a result, despite the almost universally accepted moral maxim that any "unnecessary" animal suffering ought to be prohibited, the balancing system prescribed by animal welfare laws ensures that virtually any use of animals is deemed to be "necessary" irrespective of the trivial nature of the human interest involved or the serious nature of the animal interest that will be "sacrificed."

In such a scenario, notions like "humane" treatment or "unnecessary" suffering are merely euphemistic indications of the success or failure of conduct in facilitating the exploitation of animal property. For example, scientists have on numerous occasions conducted experiments in which they subject conscious, unanesthetized animals to intense heat, supposedly in order to learn about burns. Indeed, I have a video I show to law students that depicts an actual federally funded experiment in which experimenters at a prestigious institution burn a large portion of the body of a conscious unanesthetized pig in order to study the effects of the pig's subsequent eating habits. This is not considered "cruel" or "unnecessary," because it facilitates an institutionalized form of exploitation that is considered legitimate. The question whether the conduct is "necessary" is decided not by reference to some moral ideal but by reference to norms of exploitation already deemed legitimate. If, however, an adolescent performs the exact same act, the act may be punished (albeit with a relatively minor sanction under the most punitive scenario) as "cruel," not because the actions in the two cases are different—indeed, there is no difference in the *quality* of treatment in the two cases—but because the action by the adolescent does not facilitate the normative, "legitimate," institutionalized exploitation of the animal. In institutional use, the people who exploit animals (who are in most cases also the owners of those animals) determine that there are benefits to that animal use, and the law accepts that determination. But if "cruelty" or the "necessity" of pain, suffering, or death is determined not by conformity of the conduct to some abstract standard but by the animal owners' determination of the benefits that will come from such conduct, then, unless the property owners are not acting rationally (in that they have failed to maximize the value of their animal property), the law will in *all* cases think that their conduct is justified. It is *their* property, and they are using their property in the most cost-effective way in order to maximize its value.

Property rights in animals have historically been allocated to people, and animals remain property because that allocation of rights is thought to maximize the value of this particular type of property (nonhuman animals) to property owners (human animals). Our allocation to humans of rights in the bodies of animals precisely reflects our belief that it is more efficient to relegate animals to property status, with all of the consequences that are entailed and *because* of all the consequences that are entailed, than it is to value animals for themselves and to accord them dignity and respect. Concern for animals is not "cost-justified." The fact that we allocate property rights in animals means that we do not value the animals in themselves—as something not quite persons but closer to that status than to things—or that we do not value animal protection (or regulations that limit the use of animal property) beyond what is necessary to ensure the efficient exploitation of animals for its own value.

The property status of animals maximizes the wealth of animal resources in that the property status of animals is necessary for a market in which there are offering and selling prices for animals. Indeed, the notion of the productive value of animals would make no sense were it not for their property status, and this value can only be measured by human beings—which is to say that the property status of animals and their productive value are inextricably intertwined. Since animals are the property of their owners, and since we assume that the owners of property will, all things being equal, seek to maximize the value of their own property, the law relies to a great extent on self-governance to ensure that animals are provided with the level of welfare needed to ensure their most efficient exploitation. For example, vivisectors routinely argue that it is absurd to worry about animal abuse in labs, because researchers who regularly or systematically "mistreated" their animals would not get good data from the animals. But the production of good data is no guarantee that the treatment in question is not "mistreatment." "Mistreatment" is a normative word, not a scientific label. To say that there are good data may mean only that the data are deemed reliable *despite* what may be called, as a moral matter (though not necessarily a scientific matter), mistreatment. Moreover, the argument about reliability of data is illustrative of the general proposition that rational people would not so use their property as to defeat the purposes for which the property is being used in the first place. And the intuitive appeal of that rather commonsense position is one reason why, in social systems that have very strong property notions, the law generally allows the owner of property to determine what uses she makes of her property.

Even regulation of property uses for common purposes is ideally supposed to maximize overall social wealth. In some cases, the owner of property may be entitled to compensation if property (usually real property) is taken outright or its use is regulated to such an extent that courts deem that a constructive taking has occurred. Regulation of the use of animals is the only property regulation that is, at least ostensibly, intended to "benefit" the property and, at least as far as some people (those who value animal protection above the level that will facilitate exploitation) are concerned, not intended exclusively to maximize social wealth. For example, although certain laws prohibit the destruction or alteration of buildings that are designated as "landmarks," such laws cannot be characterized as conferring a benefit on the building or structure; rather, the purpose of such laws is to ensure that these buildings and structures will be available in a particular form for the enjoyment of future generations of human beings. When the law attempts to regulate animal property use in a society that, like ours, has a very strong commitment to protecting private property, and aggressively attempts to tie moral issues to market behavior, those regulations will seek to achieve the optimal level of restriction given the value of the property and the overall social wealth that will result from that regulation.

For the most part, however, the suffering of animals represents a truly "external" cost of animal use because there is no easy way to quantify that cost and to "internalize" it for purposes of determining what course of action best serves the goal of economic efficiency. As a general matter, cost-benefit calculations concerning animal welfare regulations do not even purport to measure benefit from the point of view of the animals, because, as property, the animals have no entitlements protected by right or otherwise. Rather, any assessment of the social benefit of animal welfare regulations is understood in terms of the benefits that humans perceive to come from such regulation. The USDA, which enforces the federal Animal Welfare Act has noted, in connection with assessing the desirability of additional federal regulation of animal experimentation, that "animal welfare is an anthropomorphic attribute" that requires measurement of the "increase in the level of *public perception* [of] animal welfare as the level of stringency of the regulation also increases." Such measurements involve a "lengthy and cost prohibitive study of marginal increases in social welfare or utility."[71]

The tension between the perceived need to maximize the value of property—in this case, animal property—and the costs of regulation of property use is resolved with standards of animal welfare that will, for the most part, be determined not by some moral ideal but by some measure of perceived economic utility. "Unnecessary" suffering or "cruel" treatment will come to be understood as that suffering which does not serve some *legitimate* purpose. And without any notion of absolute prohibitions on the use of animals, all uses of animals that generate social wealth will be regarded as legitimate. To put it another way, "humane" treatment and "unnecessary" suffering are determined by what will most productively facilitate particular forms of animal exploitation. If the treatment objected to results in the infliction of suffering but that suffering facilitates the particular use and generates social wealth, then the use, however savage or barbaric, will not only be permitted but will be considered "humane"—even though the conduct is considered "inhumane" with respect to virtually all uses of the term in ordinary-language discourse. If there is no recognized social benefit that occurs as the result of the use, and if the use is regarded as "gratuitous," then the law may proscribe that use because the use decreases overall social wealth with no offsetting benefit to humans, or no benefit that is recognized as "legitimate." A clear statement of the classical welfarist position is articulated by Wayne Pacelle of HSUS: Pacelle describes HSUS as wanting to eliminate the *"gratuitous* harm done to animals by humans."[72]

This analysis also indicates why animal advocates do not prevail in most challenges to such standards: once a court accepts that a particular use of animals facilitates the efficient exploitation of the animals involved, the court will generally not require that the animal owner do *more* in the way of animal protection. Courts reject attempts by non-owners to impose restrictions that are not cost-justified, because in light of the property status of animals, and in light of how capitalist legal systems treat property (including deference to property owners as the parties best able to assess the value of property), courts have no way of interpreting the normative notions of "humane" treatment or "unnecessary" suffering apart from notions of what will best facilitate the use of the animal for those purposes that are regarded as "legitimate" or as socially acceptable. If we assume, as we do, that property owners are the parties best able to value their property, and if we assume, as we do, that it is difficult to quantify the social benefit of increased animal welfare, then any changes to the regulatory scheme that depart from these assumptions will be regarded, probably correctly, as diminishing the efficient use of animal resources. I refer to this version of animal welfare theory, represented in the law of the United States (and to a considerable degree in all Western countries), as *legal welfarism* in order to distinguish the law of animal welfare from more protective versions of animal welfare, such as that defended by Garner or Singer, which are far more progressive than what is required under extant laws.

An application of this theory of legal welfarism may help to illustrate the point better. The example that I use involves anticruelty statutes, which at least some new welfarists regard as an important source of animal protection.[73] For example, Ingrid Newkirk, in defending animal welfare, argues that anticruelty statutes have now compelled "society to accept that cruelty to animals . . . is more than wrong, it is illegal."[74] Contrary to what is commonly thought, however, these statutes do not have as their primary purpose the protection of animals. A close examination of anticruelty laws indicates that they have an exclusively humanocentric focus, and to the extent that they impose duties on human beings, these duties give rise to no corresponding rights for animals. Rather, anticruelty statutes *reinforce and support the status of animals as property.*

The rationale for anticruelty statutes is, for the most part, that cruelty to animals has a detrimental impact on the moral development of human beings. But this rationale demonstrates clearly that the anticruelty laws regard the animal in *instrumental* terms; that is, we are obligated to treat animals well, not because justice requires that we do so, but because we are more likely to ill-treat other people if we do not.

In addition, the interpretation of anticruelty statutes has always protected property interests in animals and protected nonanimal property interests as against animal interests. For example, animal cruelty may be justified when it is necessary to "assist development or proper growth, fit the animal for ordinary use, or to fulfill the part for which by common consent it is designed."[75] So, for example, the branding and castration of animals, and the killing of animals for food, either in slaughterhouses or for sport, are generally explicitly exempted from the scope of the statutes, as are experiments involving animals.

Moreover, the law has *always* allowed the imposition of pain or even death on an animal as part of training or disciplining an animal. In one case, for example, a court held that although a dog is not a "beast of burden," it is "not cruelty to train and subject him to any useful purpose. His use upon a 'treadmill' or 'inclined plane' or in any mode by which his strength or docility may be made serviceable to man, is commendable and not criminal."[76] Many of the reported cases involve killing or maiming animals in order to protect (sometimes very minor) property interests, and courts almost always permit injuring animals to almost any extent in order to protect property. For example, in a 1981 case, the defendant shot and killed a dog he found destroying Easter baskets that he had purchased for his children, and the court held that the action was not punishable under the anticruelty law, which contained an exception for killing animals posing a threat to "any" property.[77]

Cases involving anticruelty statutes very often are interpreted in light of the presumption, referred to above, that property owners will not, out of self-interest, treat their own animals cruelly. In a 1962 case, for example, the defendant, who operated a traveling circus and roadside zoo, was convicted of animal cruelty because the animals were not being maintained in a humane condition. The conviction, however, was reversed; the county court held that although the court felt "sorrow" for the animals, the defendant had "expended large sums of money" on them and was "certainly not about to impair his investment by improper food and shelter." The court added that "even though some of the southern planters before the Civil war may have cruelly treated some slaves, on the other hand, the slave that produced was well fed and housed by reason of their livelihood to the planter."[78] And anticruelty statutes have never prohibited the killing of one's own animals, even though such killing could not be considered necessary.

For the most part, anticruelty statutes exclude most types of animal abuse as long as the treatment in question is part of institutionalized exploitation. To say that animal exploitation is "institutionalized" is to say that there is a social recognition that the activity of which the exploitation is a part has some legitimate value for human beings. To put the matter another way, institutionalized exploitation is that which society, or an *empowered* part of society, has recognized as an economically efficient use or as an activity whose costs, including the "external" cost of animal suffering and death, are outweighed by the benefits to the property owners. Once an activity is regarded as legitimate, animal killing or suffering that occurs as part of the activity is acceptable, and the balancing supposedly required by anticruelty statutes has been implicitly predetermined and the animal loses. By virtue of falling within the scope of some socially acceptable conduct, the activity is *assumed* to be "humane" or "necessary." The only activities that are prohibited under such a scenario are those that produce no socially recognizable benefit. But in a society whose norms permit "benefit" to include, for example, the pleasure that comes from shooting live pigeons for "sport," virtually nothing will suffice to constitute a violation of anticruelty statutes.

A review of the actual operation of these laws indicates clearly that they fail to prohibit any use of animals that forms a part of any traditionally accepted activity. In those rare instances in which conduct is adjudged to constitute cruelty, the conduct usually does not involve any economic benefit or involves other opportunity costs that are deemed to be unacceptable, such as the moral approbation connected to the gambling or drug use that occurs at animal fights, which are technically prohibited in some places. Those few activities in which the gratuitous infliction of suffering is deemed "cruel" usually represent a socially undesirable use of property because overall social wealth is diminished. As Justinian said of Roman slavery, "It is in the public interest that nobody should treat his property badly."[79] This is why the original prosecution of Taub for his actions concerning the Silver Spring monkeys did not really vindicate any *rights* of the animals, however indirectly. Taub was prosecuted not for *what* he did to his animal property but for *how* he did it. No one challenged Taub's right to do whatever was necessary to perform the deafferentation experiments; what was challenged was Taub's allowance of pain and suffering that did not serve any legitimate interest of a rational property owner. He treated his property "badly," as it were, not by ignoring any interest his property had in not being involved in those painful experiments, but rather by treating his property in a way that rendered his own science procedure and data unreliable and thus diminished the value of the property.

The protection of institutionalized animal exploitation is effected in different ways by anticruelty laws. Some statutes require a particular mental state, or *mens rea*, such as malice, that is virtually impossible to prove when the defendant is engaged in "accepted" or "customary" or "traditional" behavior.[80] Other statutes contain explicit exemptions for activities such as hunting, trapping, fishing, farming, and biomedical research.[81] Perhaps most important is that many anticruelty statutes only prohibit the infliction of "unnecessary" or "unjustified" cruelty, and these terms are interpreted, as I noted above, not by reference to some abstract moral standard but in light of the conduct's relation to some socially accepted activity.[82] Finally, virtually all anticruelty statutes impose very minor punishments, and law enforcement personnel are often unwilling to enforce the law even in clear cases.

I do not mean to suggest that anticruelty statutes are completely worthless; they are used from time to time to benefit animals. In light of the hundreds of cases that protect the most vicious abuse of animals, however, to suggest, as do some of the new welfarists, that these statutes have compelled society to accept that cruel conduct is not only wrong but illegal is not only inaccurate but *absurd*.

The foregoing throws new light on Garner's position. First, Garner misunderstands the nature of the law regulating animal welfare in both the United Kingdom and the United States. Garner maintains that no one would "seriously" defend the position that "the painful death of any amount of animals" is justified only "to provide entertainment" for human beings, and he maintains that the orthodox animal welfare position is that the human interests involved must be "significant" relative to the animal interests that are to be abrogated.[83] Garner is correct to observe that traditional animal welfare theory—*in theory*—requires "significant" human interests. He is incorrect insofar as animal welfare—*as applied in the context of legal welfarism*—has no way of interpreting the "significance" of animal interests except in terms of the value of animal property to human beings. As a result, although most people are uneasy about defending the killing or suffering of animals for the sole purpose of providing "entertainment," animal welfare laws explicitly permit such killing and suffering. Despite what Garner regards as the orthodox moral position accepted as a normative manner by most persons, animal interests are routinely sacrificed for trivial human purposes.

Second, Garner argues that the "unnecessary-suffering" standard is flexible and that evolving moral views about animals will result in more and more activities being deemed "unnecessary." And yet he presents no empirical proof—and I suspect that none is to be had—that this is the case: and, as I have argued above, it is difficult, in light of the structural limitations imposed by a system that supposedly requires the balancing of the interests of human property owners against the interests of human property, to understand *how* this evolution could occur. Garner maintains that through application of this "necessity" standard, "some of the worst excesses of animal abuse" have been eliminated, but he also recognizes that welfare reforms are often eviscerated because "animal welfare often takes second place to cost cutting." And, as I mentioned earlier in the chapter, he acknowledges that even in Great Britain, where the animal welfare movement was born and where its major proponents have worked, "much of the animal welfare agenda has been obstructed and it is difficult to think of legislation improving the welfare of animals that has seriously damaged the interests of animal users." He also states that "the animal protection movement has made relatively little progress in influencing decision makers." Garner argues that there are many reasons for this, including the fact that the resources available to animal exploiters to defend their uses far outstrip those available to animal advocates, as well as the fact that in a capitalist society government regulation "is constrained by the need to retain the confidence of the business community (secured by not threatening their interests) since their chances of retaining power depend largely upon the state of the economy."[84] Whatever the reasons, the fact remains that even Garner is highly ambivalent about the successes of animal welfare.

Indeed, a particularly troubling flaw in any "evolutionist" argument about the relationship between animal welfare and the abolition of animal exploitation is the emergence of factory farming. Since approximately 1950, increased consumer demand has resulted in a complete transformation of animal agriculture. Animals, which were once raised primarily on small farms that allowed the animals some opportunity to satisfy natural desires, such as grazing for cattle and nesting for hens, are now raised under conditions that are labeled as "factory" farming or "intensive" farming. Egg-laying hens are crowded into wire cages— four to a cage roughly the size of a record album—in which they live their entire lives. Pigs are raised in stalls that are stacked on top of each other. Dairy cows are confined in barns in which they are forced to stand in the same position virtually all of the time, or they are shocked by a mechanism that runs along each row of cows to keep the cows from moving backward more than few inches. The list goes on and on, and the treatment of animals raised and slaughtered in these conditions is morally indefensible.[85] Yet, this worldwide transformation of animal agriculture—and the hideous suffering that it brought—all occurred while the "unnecessary-suffering" standard was, in Garner's view, the morally orthodox position accepted by just about everyone. If, as Garner maintains, the "unnecessary-suffering" standard is, indeed, flexible enough to eliminate the "worst excesses" of animal exploitation, it is difficult to understand how animal agriculture, which represents by far the largest number of animals exploited in an institutionalized context, transformed in the way that it did. Moreover, the fact that the "unnecessary-suffering" standard was ineffective in stopping or modifying intensive agriculture as its practices emerged and the fact that animal welfare has been similarly unable to effect any regulation of these practices after the fact speak volumes about the practical utility of animal welfare. Interestingly, although he claims to be inclined more toward the rights position, Garner defends an animal welfare theory ostensibly because it accords more with "practical" politics.[86] Similarly, Kim Stallwood claims that to seek the abolition of animal exploitation is "utopian" and that we must instead compromise in favor of reform in order to be "pragmatic";[87] but neither Garner nor Stallwood seem able to demonstrate that animal welfare is a "pragmatic" means to any end except the continued—and exacerbated—exploitation of animals.

Third, it is difficult to understand Garner's view that the "necessity" standard lends itself to an evolution from regulating animal exploitation to prohibiting it at least in some of its forms. As I argue later, to prohibit a form of animal exploitation, as opposed to regulating that exploitation, is, at least in some circumstances, to recognize that animals have interests that *cannot* be traded away irrespective of the benefits that are expected to inure to human beings (or, in particular, to the owners of animal property). If, however, the system structurally resists moving beyond those regulations that owners think are not cost-justified, the system is highly unlikely to recognize any protection of animal interests that is not explicitly tied to assessments of animal valuation made by animal owners.

Garner's own discussion of efforts by British "radicals" to get certain types of research prohibited as part of the 1986 legislation that revamped the regulation of vivisection supports my point. Garner argues that although these demands were "reasonable, and ultimately achievable," the "radicals" were unrealistic and the demands "were never going to be acceptable," because "in the present climate no parliament will prohibit research on animals for medical purposes."[88] But

Garner acknowledges that the uses targeted by the radicals, which included weapons tests and cosmetic tests, were "symbolic" because the targeted uses constituted such a ' small percentage" of animals used in experiments.[89] The reluctance to accept the "radical" demands, which Garner characterizes as "reasonable," "ultimately achievable," and "symbolic" in light of their numerical insignificance, does not provide hope, as Garner argues, that the "necessary-suffering" standard of animal welfare is sufficiently flexible to accommodate evolving notions of "humane" treatment and, eventually, even prohibitions of particular animal uses. On the contrary, the events, *as Garner describes them,* far more strongly support the view that animal welfare is incapable of providing regulation that goes beyond minimal standards to ensure that animals live long enough or remain "healthy" enough so that we may exploit them as efficiently as we can in light of their status as the property of their owners.

The Characterization of Welfarist Reforms as Creating "Rights"

Andrew Rowan, who explicitly adopts the view that welfarist reforms "evolve" into progressive social change for animals, claims that a "wide range of animal protection positions could be couched in rights terminology. For example one could claim that an animal has a right not to be cruelly treated."[90] The Animal Legal Defense Fund (ALDF) seeks congressional enactment of an animal "bill of rights" that would recognize the "right" of animals to be free from "exploitation, cruelty, neglect, and abuse." Regulatory laws such as state anticruelty statutes and the federal Animal Welfare Act require that animals be treated "humanely" and be free of "unnecessary" suffering. Rowan and ALDF would maintain that such laws create a *right* of "humane" treatment and a *right* to be free of unnecessary suffering.

The problem with the Rowan / ALDF view is that supposed "rights" generated by welfarist reform are really nothing more than "rights" to have animal interests evaluated under the welfarist structure. Animal welfare purports to balance animal interests and human interests, but animal interests, because of animals' property status, are *necessarily* sacrificed in all cases except where the sacrifice is seen to serve only a gratuitous waste of animal resources. To say that an animal has a "right" to such treatment would be tantamount to maintaining that the animal is entitled to have her interests balanced against the competing interests of humans, which is nothing more than what is dictated by animal welfare laws (and animal welfare theory) in the first instance.[91] The anticruelty laws do not, for the most part, prohibit *any* particular treatment of animals, however much pain is inflicted on the animals and whether or not the treatment results in the death of the animals.

Philosopher Joel Feinberg argues that a right is a "valid claim," which is "a decisive case, invulnerable or conclusive. As such it is a morally sufficient title and an extremely valuable possession, neither dependent on nor derivative from the compassionate feelings, propriety, consciousness, or sense of *noblesse oblige* of others."[92] He uses as an example the "right" to humane treatment, which, he believes, can be guaranteed by an institutional or legal rule and can be recognized on a moral level alone or in addition to legal and institutional levels. Again, for the same reason that Rowan and ALDF misunderstand the fundamental nature of rights, Feinberg's analysis fails to consider that any such "right" that is part of the institutionalized exploitation of animals is not going to be a "valid claim," which is what Feinberg intends to describe.

The logical deficiency can be demonstrated by reference to the federal Animal Welfare Act. AWA standards seek to ensure good animal *husbandry,* that animals used in experiments, for example, are provided with wholesome food and water, and clean air and cages. These standards, however, merely reflect and reinforce the property status of animals and the social concern that animal resources not be wasted. The act places no limits on the *types* of experiments that can be done; to the extent that animals have interests, the act allows for *all* of those interests to be "sacrificed" as long as experimenters believe some "benefit" will result from the animal use. The act imposes no limits on the character of this benefit, which may consist in nothing more than satisfying the curiosity of experimenters, which, of course, imposes no real restriction at all. To say that animals have "rights" under the act is, again, to say that they are entitled to have their interests—which can be traded away for *any* supposed benefit for humans—weighed against the interests of humans. But this is to say that they have a "right" to have their interests weighed within a welfarist framework that systematically devalues their interests. The use of "rights" talk in such contexts is misleading because it implies that there is some protection afforded in addition to whatever protection (or lack thereof) is provided by animal welfare—and that is not the case.

Institutional animal exploiters object to any restriction on the use of their animal property that does not facilitate the exploitation of that property. For example, the research community generally supports the Animal Welfare Act, but that act is intended only to provide for a level of care that is consistent with the extraction of valid data from animal property used in experiments. In addition, animal exploiters favor leaving standards for "humane" conduct vague rather than defining specific conduct as "humane" or "inhumane," even when there is very little difference between the two. A specific standard might read, "Animals must be given three feet square of floor space in caging"; the more vague standard would read, "Animals shall be provided with 'humane' housing, including adequate cage space." There is always an opportunity cost measured by compliance costs imposed on property owners by the specific standards. The vagueness of the more general standard would normally create uncertainty for property owners, but given salient aspects of the regulatory scheme, such as the assumption that property owners are best situated to decide the value of animal property, and the general lack of enforcement, the uncertainty of the general standard does not increase costs for animal property owners. In addition, the general standard allows property owners to depart from what would be required even by minimal specific standards in particular cases in which the owners believe that less care will still allow for maximum economic exploitation of animals.

Animal Welfare and the Thirsty Cow

In light of the failure of animal welfare to lead to animal rights, it is inviting to speculate why so many well-meaning people nevertheless persist in their almost religious conviction that incremental welfarist reform will facilitate the ultimate abolition of exploitation. One possible explanation may be found in an example offered by Ingrid Newkirk, who argues that every welfarist reform "can only bring us closer to our ultimate goal." Newkirk and other new welfarists maintain, for example, that laws that require watering of cattle awaiting slaughter are "steps in the right direction" and act as a "springboard into animal rights." Newkirk speaks from this position when she notes that certain animal advocates refused to support these laws, claiming that they were opposed to animal agriculture altogether and would not support a law that required the watering of animals awaiting slaughter. Newkirk argues that she "cannot imagine how those vegetarians with clean hands, who declined to help, could explain their politics to the poor cows, sitting in the dust with parched throats."[93]

Newkirk uses a powerful image—a thirsty cow awaiting slaughter—and asks us to put ourselves in the position of determining whether to give the cow water. When confronted face to face with suffering of that kind, many people would feel an obligation to minimize the suffering of the cow even if they were avid meat eaters. I assume for present purposes that we are obligated to give water to a thirsty cow. But to say that we have an obligation to give the cow a drink of water in order to minimize her suffering does not in any way support the position that we ought to support animal welfare because it also seeks to minimize suffering. This confusion—between the "micro" and "macro" moral issues presented in situations like the one Newkirk describes—has accounted for much confusion among animal advocates.

Assume the following hypothetical: You are a guard working in a prison in which completely innocent people are jailed and tortured by government security forces for no reason other than the difference between their political views and those of the government. You disagree with the treatment of the prisoners, but you feel that there is not much that you can do, and, indeed, you try your best to ensure that the prisoners under your guard are treated well. You avoid direct participation in any torture or physical mistreatment of the prisoners. One day, one of the prisoners, who is obviously very thirsty, asks for a drink of water. You feel that you have an obligation to minimize the suffering of the prisoner, and you give the person a drink of water.

And on yet another day, you decide that this institutionalized violation of basic human rights is not merely disagreeable to you, but that you want to seek the complete abolition of the torture and imprisonment of political prisoners. Your fellow guards try to talk you out of it; they argue that you can reduce the suffering of prisoners with whom you come in contact by treating them kindly. Although you certainly want to reduce the suffering of these unjustly imprisoned people, you believe that their suffering is caused by the unjust institution. What is needed is the elimination of the unjust institution that causes the suffering and deprivation of other interests that together define the minimal conditions of what it means not to be treated exclusively as a means to an end—in this case, the end of the police state that imprisons people for their political speech. Indeed, you reply to your fellow guards that even if the prisoners were not tortured, and even if they had relatively nice lives, their interests in liberty would be violated by their unjust imprisonment alone, which, although not painful, would still represent a serious deprivation of fundamental interests other than that in being free from suffering.

Now assume that you quit your job as a guard, form a human rights organization, and begin to seek legislation to rectify the situation. It seems that there are at least two options that are open to you to pursue your goal. First, you could pursue legislation that would require that all political prisoners receive a drink of water periodically, except when the warden of the prison made a determination that compelling state security interests made it "necessary" to deprive prisoners of water. And then, after you secured that law, you could seek another law that would ensure that when a prisoner was tortured, all efforts would be made to see that the prisoner was tortured "humanely," and specifically that no prisoner would be tortured in excess of two hours per day except when the warden deemed it "necessary." You might lobby hard for a provision that requires any such "necessity" determination be approved by a committee of state security police, all of whom support the principle that prisoners need to be treated in this way in order to have a healthy state but all of whom claim to endorse the view that prisoners ought not to be subjected to "unnecessary" torture, which is understood as that torture which is done for gratuitous purposes (the sadism of those who conduct the torture) and cannot be justified by the goal of state security.

Alternatively, you could pursue measures that are aimed directly at the institutionalized exploitation—the practice of imprisoning, torturing, and killing people solely to benefit a corrupt regime—such as mounting a campaign of public education aimed at persuading the population that such practices exist and should be abolished. Or you could organize constant but peaceful demonstrations of local residents at locations where political prisoners are kept.

The difference between these two approaches is clear: In the first case, you focus exclusively on the interest of the prisoners in avoiding pain and suffering, which seemed a perfectly appropriate response while you were a guard, and you generalize that legal and social change ought to do on the macro level what you did in the prison on a micro level. In the second case, you continue to be concerned about pain and suffering, but you approach the matter as one in which the pain and suffering is a direct result of institutionalized exploitation that treats people exclusively as means to the end of a corrupt political regime and that seeks to justify the deprivation of all of these interests on the good consequences (public order, suppression of "radical" ideas, and the like) that supposedly result from the imprisonment, torture, and killing of these people. Accordingly, you conclude that seeking only to "reduce" suffering as a way of eradicating the institution will probably be counterproductive. When I am confronted with the thirsty prisoner, I am deciding an issue of morality on a micro level that concerns how I respond to humans or other beings when I am confronted with their suffering—especially when their suffering is the result of a socially sanctioned, institutionalized deprivation of all of that person's interests. What I then urge on a macro level of legal change or social policy change is, at least arguably, a completely different matter. My decision to offer water to the prisoner does not necessarily indicate that I ought to try to secure laws that purport to achieve that reduction of suffering on an institutional basis, by, for example, providing a glass of water to each prisoner on the way to execution.

What these examples illustrate is that animals (and people) have different sorts of interests. As a political prisoner, I most certainly have an interest in avoiding the pain and suffering of torture. But I most certainly have other interests as well, foremost among them an interest in not being a political prisoner in the first place, an interest in not being treated as a mere instrumentality and in not being part of the institutionalized exploitation that causes the suffering. When a guard responds to my thirst, the guard recognizes and respects my interest in avoiding pain and suffering. But once the guard recognizes that I have an interest in eradicating an institution of injustice that is *unjustly causing the suffering in the first place*, then in order to do something about the institution of exploitation, it is necessary to secure the respect for these other interests. After all, even if I was not tortured or subjected to thirst and hunger—that is, even if my interest in pain and suffering was respected completely—I would still be a prisoner, and my interest in liberty would remain unsatisfied. Newkirk recognizes that animals have an interest in not suffering, but she, along with other new welfarists, does not recognize that other interests are at stake or that the suffering she seeks to reduce is part of institutionalized exploitation that explicitly condones whatever level of suffering is required to fully exploit the animal property.

To put this matter in terms of the structural defects of animal welfare discussed above, the problem is that once the new welfarist tries to generalize the understandable reaction to the individual thirsty cow who crosses her path, she finds herself trying to obtain laws that will "reduce" the suffering of animals who are regarded as property, laws that define "inhumane" levels of suffering as those—and, for the most, *only* those—that do not serve some legitimate "social" purpose. And in a society like ours, in which property rights are understood as equivalent in importance to rights of personal security and personal liberty, and in which respect for the autonomy of the property owner is itself a value that plays a central role in the culture, virtually *any* purpose will justify the imposition of pain, suffering, distress, and death on animal property. As a result, the new welfarist is constantly chasing her own tail, as it were, seeking the "springboard into animal rights" through laws, like the federal Animal Welfare Act, that "reduce" the suffering of animals that is made possible through a socially sanctioned institutionalized form of exploitation that allows the sacrifice of *every* animal interest, however fundamental, to satisfy *any* human need, however trivial. The new welfarist is caught in an endless spiral of trying to reduce suffering within an institution that structurally permits virtually unlimited suffering to be imposed in virtually unlimited ways.

The new welfarist is constantly arguing that particular suffering is not justified; the institutional exploiter is constantly arguing that only wholly gratuitous suffering is not justified. Like the mythical hydra, the body of institutional exploitation produces "new" types of suffering as soon as older ones are removed. Even if the welfare system recognizes in some limited way the interest an animal has in avoiding pain and suffering, that recognition does not establish any respect for the inherent value of the animal and establishes no enforceable limits on *what* can be done to animals. So, for example, although we have as a society long accepted that "unnecessary" animal suffering is morally wrong, and although welfarist reformers have tried for two centuries now to implement that moral view, the most heinous form of institutionalized exploitation of animals in history, both in terms of numbers of animals used and the treatment of animals, has arisen in the past thirty years. In short, effort to reduce the pain and suffering involved in institutionalized exploitation ignores the reality of legal welfarism and, in and of itself, does nothing to eradicate the underlying institutions that violate the interest of the animal in not being treated exclusively as a means to an end. Institutionalized animal exploitation will—and *is supposed to*—produce endless animal pain and suffering in contexts that are limited only by the desires of property owners.

Although the approach of the new welfarists can provide busywork for endless numbers of people, thus creating the illusion that there really is some viable and effective social protest movement for animals, the result is clear: despite three hundred years of sincere, dedicated people trying to promote animal welfare, we are no closer to the abolition of these institutions of exploitation than we were three hundred years ago, and these institutions are probably more entrenched than they have ever been. Institutionalized exploiters—property owners— will continue to accord to nonhumans the lowest level of treatment that will facilitate the exploitation of the animals as property. Trying to reduce pain and suffering through laws and regulations will, even in the unlikely event that such efforts are successful, eliminate virtually nothing because there is nothing to stop property owners from subjecting their animal property to the same level of pain and suffering in some other context. That is the problem. As long as animals are property, there is no baseline below which their treatment cannot fall (other than that which distinguishes "use" from "waste" of animal resources).

These structural defects of animal welfare theory help to explain why any obligation to reduce suffering on the micro level should not be generalized or universalized on a macro level. When we generalize about our obligation to reduce the pain and suffering of human beings, we invariably seek to eliminate the *cause* of the pain and suffering and not just the pain and suffering itself. If our concern is that the pain and suffering is the consequence of an institution that is in itself unjust, then our obligation on the macro level is to eliminate that institution, not merely to reduce the pain and suffering that are *inherently and inevitably* produced and "justified" *whenever* the institution identifies that pain and suffering with human "benefit."

Finally, animal advocates who adopt a welfarist or new welfarist approach will try to pass laws to ameliorate some level of suffering within the institution; but in an effort to be "moderate and respectable," not only will they go no further in their demands, but they may even promote the change as one that will *help* the exploiter, as Temple Grandin, an avowed welfarist, urges in connection with her "humane" slaughter practices, which, she claims, will make the meat business more profitable.

Conclusion

In this chapter, I have argued that one of the notions central to new welfarism—that animal welfare reform can and does lead to the abolition of animal exploitation—is mistaken. The empirical evidence indicates that welfarist reform does not work, and its structural defects arguably make it impossible for welfare theory *ever* to play the role envisioned by the new welfarists. Finally, the belief of new welfarists concerning the supposed causal link between animal welfare and animal rights may be traced to a confusion concerning micro and macro levels of moral theory.

CHAPTER Six

Is Animal Rights a "Utopian" Theory?

The modern animal movement has assumed that animal rights theory is "utopian" and does not provide a blueprint for incremental change that is qualitatively different from welfarist reform. For example, PETA's Ingrid Newkirk dismisses animal rights as involving an "all-or-nothing approach" that requires nothing less than the immediate cessation of all animal exploitation and that cannot accommodate incremental change different from that pursued through welfarist reform.[1] Similarly, Animal Rights International's Henry Spira maintains that animal rights theory requires an "all-or-nothing" approach and that "if you push for all or nothing, what you get is nothing."[2]

At least some scholars come to much the same conclusion about the supposedly unrealistic nature of animal rights theory—and the supposedly realistic nature of animal welfare reforms. For example, Bernard Rollin believes that incremental change is the only realistic approach and that incremental change *means* welfarist reform. Rollin claims that in the United States "we have never had a social and moral revolution that was not incremental." In the context of discussing animal experimentation, he argues that although he endorses the rights view, that view is "utopian and socially and psychologically impossible in our culture." As a result, Rollin endorses incremental change based on welfarist reform that would ensure that the benefit to humans of exploiting animals "clearly outweighs the pain and suffering experienced by the experimental animals."[3] Robert Garner claims to be "more convinced by the protection afforded to both humans and animals by rights" than alternative theories, but endorses the view that "any significant human interest outweighs any (sum of) significant non-human interests" because his book "is primarily a book about *practical* politics."[4] Garner argues throughout his book that incremental welfarist reform is the only "practical" way to achieve greater protection for animals.

As I observed earlier, this notion that rights theory cannot provide a plan for realistic incremental change is related to Singer's view that rights theory, in order to be applicable in a practical sense, requires "complexities," such as the formulation of very detailed rules or the establishment of ranking structures for rules to resolve conflicts.[5] According to Singer, rights theories represent "ideal" systems that are "all very noble in theory but no good in practice."[6] Singer claims that rights theories as a general matter are unrealistic because, unlike his own theory of utilitarianism, the former fail to take into account the consequences of actions in differing circumstances. The new welfarists echo this view, adopting Singer's rhetoric, endorsing his utilitarianism as a "realistic" approach to animal exploitation, and labeling rights theory as "utopian" and unworkable.[7]

I have argued that animal welfare theory will not lead to animal rights. It is now necessary to consider whether animal rights theory cannot provide an acceptable alternative to animal welfare.

To the extent that the criticism of animal rights theory is based on the supposed inability of that theory to provide a practical program for incremental change, the same could be said of the utilitarian theory of Singer. As I argued earlier, Singer espouses a theory of act-utility informed by the principle of species equality, but with regard to the day-to-day activities of the animal movement, he seems unable to provide any guidance beyond encouraging *all* approaches, from the most moderate to the more progressive. Singer accepts a version of new welfarism that fails to reflect any aspect of his overall theory, and his prescription for incremental change is consistent with neither act-utility nor equality.

In this chapter, I evaluate Singer's claim that relative to his own utilitarian view rights theory, as illustrated in Regan's work, lacks normative guidance. The new welfarists claim that rights theory is simply abstract idealism that cannot provide any sort of "realistic" solution to the problem of animal exploitation. This version of the "utopian" criticism may take different forms; most notably, it is claimed that rights theory fails to provide for a theory of incremental change and therefore requires an "all-or-nothing" solution, which is unrealistic. Singer himself claims that rights theory without the complexities of very definite (and often controversial) formulations and complicated and equally controversial ranking structures for conflicts between rules is too indefinite to provide any normative guidance. For this reason, and for the reason that the new welfarists have ostensibly embraced what appears to be Singer's prescription for incremental change, it is important to examine Singer's criticisms of rights theory.

The Three Components of Moral Theory

The philosophical theories—animal rights theory and utilitarianism—have three components. The first component is what the theory *ideally* seeks. That is, what state of affairs would the theory want to achieve were all other things equal? Rights theory (or rather a theory of basic rights for animals) seeks the abolition of all institutionalized animal exploitation. Singer's utilitarianism seeks a state of affairs where (1) all decisions about what is good or bad are determined by which action will maximize the desirable consequences for all affected, and (2) interests of animals that are equal to interests of nonhumans are given equal consideration. For purposes of shorthand, I use the term "ideal component" when referring to this part of moral theory.

The second component of the moral theory does or does not provide normative guidance to the individual about *what, if anything, the individual moral agent ought to do in terms of what theory ideally requires.* That is, what concrete moral guidance, if any, does the theory prescribe for individuals who purport to accept the ideals of the theory? Regan's rights theory requires the abolition of institutionalized animal exploitation as a social practice, but does that theory also prescribe what the individual should do in light of the fact that the ideal state (the abolition of institutionalized exploitation) has not yet been achieved? I use the term "micro component" when dealing with this part of moral theory. This usage parallels that which appeared earlier, when I argued that new welfarists point to situations on a micro level in which it is clear that a human ought to reduce the suffering of a nonhuman, such as the situation presented by Newkirk's thirsty cow, and that they then extrapolate from this obligation on the micro level an obligation on the macro level as well. I consider the micro component of a moral theory to be that which addresses obligation on the micro level, that which prescribes what individuals ought to do on the micro level to implement the ideals of the theory.

The third component does or does not provide a plan for *incremental* change to achieve the state of affairs required under the ideal state. Does rights theory provide a prescription for moving law and social policy in the direction of the ideal state of affairs (the abolition of all institutionalized exploitation) in addition to providing normative guidance for moving the individual (the subject of the second component)? I use the term "macro component" when dealing with this part of moral theory. This usage, like that of "micro" to describe the second component of moral theory, reflects the same distinction that I drew in analyzing the confusion by new welfarists of micro and macro levels of moral obligation. The new welfarist often argues that what the individual is obligated to do on the micro level (e.g., alleviate the suffering of the thirsty cow) is what the movement ought to pursue on the macro level as a legal or regulatory matter (e.g., support laws and regulations that require that cows be given water on the way to slaughter) or as a social matter (e.g., educate society to be morally concerned about that issue apart from the overall institutionalized exploitation of animal agriculture). The macro component of moral theory addresses obligation on the macro level and prescribes what, if anything, a social movement should seek to do on a social, political, or legal level to implement the moral ideals in the society generally, through, for example, education or legislation intended to change social institutions that support animal exploitation.

An example may help to put this tripartite scheme in perspective. Assume that my overall goal is to achieve a completely pacifist world in which there is no violence. The ideal component of my theory requires that there be no or practically no acts of violence. The micro component of this theory may require that I not respond violently to others irrespective of provocation. The macro component of the theory may prescribe legislation that eliminates various forms of violence (e.g., a law that forbids the manufacture of guns). These are three very different aspects of moral theory.

The Clarity of the Ideal and Micro Components of Rights Theory

The ideal component of moral theory requires that we ask what the theory envisions as the ideal state that would be achieved if the theory under consideration were accepted. For Regan, the answer is quite clear; rights theory is about the abolition, not the regulation, of institutionalized animal exploitation. Regan objects to the treatment of animals exclusively as means to ends; or, to put the matter in legal terms, he objects to the property status of animals, which allows all of their interests, including their basic interest in physical security, the prerequisite to the meaningful recognition of other interests, to be bargained away as long as there is some sort of human "benefit" involved. Acceptance of Regan's theory would necessitate the complete abolition of those forms of animal exploitation that are dependent upon the status of animals as human property. These activities would include using animals for food, for experiments or product testing, for clothing or entertainment, or using animals in any other way that fails to respect the inherent value of the animal.

For Singer, the answer is also clear—at least in terms of a formal statement of Singer's long-term goal. That is, Singer, as an act-utilitarian, wants to see a world in which the rightness or wrongness of all decisions concerning animals is determined by the principle of act-utility, a world in which we perform that action which maximizes the desirable consequences (e.g., reduction of suffering, maximization of pleasure and preference-satisfaction for those animals that have a sense of the future). In making this assessment, we must make sure that we do not discount the value of any party as a result of a morally impermissible criterion, such as race, sex, or *species*, either in assessing the competing interests in the first place or in weighing those interests. We must, according to Singer, accord equal consideration to equal interests.

On one level, *both* of these theories can be said to represent a "utopian approach in that both theories describe ideal states that are far removed from the present reality of the human/animal relationship. Neither ideal will be realized without a profound change in the current state of affairs, and that change is very, very unlikely to happen overnight. In their ideal components, then, both theories describe "utopian" states that are far removed from the world in which we presently live.

On another level, however, Regan's theory provides a rather vivid description of the ideal state of affairs, whereas Singer's does not. The *clarity* of the ideal state is important because that clarity will help to inform the individual how to behave on the micro and macro levels of moral decision. It is easy to identify the practices to which Regan objects, given that his target is the institutionalized exploitation of animals. Regan's overall prescription that we stop using animals exclusively as means to human ends and that we recognize that some animals are subjects-of-a-life would eliminate the overwhelming portion of what Regan regards as violations of the rights of animals. There may, of course, be some "hard cases," but under Regan's theory, institutionalized animal exploitation can *never* be justified, irrespective of consequences, just as human slavery can never be justified, irrespective of the supposedly beneficial consequences that would occur were we to enslave humans.

Similarly, rights theory does provide more guidance on the micro level than Singer's criticisms would suggest. Just as rights theory condemns the institutionalized exploitation of nonhumans as a matter of social practice, it similarly condemns *at least* the direct participation in animal exploitation. After all, if a person advocates the abolition of human slavery because the institution of slavery is unjust, that person will presumably also conclude that individual ownership of human slaves is violative of the rights of the slaves, since slaves can only participate in the institution of slavery by being owned by *an individual*. Similarly, the individual participates directly in the institutional exploitation of animals by eating meat or dairy products, or wearing animals, or using them in experiments.[8] These institutions do not exist except by virtue of individual moral agents who choose to participate directly in the institutionalized exploitation.

This is not to say that there will not be difficult moral questions remaining. It is impossible completely to avoid participation in institutionalized animal exploitation in light of the fact that virtually every aspect of our lives is involved in some way or another with the institutionalized exploitation of some animal or another. So, the rights advocate is faced with the decision, for example, whether to use a drug that has been tested on an animal, just as the opponent of human slavery is faced with the decision whether to travel upon roads in the southern United States, many of which were laid originally with slave labor. But that does not mean that the rejection of institutionalized animal exploitation does not resolve *many* of the moral questions that confront us. For example, I argued earlier that accepting the view that animals should not be regarded exclusively as means to ends does not prohibit, and arguably requires, my attempt to alleviate the pain or suffering of any victim of institutionalized exploitation I can directly affect by my action. In such a circumstance, I am acting affirmatively to ensure some aspect of treatment that would be required were we *not* to regard the animal as a means to an end, and my assistance does not in any way constitute an endorsement or support—directly or indirectly—of the institutional exploitation at issue. Similarly, if animal rights means anything, it means that as a society *and as individuals* we can no longer countenance the institutionalized killing of animals for food, any more than we can justify performing experiments ourselves, or wearing clothing made from animal skins or pelts.[9]

There is no mystery to the greater clarity of the ideal and micro components of Regan's theory, even if Singer is correct to note that rights theory as a general matter is very complicated (though no more complicated than utilitarian theory). Regan certainly does not intend to argue against exploitation as some general notion. For example, he talks about how we "use" others for skills and talents that they have and that benefit us. What Regan opposes is not exploitation per se, but *institutionalized exploitation* that represents the treatment of animals *exclusively* as means to human ends. What animal agriculture or vivisection or the use of animals for clothing or entertainment represents is the notion that the most fundamental animal interests in their physical security and liberty may be sacrificed simply because an aggregation of consequences that is thought to represent human "benefit" justifies the sacrifice. It is this institutionalized exploitation, which represents the systematic and structural violation of a variety of animal interests, including, *but not limited to*, the interest in avoiding suffering, that causes the suffering in the first instance. Indeed, and as I have mentioned many times earlier, these institutions of exploitation explicitly maintain that the violation of such interests is *always* justified as long as there is sufficient benefit.[10]

Regan's theory is more aptly described as a theory of "basic" or "absolute" rights, but it must be understood that Regan does not purport to describe a theory of rights beyond the "basic" right not to be regarded exclusively as a means to an end. Although the notions of "basic" and "absolute" rights are discussed in much philosophical literature, their most lucid presentation for present purposes may be found in the analysis presented by Henry Shue in his book *Basic Rights*.[11] According to Shue, a basic right is not a right that is "more valuable or intrinsically more satisfying to enjoy than some other rights."[12] Rather, a right is a basic right when "any attempt to enjoy any other right by sacrificing the basic right would be quite literally self-defeating, cutting the ground from beneath itself." Shue states that "non-basic rights may be sacrificed, if necessary, in order to secure the basic right. But the protection of a basic right may not be sacrificed in order to secure the enjoyment of a non-basic right." The reason for this is that a basic right "cannot be sacrificed successfully. If the right sacrificed is indeed basic, then no right for which it might be sacrificed can actually be enjoyed in the absence of the basic right. The sacrifice would prove self-defeating."[13] Shue emphasizes that basic rights are a prerequisite to the enjoyment and exercise of nonbasic rights and that the possession of nonbasic rights in the absence of basic rights is nothing more than the possession of rights "in some merely legalistic or otherwise abstract sense compatible with being unable to make any use of the substance of the right."[14]

Although Shue identifies several basic rights, the most important of these is the "basic right to physical security—a negative right not to be subjected to murder, torture, mayhem, rape, or assault." While acknowledging that it is not unusual in a given society that some members of at least one disempowered group receive less physical protection than others, Shue argues that "few, if any, people would be prepared to defend in principle the contention that anyone lacks a basic right to physical security."[15] If a person does not enjoy the basic right to security and may be murdered at will by any other person, then it is difficult to understand what *other* rights that person might enjoy. Most of the time, discussions about rights occur in the context of discussions of human rights, and these discussions do not concern whether we should be able to kill and eat *people*, or whether we should be able to use *people* in experiments to which they have not given their informed consent, or whether we should be able to use *people* in rodeos or exhibit *people* in zoos. It is assumed—at least under the law of most countries and at least in the moral views of most people—that people have certain rights, or, at least, that they have certain interests that cannot be compromised irrespective of consequence.

Shue is certainly correct to note that we always assume that humans have basic rights to physical security, whether or not there are social differences in the actual distribution of the right. In other words, recognition of the basic right of physical security is a right *as a matter of law* whether or not the state enforces this right in an evenhanded manner. In the case of animals, however, the situation is precisely the opposite. We talk informally about the rights of animals, but animals do not have the basic legal right of physical security, and *as a matter of law* they cannot possess it. Animals are regarded as the property of their human owners, and property is not entitled to basic rights. Moreover, because animals do not have the basic legal right of physical security (or any other basic rights), it is senseless to talk about animals having legal rights at all.

Given that property status is inconsistent with the possession of basic rights, as long as animals are regarded as property, the achievement of animal rights will remain impossible. If animals are to have any rights at all (other than merely legalistic or abstract ones to which Shue refers), they must have certain basic rights that would then necessarily protect them from being used as food or clothing sources or as the objects of experimentation. If animal rights require at a minimum the recognition of basic rights as Shue understands them, then animal rights may very well entail an "all-or-nothing" state of affairs because, at a minimum, they requires the *complete* rejection of the status of animals exclusively as means to human ends.[16]

The basic right that Regan argues for—that animals not be treated *exclusively* as means to ends—can be understood and described in legal terms as the right of an animal *not to be regarded as property*. To speak of something that may be treated *exclusively* as a means to human ends is to describe that which is property and that which cannot have any relations with anyone or anything else within the legal system. To say that "X is a piece of property belonging to Y" is equivalent to saying that "X can be treated exclusively as a means to Y's ends."

Regan is seeking to focus our attention on the institutions of exploitation that systematically and unjustly disregard the constellation of interests that constitute the *minimal* conditions for "personhood." This follows from Regan's concern with establishing animals' basic right not to have their interests tradable whenever human owners demand the "sacrifice." And this is perhaps the most important distinction of Regan's theory for purposes of understanding how an animal rights advocate should approach practical efforts to achieve justice for animals.

A central feature of Regan's rejection of utilitarianism is his rejection of the utilitarian's concern about the animal's pain and suffering *to the exclusion of all other interests*. As Regan describes throughout the book, the utilitarian, and in particular the act-utilitarian, tries in each case to minimize pain and suffering. Although both understandable and laudable, this approach, Regan argues, completely ignores the animals' other interests that are simply not a part of the utilitarian calculus. For example, Regan claims that—and Singer confirms this explicitly in the second edition of *Animal Liberation*—as far as the utilitarian is concerned, as long as animals are raised for food "humanely" and are killed "humanely," and as long as a second animal is brought into being when the first is "humanely" slaughtered, there is no moral objection. But for Regan, even "happy" slavery is *slavery*. So, even if the farm animals are "happy" animals, they are still part of an overall institutionalized exploitation of their interest in not being killed for food. This is similar to the prison-camp example that I used earlier. Even if the prison camp is operated without torture or execution and all prisoners are fed properly and even provided with considerable amenities, there is still something wrong about an institution that deprives people of their liberty based on their political beliefs alone. What Regan argues is that there are interests other than the interest in avoiding pain and suffering and that the deprivation of this and other fundamental interests is *implied* by the treatment of animals *exclusively* as means to ends.

Clarity, however, is a relative value, as is the normative force of a particular moral theory. In order to see how clear the ideal and micro components of rights theory are, it is important to compare the clarity of rights theory with the clarity provided by Singer's theory.

The Lack of Clarity of Singer's Theory

I have argued that Singer does not accept that animals (human or nonhuman) have rights. Singer's long-term goal is not the achievement of animal rights or necessarily even the abolition of all animal exploitation. Singer's theory of animal liberation requires that we reject speciesism, which would, for example, prevent the use of animals in experiments in which we would not use humans who had the same interests at stake. But beyond this rejection of species bias and the use of a theory of act-utilitarianism that would treat animal interests seriously, Singer's theory of animal liberation provides little normative guidance concerning issues of animal suffering and on the issue of the killing of animals.

Singer's utilitarian theory is different from traditional animal welfare in that Singer regards the long-term goal as animal "liberation," which is Singer's shorthand for a state of affairs that would accord equal consideration to the equal interest of animals. So, in this sense, Singer's long-term goal is arguably more progressive than the traditional welfarist approach as long as everyone is agreed to a method for describing competing interests and then are agreed to a method for weighing those interests in light of an assessment of consequences—and agreement about such matters is not easy to achieve. But Singer's theory is similar to animal welfare because it requires that we balance the interests (unprotected by claims of right) of animals against the interests of humans (also unprotected by claims of right because Singer does not think that humans have rights either) under circumstances that threaten to compromise the assessment of animal interests in any event.

There are at least six aspects of Singer's theory that portend great normative uncertainty at any level of application. For present purposes, however, I am concerned primarily with the ideal and micro components of moral theory. It is my view not only that certain aspects of Singer's theory render its ideal component far more unclear than that offered by Regan, but also that its micro component provides very little guidance to the individual in resolving those human / animal conflicts that are part of everyday life in a society in which certain sentient beings are treated as the property of others. (I stress that the purpose of this discussion is not to present and analyze critiques of utilitarianism in general, or even Singer's utilitarian theory of animal liberation in particular. Rather, I am responding to Singer's claim that rights theory is incapable of providing concrete normative guidance *relative* to that Singer claims for his view.)

First, as I discussed earlier, Singer's utilitarian theory requires some sort of empirical description of the consequences of acts. But it is often difficult to predict these consequences under the best of circumstances. Singer's long-term goal is to ensure that equal human and nonhuman interests receive equal consideration in a balancing process that is as free of speciesism as is possible. Even if animal interests were taken seriously, however, as they would be in Singer's ideal framework, consequences of actions—especially actions that purport to effect systemic changes, such as legislation—would be very difficult to assess before or after the fact.[17]

Second, Singer's theory requires that we make interspecies comparisons of pain and suffering. That is, in order to maintain that the equal interests of animals and humans ought to be treated equally, Singer's theory needs some notion of how we can measure (however imprecisely) interspecies experience. For example, he observes that a slap that would cause virtually no pain to a horse may very well cause considerable pain to a human infant. "But there must be some kind of blow—I don't know exactly what it would be, but perhaps a blow with a heavy stick—that would cause the horse as much pain as we cause a baby by slapping it with our hand."[18] The difficulties with making such assessments are obvious: it is difficult to compare pain intensity when we are concerned only with humans who can give detailed verbal reports of the sensation that they are experiencing; it becomes virtually impossible to make even imprecise assessments when animals are involved.

Third, and related to the problem of interspecies comparisons of pain and suffering, is the problem of speciesism: although Singer's analytic framework requires that we reject speciesism, he acknowledges that species differences may very well affect our assessment of various interests.[19] In some instances, these differences will be obvious, and their use will not be controversial. For example, no one (as far as I know) maintains that scholarships for higher education ought to be given to dogs, given that there are differences in the types of intelligence between humans and dogs. But in many cases in which there is a purported conflict between animal and human interests, the differences may not be as obvious, and their use may be far more controversial. For example, even if we can ascertain what type of blow, when delivered to a horse, will cause the same amount of pain as a sharp slap will cause an adult human, the question remains whose interest in avoiding the pain should be sacrificed in the case of conflict that involves suffering or distress as well. Singer claims that pain is pain irrespective of "whatever other capacities, beyond the capacity to feel pain, the being may have," but those capacities may very well be relevant to an assessment of suffering and to the ultimate determination of whose interests should be protected in the case of conflict. So there can be considerable controversy regarding the relative suffering of horse and human: Will the horse's mental capacities, which differ from those of the human, result in more overall suffering by the horse, who for a short period of time may be terrified as a result of the blow? Or will the suffering be greater in the human, who may not only experience the pain but may also experience anxiety over a longer period of time, or who, as a result of different mental capacities, may anticipate another blow or be more distressed by the blow because of memories of physical abuse suffered earlier. Singer could, of course, reply that any interest balancing requires that competing interests be characterized as accurately as possible and that accurate characterization requires taking account of individual characteristics. This is, of course, one reason why utilitarianism is such a difficult theory to apply in the real world, even when animal interests are *not* included in the calculus. When they are included, there is a tendency, as Singer's own work shows, to evaluate the characteristics of individuals by reference to species differences. This approach both invites and facilitates introduction of humanocentric notions about animal consciousness. In any event, even if the individual characteristics and capacities of particular animals or species could be ascertained with some degree of empirical certainty, it would still be virtually impossible ever to apply this framework in concrete circumstances, given the inexhaustible differences among individuals.

Fourth, when Singer turns from pain and suffering to the morality of killing animals, he again explicitly allows for consideration of individual capacities. He concludes that a "rejection of speciesism does not imply that all lives are of equal worth," because, "while self-awareness, the capacity to think ahead and have hopes and aspirations for the future, the capacity for meaningful relations with others and so on are not relevant to the question of inflicting pain—since pain is pain, whatever other capacities, beyond the capacity to feel pain, the being may have—these capacities are relevant to the question of taking life."[20] It is precisely this view that leads Singer later to conclude that it may very well be morally acceptable to eat animals who have not been raised under intensive-agricultural conditions, as long as they are slaughtered humanely, because, according to Singer, "it is not easy to explain why the loss to the animal killed is not, from an impartial point of view, made good by the creation of a new animal who will lead an equally pleasant life."[21] Once again, Singer's rejection of speciesism is tempered by his competing view that there are species differences concerning such matters as self-awareness, that an animal used for food purposes "cannot grasp that it has 'a life' in the sense that requires an understanding of what it is to exist over a period of time,"[22] and that these differences are relevant to moral assessments about killing.

Fifth, as the preceding points make clear, Singer's rejection of speciesism when "cashed out" is really quite formalistic and is almost impossible to apply in concrete circumstances because of the difficulty of assessing interspecies pain and suffering in the absence of a concomitant consideration of species differences. Part of the problem here is that there is—and should be—a tension between Singer's rejection of speciesism and his utilitarian theory. Indeed, Finsen and Finsen argue that although Singer defends a theory of utilitarianism, he "presents an important objection to the current treatment of animals that is not based on a utilitarian calculation but expressed in terms of demanding that we avoid speciesism."[23] Singer's own rejection of speciesism may not be justifiable in light of utilitarian moral theory, which is why this rejection is so carefully qualified by considerations of capacity in the assessment of overall interests in avoiding pain and suffering and in the assessment of the morality of killing animals. In any event, to the extent that Singer accepts a nonconsequential element (the rejection of speciesism irrespective of consequences) in his theory, there is an inevitable tension with his overall view that even speciesism can be morally acceptable if the aggregation of consequences so indicates. This confusion and uncertainty, and the resultant tension between rejecting speciesism and purporting to judge the morality of acts based solely on consequences, make Singer's theory even more difficult to understand and to apply.

Sixth, although Singer is an act-utilitarian, it is not even clear whether, on the micro level of moral decisionmaking, Singer requires an application of his utilitarian theory, or whether he argues for something else. It is not clear whether Singer believes the individual moral agent should pursue the action that will have the best overall consequential effect, or whether he requires only that the agent seek to reduce suffering and minimize pain. As I argue below, the reduction of suffering is certainly what Singer advocates on the macro level of social and legal change.

In sum, Singer's principle of equal consideration for equal interests may sound simple, but it is not at all clear what is required by its ideals, and practical application on the micro level is almost impossible because of uncertainty and controversy surrounding the assessment of consequences, the characterization of competing interests, and the weighing of those interests. But even if the uncertainty was reduced and the controversy diminished, the question of animal use would still have to be evaluated on a case-by-case basis. And herein lies what is perhaps the most important difference between rights theory and welfare theory for purposes of applying either to concrete situations. Singer may be correct to say that rights theory in general can become complicated in light of complex rule formulations and ranking structures to govern rights conflicts, but Regan's rights theory provides relatively clear and unambiguous normative direction at the long-term level and on the level of personal moral choice as that choice involves the institutionalized exploitation of animals. Regan argues that his long-term goal is the abolition of the institutionalized exploitation of animals, and he argues that if we accept that animals have at least the basic right not to be treated exclusively as means to human ends, then certain animal uses, such as the eating of animals, or the use of animals in experiments to which the animal cannot consent, or the killing of animals to make clothes, cannot be morally unjustified. Period.

This is not to say that Regan's theory does not leave many questions unresolved, even at the level of long-term theory. For example, even if we assume that animals have the rights that Regan attributes to them, there may very well be a conflict between human and animal rights, such as when humans seek to build for other humans housing that is needed but that will displace nonhumans. In such cases, rights theory may become more complicated because new criteria will need to be devised to deal with the rights conflict. But, for the most part, instances of animal exploitation are ruled *out* from the start in Regan's theory, whereas under Singer's view they are all ruled *in* unless Singer can demonstrate that the aggregation of consequences indicates otherwise. Indeed, even if we presume as a *prima facie* matter that most animal exploitation will also be ruled out under Singer's theory, the question whether a particular type or instance of animal use should be allowed (because it maximizes overall utility) is still open to discussion because its initial exclusion may not be justified under Singer's own theory. Singer cannot have such a bright line, because, as an act-utilitarian, he cannot argue that any instance of institutionalized exploitation is *always* wrong.

Rights and Welfare in the Macro Component of Moral Theory

Any response to the claim that animal rights theory is "utopian," "unrealistic," or "absolutist" also requires an examination of the macro components of these various theories in order to determine what each prescribes to achieve the ideal state of affairs for animals, beyond personal changes in lifestyle. It is a central tenet of new welfarism that rights theory represents an "all-or-nothing" approach that cannot provide a theory of incremental change. If, the argument goes, rights theory regards complete abolition as a societal ideal, and as a matter of micro-level personal behavior, then the rights advocate *cannot* affirmatively seek any change short of complete abolition without acting in conflict with rights theory. Since there is no realistic possibility of complete abolition anytime soon, rights theory is dismissed as "utopian" in that it seeks an ideal state without a corresponding theory about how to get there.

I have been unable to find a single instance in which animal rights advocates support the notion there is any possibility of overnight abolition of all institutionalized exploitation. The only way that such an effort could succeed was if huge numbers of people were willing to rise up in what would probably be a very violent confrontation given the large numbers of people who are involved in institutionalized exploitation and the capital that they control. But if there were a sufficient number of animal advocates to make such a scenario even remotely likely, I suspect that the confrontation would be unnecessary because that number of people (and it would have to be a most considerable number) would be able to effect dramatic changes in the treatment of animals through political means and would not have to resort to a violent revolution. That is, nothing short of a revolution could effect in "one move," or anything like it, the ideal state conceived under rights theory, but that revolution would require such considerable participation that it would obviate the need for itself. Advocating it, therefore, would not only be "utopian"; it would be silly.

I have been unable to find anyone who argues that the animal rights advocate is somehow committed to violent revolution. Robert Garner argues that rights theory *can* support "extreme forms of direct action in defence of animal rights," although "Regan himself fails to draw the revolutionary conclusions that appear logically to follow from his philosophical arguments." Instead, Regan extols "the virtues of Gandhian principles of non-violent civil disobedience," which Garner pejoratively likens to threatening to scream until one makes oneself sick.[24] But Garner *does not* argue that rights theory compels any particular "extreme forms of direct action," and he fails to explain why Regan cannot carry forward revolutionary conclusions in a nonviolent manner. In any event, I do not think that anything about the macro component of rights theory clearly requires the individual to seek social and legal change that will lead to the abolition of all animal exploitation, although the micro component does direct the individual not to participate in those institutions of exploitation. Indeed, some of the reasons Regan gives in support of Gandhian nonviolence may be reasons against any incremental action that includes violence against humans or nonhumans, or even against property crimes that do not involve removing animals from harm's way.[25]

To suggest that *any* animal rights advocate is maintaining that we can achieve "total victory" in "one move" is simply ridiculous. If an advocate of animal rights is going to advocate on behalf of legal or social change on the macro level at all, *the rights advocate has no choice but to support some sort of social change.* And on at least two levels, rights theory prescribes a very definite theory of incremental change. First, by requiring that individuals eschew animal products in their own lives (as a matter of the micro component of moral theory), rights theory implicitly contains a prescription for achieving the ideal state through the incremental means of more and more people who do not participate directly in institutionalized animal exploitation as a result of this micro-level obligation. Second, it is certainly consistent with rights theory to pursue educational efforts through traditional and non-traditional means—such as demonstrations, non-violent civil disobedience, and the like, directed toward persuading more people to recognize their micro-level obligations—and to demand the cessation of institutionalized animal exploitation as a political matter. Non-violent civil disobedience may also be used to protect individual animals, which is also consistent with rights theory. Boycotts of products and companies directed at the eradication of institutionalized exploitation can also be regarded as incremental change that is totally consistent with rights theory. In sum, advocating on behalf of complete and immediate abolition is itself incremental and completely consistent with rights theory.

The problem is that the new welfarists believe that the primary types of meaningful incremental change are legislation, administrative regulation, and judicial decision, which new welfarists see (mistakenly) as causally related to the abolition of animal exploitation. These changes, however, will necessarily fall short of complete abolition, and the question becomes whether advocating on behalf of, or otherwise supporting, any measure *short* of complete abolition is, as the new welfarists maintain, inconsistent with rights theory.

Incremental Change and Insider Status

Based on the structural defects of animal welfare and of the legal and political institutions that brandish the property status of animals in enforcing some version of animal welfare, there are probably some compelling reasons for animal rights advocates to spend their limited time and resources on incremental changes achieved through various forms of education, protest, and boycotts. The primary reason is that judicial or legislative change sought by formal "campaigns" requires some sort of "insider" status as discussed by Garner. Once an animal advocacy group decides to pursue activity other than public education, or, more precisely, once the group decides that it wants to have an affect on legislation or regulatory policy, it becomes necessary to seek "insider status" in order to "achieve access to government" and "to influence policy makers." Garner states that it "is easy to see why insider status is valued so highly. Access to government gives groups an opportunity to influence policy development at the formulation stage, thereby avoiding the difficult and often fruitless task of reacting against government proposals" that "are unlikely to change fundamentally" once they are formulated.[26] Garner recognizes that this "insider" status may be used to marginalize animal advocates through, for example, the creation of government advisory bodies that do little, if anything, but that give the mistaken impression that animal concerns are being taken seriously. Nevertheless, he holds to the view that "insider status can allow pressure groups to have a significant input into the formulation of public policy." This insider status, however, is largely dependent upon a group's being perceived by government as "moderate and respectable." Garner observes that although moderation and respectability are relative terms, "it is clear that the radical demands of the 'rights' faction of the animal protection movement are not regarded as acceptable enough" to give rights advocates "insider" status.[27] Garner argues that insider status is necessary for animal advocates to be effective, yet he states explicitly throughout his book that despite moderate status that animal welfarists have enjoyed, "the animal protection movement has made relatively little progress in influencing decision makers."[28]

As I indicated earlier, the modern American animal movement, with the exception of the Animal Liberation Front and similar groups, has, from its inception, demonstrated a strong desire for the "insider" status of which Garner speaks. In discussing American animal advocacy groups, Deborah Blum observes that "most of the animal advocacy groups work within the system: even PETA lobbies in Congress."[29] As Finsen and Finsen note, PETA, once the most "radical" of the American animal groups, has now opted for an image as "professional, savvy and smart" and "believes that this 'professionalization' of the movement" is essential to its success.[30] And, as noted earlier, the federal Animal Welfare Act amendments of 1985 were supported by a broad spectrum of "rights" and "welfare" groups.

Much of Garner's discussion of "insider" versus "outsider" status occurs in the context of his discussion of explicit intramovement debate about the rights/welfare conflict in Britain; for the most part, this is a debate that has not yet occurred on a remotely similar scale in the United States, because to seek such debate is to incur from many American animal advocates recrimination as being "divisive."[31]

Garner assumes that "insider" status is desirable, although he does acknowledge that "there is a danger here of giving the impression that all forms of insider dealing with the government are valuable."[32] And though he does recognize that groups may be seriously compromised by efforts to achieve such status, he assumes that "there are advantages in the compromise approach." Garner argues that in the absence of such compromise there might be "fewer and weaker animal protection measures" and that compromise may claim responsibility for "improvements in the way animals are treated . . . in the short term."[33] Indeed, Garner dismisses the notion that anyone would *not* want "insider" status: he claims that "most groups . . . want to achieve access to government even if they will not admit as much." He remarks that "some groups might *want* to be outsiders, as no doubt some motorists might *want* to drive a ten-year-old car."[34]

But whether to pursue "insider" status as Garner understands that notion is at least one of the issues that needs further consideration: should the advocate of animal rights seek "insider" status when, as Garner acknowledges, such insider status comes only when the animal rights advocate is willing be "moderate" in demand and "respectable" in presentation? It is, of course, not particularly difficult to understand why "insider" status is particularly problematic when considered in the context of animal rights theory. Insider status requires negotiation and compromise with those on the inside of legislative and executive branches of government. Again, no one seriously doubts that one of government's primary functions, especially in a capitalistic economy, is to protect *property* rights. And animals are a most important species of *property*. It is unlikely that any society with strong property notions[35] will be inclined to compromise property rights for solely or primarily moral concerns.

There is a fundamental political difference between the rights position and the welfare position. The rights position is essentially an *outsider* position; it is the position of social protest that challenges basic social institutions that have facilitated the exploitation of nonhumans.

As I noted in Chapter One, animal welfare does not require fundamental changes in industries that exploit animals, whereas the ethic of animal rights clearly does. Rights advocates are trying to change—and in many cases ultimately trying to *end*—the operation of institutionalized animal exploiters. The welfarist seeks to influence the system from the inside as one of the participants in the system. When Garner makes the observation that those who accept the status of outsiders are like those who claim to be content to drive ten-year-old automobiles, he fails to understand that for at least some people a choice about fundamental moral issues is different from a decision about automobiles.

"Insider" Status and Movement "Unity"

Garner argues that welfarist reform has been hampered by a lack of unity because a "crucial factor which plays a significant part in a government's attitude towards a group is the extent to which it is united. A group or set of groups involved in the same issue area who are divided, unsure of their objectives and turned in on themselves, are unlikely to be taken seriously by decision makers."[36] Garner discusses at length the division that occurred in Britain concerning the Scientific Procedures Act of 1986. According to Garner, the impetus for the act came from moderate animal welfarists, whose position was "that the infliction of pain on animals in the laboratory should only be allowed in exceptional circumstances when 'it is judged to be of exceptional importance in meeting the essential needs of man or animals.' "[37] The welfarists also sought greater public accountability on the question of animal use in laboratories. The British government rejected the welfarist approach, maintaining that "only when animals were found to be 'suffering severe and enduring pain' must a particular procedure be terminated." "Radicals" formed the Mobilisation for Laboratory Animals Against the Government's Proposals, and opposed the legislation in part because it did not abolish, but rather regulated, animal use in product and toxicity tests and in military, psychological, and drug addiction experiments. The welfarists negotiated with the government, but the "radicals" chose to remain outsiders. The result was that the welfarists persuaded the government to provide public accountability (in the form of a government review committee), but the government continued to refuse to accept the welfarist proposal that animals be used only when the benefits rose to the level of "exceptional importance." The radicals, Garner argues, had "missed the boat" because their proposals were unacceptable anyway and because they were not involved in the formulation stages, as were the welfarists.[38] The welfarists were "insiders" and got something done; the radicals were "outsiders," and their advocacy on behalf of abolishing, rather than regulating, certain procedures was ignored by the government and the "insider" animal welfarists. Garner's view is that more could probably have been accomplished had all segments of the animal advocacy community been united. It is, of course, difficult to understand precisely *how* such unity could have been achieved, since at least some of the parties involved assumed diametrically opposed positions.

Rowan makes similar observations. But these divisions among animal advocates notwithstanding, there is no evidence that such divisions are even partly responsible for the pathetic state of the law as it concerns animals.[39] An examination of a particular case illustrates the point. In the early 1980s, several animal groups, most notably United Action for Animals (UAA) and Friends of Animals (FoA) promoted alternatives to animal use, and they succeeded getting a bill, H.R. 556, called the Research Modernization Act, introduced in Congress in 1981. H.R. 556 required (1) the establishment of a center for research into alternatives to the use of live animals in research and testing that would also disseminate information about alternatives to government, academic, and private animal users; (2) the establishment of courses and training programs concerning alternatives; (3) a prohibition on the use of any federal funds for animal tests in situations where the center has identified scientifically valid alternatives; and (4) expenditure by each federal agency involved in animal use and represented in the center of no less than 30 percent of its annual budget on alternatives research, development, and education.[40] H.R. 556 generated vehement opposition from the research community and was not enacted.

According to Rowan, the "bill was gutted by Congress because the legislators could not accept its radical demands."[41] Granted that the act was more progressive than the federal Animal Welfare Act, it is nevertheless something of a stretch to call the legislation "radical." To say that Congress refused to accept the so-called radical demands neglects the fact that the *scientific community* (including those in industry)—the animal users and animal property owners—opposed the Research Modernization Act. Indeed, Congress held hearings in 1981 on several bills, including the Research Modernization Act. Most of the criticisms of specific bills (as opposed to the overall issue of regulating animal use) were directed against the Research Modernization Act by various animal users.[42] Congress capitulated to pressure from animal users, and Rowan's claim that Congress rejected the "radical" law, although technically true, does not state *who* caused Congress to reject the law in the first place.

What is interesting for present purposes, however, is that Rowan analyzes this as a situation where movement disunity decreased the chances for successful legislation, and he attributes the disunity to UAA and FoA, suggesting divisions between animal advocates "ultimately destroyed the slim chance of congressional action." The Humane Society of the United States (HSUS) did not support the Research Modernization Act, because HSUS had decided that, based on discussions between Rowan, then employed by HSUS to do outreach to the scientific community, and that community, HSUS would lose its credibility in the scientific community if it supported the act. UAA and FoA criticized HSUS publicly for this action. According to Rowan, UAA and FoA "wrongly" accused HSUS of "collusion with the 'forces of darkness.' " Rowan admits that HSUS did not support the Research Modernization Act, and he admits that it withheld support because the scientific community opposed the bill and HSUS had determined that it was more important for HSUS to retain credibility with the research community. Whether one chooses to say HSUS was in "collusion with the 'forces of darkness' " or, perhaps a little less colorfully, "HSUS decided withhold support from support a piece of legislation because the research community opposed it" is, as far as I can tell, a matter of style and not much more. In any event, Rowan argues that animal exploiters "watched in satisfaction as the actions of UAA and FoA clearly demonstrated to key congressional aides the deep divisions within the humane movement, and ultimately destroyed the slim chance of congressional action in 1982."[43]

Such examples are paraded endlessly by Rowan, Garner, and others in order to demonstrate that the success of animal advocates in achieving insider status depends on the extent to which they are united, and the "radicals" (in the above example, UAA and FoA) seem to behave in ways that preclude such unity. But a closer examination of the above example indicates that the attribution of blame to the "radicals" is odd, to say the least. UAA and FoA had succeeded in getting the Research Modernization Act introduced. Industrial and academic animal users objected to the bill for obvious reasons. They approached Congress unified in their opposition. But that is hardly surprising. Whatever differences may exist between various animal users, they have a strong interest in not having the law regulate their use of animal property. Indeed, this narrow common interest explains why animal research advocacy organizations, such as the National Association for Biomedical Research (NABR), frequently report updates about the efforts of animal advocates to reform animal agriculture or the use of animals in entertainment and praises the efforts of animal exploiters to defeat such efforts. In theory, not only should NABR be completely disinterested in what animal advocates are doing about slaughtering animals for food, but NABR should probably *support* such efforts, since no vivisector with any knowledge of nutrition would maintain that eating animals is "necessary" in the way that using animals in science is "necessary." And no one (vivisectors included) would maintain that using animals in entertainment is "necessary." But it seems as though the scientific arguments based on the supposed "necessity" of using animals in experiments melt before the *common interest of property users to be as free as possible of governmental regulation of property use.* Not only does the government act to protect property interests, but the groups that use animal property have a narrow but strong common interest in preserving that protection. Their primary focus is on opposing governmental regulation of property *irrespective of the use.*

In any event, HSUS opposed the Research Modernization Act because the research community opposed it. To the extent that there was disunity in this example, it was disunity that was caused by HSUS, and it occurred because HSUS wanted to retain credibility with the research community. Had UAA and FoA "behaved," the legislation would not have been successful anyway, because the research community opposed it, they opposed it in a unified way, and they voiced their objections as insiders to a political establishment that serves property interests. In fact, had UAA and FoA truly "behaved," both sides could have maintained a pristine unity in the torpor of inaction because the bill would never have come before Congress for debate and consideration in the first place. That is the whole point, and Rowan appears to miss it.

To the extent that insider status is dependent upon a unified position to any degree, that unity will almost invariably be greater among property users, who, despite differences, will agree on the narrow and crucial issue of the undesirability of property regulation.[44] This concern overshadows other moral concerns, so that vivisectors will, as they have, form at least intellectual alliances with furriers and orangutan trainers in common opposition to animal advocates who would seek to impose regulations on their property use that are not cost-justified. As long as the research animals are providing data that are regarded by scientists as reliable, any further required expenditure for animal welfare is a restriction on the use of property that is not cost-justified. As long as the orangutans are fit to perform, any further protection is a regulation of use of animal property that is not cost-justified. Whether you are doing AIDS research or training orangutans, you have a strong common interest in opposing any regulation on the use of your property that you, as a property owner, think is not cost-justified. After all, in light of the fact that you are using animals in experiments in the first place or you are using them to entertain people in casinos, you have already decided the basic issue about the morality, *per se*, of using animals in these ways; and, as a rational property owner, there is simply no reason for you to agree to welfare protection that exceeds the level necessary to ensure that your animal property yields the benefits that you seek. In any event, property owners—especially the owners of economically significant property, such an animals—have a strong incentive to protect this overriding concern.

These property interests, which in the case of animal property involve some of the most powerful economic actors, such as agribusiness and drug companies, will voice their concerns to a political establishment that must pay close attention. After all, the right of property ownership and relatively unimpeded exploitation of property is regarded not only by these powerful interests but by average citizens as among our most important rights. Although relatively few Americans feel that the ownership of guns is a right that should not be burdened at all, those relatively few enjoy strong lobbying support from the National Rifle Association, which, with the agribusiness and research lobbying groups, is among the most powerful of lobbies. The result is that despite the high cost that we as a society pay in terms of injuries caused by guns, we have yet to enact any meaningful restrictions on this form of property, and we tolerate this state of affairs in large part precisely because, although most of us may not feel strongly about gun ownership, we do feel strongly about ownership in general. We are reluctant, except under extraordinary circumstances, to tread on the property rights of any owners for fear of establishing problematic precedent.

Just as animal exploiters, despite their differences, will almost always unify to protect their property interests, animal advocates will just as invariably be divided *at least along the rights/welfare line*.[45] For the reasons discussed earlier, animal welfare as embodied in current American law is structurally unable to accommodate claims of animal protection that require action that transcends what property owners think is the "best" use of their property. And this is why, despite a great deal of animal welfare legislation, there have been no serious inroads made into institutionalized animal exploitation. As long as animals are property, this state of affairs will never change.

Moreover, the welfarist prescription that we effect macro change that "minimizes" or "reduces" animal suffering is a recipe for confusion. Just as everyone agrees that there should be no "unnecessary" suffering, everyone has an interpretation of "necessity." It is no wonder that welfarists are often divided among themselves—something that Rowan and other commentators discuss to a considerably lesser degree. They understandably cannot agree on what constitutes "necessity" given that such determinations invariably rest on ideological notions about the human/animal relationship and the moral status of animals. As I have argued throughout this book, the organized animal movement at least at the national level has been long on rhetoric but short on theory. As a result, not even they can agree on broad theoretical notions to inform the meaning of "necessity." To the extent that the welfarists themselves realize this, they are tempted to abandon theory altogether and claim that as long as the *individual moral actor* thinks that change on the macro level will reduce suffering, then it is "elitist" to have any standards against which to evaluate this claim. But this complete rejection of theory leaves the content of "necessary" suffering to interpretations that are consistent with institutionalized animal exploitation. This explains why researchers and supposed animal rights advocates both endorse the "three Rs" and why the president of the board of directors of the *Animals' Agenda* sees no inconsistency in also serving as the editor of the *Journal of Applied Animal Welfare Science*. But it also explains why the state of animal exploitation is no better today than it was one hundred years ago, and is, indeed, probably worse, considering the numbers of animals exploited in the relatively recent phenomenon of intensive agriculture. There can be no unity around the welfarist platform because, according to the view that *any* exclusion is "elitist," there can be no way to exclude—or even to identify—the animal exploiters. If there is anything "utopian," it is the view that people who have no ideological views—beyond the amorphous and ultimately meaningless views that we ought to "help" animals, or "care" for animals, or treat them "humanely," or prevent them from "unnecessary" suffering—can agree on *anything*.

As long as animals are property, insider status is almost always what Garner refers to as "phoney." The best that the moderate insider will be able to do in the overwhelming number of cases is to ascertain what level of property regulation will be agreed to by property owners as acceptable, and not much more. Garner is correct to say that only those who articulate "moderate and realistic aims pursued in a conciliatory and calm fashion" will achieve insider status, but that status in this context means only that its possessors will have the ability to promote those changes that are going to be acceptable to the unified opposition of property owners, whose interests are protected conscientiously by the government in any case. It should, then, come as no surprise that "radicals" do not see this arrangement as even potentially promising and so stop supporting it. To call such unwillingness to participate "divisive" or to argue for the desirability of unity under these circumstances is to make an argument in favor of unity, but merely to restate support for welfarist reform in opposition to the rights approach.

New welfarists assume that incremental change *means* change that depends on access to, and negotiation with, government decisionmakers. But that is simply a consequence of their acceptance of the legitimacy of welfarist reform in the first place. An animal rights advocate may reasonably conclude that attempting to secure insider status is, because of the structural defects of animal welfare, counterproductive. In the cases cited by Garner and Rowan, movement "unity" would have meant merely that those who agreed with the rights view should not have expressed their views and their disagreement with the welfarist approach. And had these rights advocates complied, and had they acted in a unified way, the result would have been the same anyway. The whole point is that the *legal system structurally limits the scope of reform to what is dictated by the instrumentalist position.* The best that can be hoped for is that on rare occasions a strong radical presence may help to nudge welfarist reforms in the direction of providing protection that slightly exceeds the level that would be provided pursuant to the orthodox position.

In any event, the animal rights advocate may decide that, in light of limited time and resources, incremental change (beyond change in one's lifestyle on the micro level) should be effected through education, protest, demonstrations, and boycotts, most of which can be conducted without seeking or obtaining any insider status. The insider position is relevant primarily to those who believe in the legitimacy of the structure to which one seeks access. And the structure presently regards animals as the property of humans and does not even possess a theoretical framework for assessing those interests in any other way. To put the matter another way, animal welfare, which rests on the assumption that animals are property, is structurally incapable of qualitatively altering the property status of animals. Under these conditions, a decision to remain an "outsider" who seeks incremental change indirectly through education, protests, or boycotts, or through campaigns that do not depend on legislation or administrative regulation, is completely defensible. Moreover, this position is not "utopian" in the sense that it leaves the animal rights advocate without anything practical to do on a day-to-day basis. The strategic plate of the animal rights advocate is quite full, but her activism does not take the form of seeking insider status within a political framework that will structurally and systematically sacrifice the most basic animal interests to ensure and to increase the value of animal property. Rather, her activism consists of "outsider" conduct. It is, of course, not surprising that new welfarists have regarded my view as problematic, because, as I have indicated, a central tenet of new welfarism is that welfarist reform through the legislative and regulatory process is not only desirable but *necessary* in that it is the only way that we will move toward the goal of abolishing animal exploitation altogether. I have argued that the assumptions that support this view are wrong because the legal status of animals as property precludes taking animal interests seriously, and that the empirical results of animal welfare support the view that animal welfare is ineffectual.

Moreover, insider status is a matter of degree, and, as Garner correctly notes, to the extent that rights advocates negotiate and compromise, they cannot engage in aggressive public campaigns that "alter the social climate and directly confront those economic interests who benefit from the use of animals."[46] This provides yet another reason that the rights advocate may avoid altogether putting her activist energies into trying to obtain insider status. A good argument can be made that attempts to seek insider status and new welfarism are inextricably connected, and that the radical character of the movement will dissipate proportionately with efforts to seek insider status.

Even if the rights advocate agrees with this analysis and concludes that she is better advised, at least at this stage of things, to pursue incremental change through protests, demonstrations, and boycotts, there is an important matter that has yet to be discussed. The rights advocate may aim her educational efforts (in whatever form) at getting people to accept the philosophy of animal rights—that is, she may urge people to accept the ideal that all animal exploitation ought to be abolished and urge them on a micro level to become vegetarians or to eschew animal products. In this case, the advocate does not really need a theory of incremental change per se beyond the view that change will come incrementally only as more and more people adopt abolitionist moral views and implement those moral views in their own lifestyles.

The animal advocate is pursuing incremental change in that she is not attempting to achieve "total victory" in "one move." She recognizes that this is going to be a slow, arduous process and that if the goal of abolition is to be achieved, it will be only by incrementally convincing individuals of the rights viewpoint and the abolition that it implies, and not by securing insider status and a concomitant influence over legislation that will invariably compromise fundamental animal interests.

The question remains whether it is possible to urge something, other than the abolition of animal slavery, that is not simply welfarist reform? This question arises frequently, but not always, in the context of efforts to effect legislative or regulatory change. For example, when animal advocates protest against the practice of raising veal calves in small crates, such protest usually occurs in the context of efforts to get a law that will ban such devices. However, this is not necessarily the case; for example, the protesters may be putting social pressure (e.g., through demonstrations and newspaper ads) on a single farmer to abolish the veal crates on a particular farm. For present purposes, the issue under consideration is the same in either case: whether, and under what circumstances, animal rights advocates can urge, through legislation or education, *some* sort of change other than the immediate and complete abolition of institutionalized exploitation. After a brief digression, I return to this question.

Animal Welfare: Theory and Practice

In order to assess the claim that animal rights theory is "utopian" and cannot prescribe a practical strategy for incremental change on the macro level, it is necessary to examine the theory of incremental change advocated by the new welfarists to get some idea of what is regarded at least by new welfarists as a better, or more desirable, theory of incremental change. Unfortunately, the new-welfarist view—that any measure that, in Singer's words, "reduces the suffering of animals or enables them to meet their needs more fully" or, in Barnes's words, "minimize[s] the pain and suffering" of animals or, in Newkirk's words, helps "animals suffer less during the many years before they achieve the rights we wish for them"—fails to provide any satisfying normative guidance at all. As I have argued throughout this book, no one, *including the animal exploiters themselves*, disagrees with the view that we ought to minimize or reduce suffering. I have also argued that animal advocates, as a direct result of confusion on this point, frequently find themselves supporting the same proposals that are advocated by institutional animal exploiters, such as the welfarist principle of the "three Rs," endorsed by both Henry Spira and the National Association for

Biomedical Research, or the "humane" slaughtering principles endorsed by animal rights advocates and the American Meat Institute.

The new welfarists would, of course, object and argue that they have very definite understandings of what sorts of action will "reduce" or "minimize" suffering. But that is precisely the problem. Without any sort of theoretical criteria to delimit what incremental changes that supposedly "minimize" or "reduce" suffering are desirable, the new welfarists are *incapable* of distinguishing their program for strategic change from that of the exploiters themselves, all of whom agree that animals ought to be treated "humanely."

The problem can be illustrated clearly with the following example. Assume that animal advocates criticize experiments in which animals are burned without the benefit of anesthesia for five minutes. In response to a protest, the experimenter proposes a "compromise" under which the experiment will be conducted, but will be limited in duration to four minutes and fifty-nine seconds instead of five minutes. There is arguably a reduction of suffering. There is even more arguably a reduction of suffering if the proposed compromise duration is four minutes and thirty seconds. I would suspect that most of the new welfarists would not find this an acceptable compromise despite endorsing the view that "any" measure that reduces suffering is acceptable. The problem is that, without any further theory, the prescription of the new welfarists is simply too general to provide *any* normative guidance. Moreover, virtually any moral theory that requires that the consequences of actions be anticipated with any sort of precision is problematic, not only because it is empirically difficult to know what the consequences will be, but because the characterization of those consequences is often controversial.

The new welfarists need some theory to differentiate their views from the views of institutional animal exploiters, who have adopted the moral rhetoric of animal welfare theory. Many of the new welfarists eschew theory in any formal sense, but it is clear that Singer's utilitarian theory of animal liberation has been loosely adopted by the new welfarists. Singer does not, like most new welfarists, view the long-term goal necessarily as the abolition of animal exploitation (it would depend on whether abolition satisfied the principle of act-utility), but he presents a philosophical theory that he argues requires the elimination of *much* animal exploitation and that provides a theoretical justification for pursuing incremental change that "minimizes" or "reduces" animal suffering in the short term.

It is, however, difficult to understand precisely what this theory is or how it relates to incremental change. Singer desires as a long-term goal a treatment of animals that would be dictated by a theory of act-utilitarianism informed by the principle of equal consideration for equal interests. That is, if Singer were able to construct his ideal moral world for animals, animals would be treated so as to maximize the pleasure and preference satisfaction for all beings affected. In determining this treatment, the moral agent would accord to animal interests as much consideration as the equal interests of human beings. Putting aside the practical problems I have already identified with the real-life application of this theory, one can perceive in Singer's position two separate elements: (1) endorsement of the principle of act-utility, according to which individual acts (and not classes of acts) are to be tested against the principle of utility; and (2) endorsement of the principle of equality, according to which the equal interests of beings are accorded equal consideration without reference to considerations of race, sex, *or species.*

It is difficult to understand how Singer relates these notions to his view that animal advocates ought to support *any* measure they think will reduce suffering. Both aspects of Singer's theory are conspicuously absent from this prescription. Singer does not seem to subject any particular incremental measure to any analysis using either aspect. He does not, for example, require that any particular incremental measure reduce suffering *more* than possible alternatives. He does not even urge that as a *proactive* measure animal advocates should assess the competing options and pick the one that will reduce suffering the most. Part of the problem is that it is difficult to know what the consequences of various options will be if the primary or sole concern is the reduction of animal suffering. After all, whether the federal Animal Welfare Act reduces animal suffering is anyone's guess; the consequences of that law in terms of reducing animal suffering could be debated forever. Recognizing these problems, Singer urges that we simply support "any" measure that "reduces suffering." But that is the same as providing no guidance on incremental measures, or at least no guidance that serves to differentiate the incremental measures that should be supported by animal advocates from the welfarist reforms that *are* supported by animal exploiters.

Similarly, although Singer's major contribution is his argument against speciesism, or in favor of according equal interest to equal considerations without species bias, he nowhere requires that this portion of his theory be applied to incremental change. Singer does not maintain that incremental changes have to be those that are untainted by species bias; and if he is going to support "any" measure that he thinks will "reduce" animal suffering, he *cannot* use the criterion. For example, many new welfarists regarded the 1985 amendments to the Animal Welfare Act as representing incremental change in the direction of animal rights. But those amendments explicitly assumed that it was morally acceptable to use animals in experiments under conditions in which similarly situated humans could not be so used. There was, however, no consideration of this by the new welfarists; nor, as far as I am aware, was any such consideration urged by Singer.

Finally, it is important not to confuse the various components of moral theory. I want to stress a notion that I discussed earlier: I am unable to discern anything in rights theory that is inconsistent with my giving water to a thirsty cow on the way to slaughter. In the first instance, it is difficult to take issue with the view that, for many people, the sight of a particular person or animal in distress evokes a desire to alleviate that distress. If I am responsible for placing and keeping the cow in this situation (in which she is awaiting her slaughter and is thirsty), I may be violating her rights because I placed her in that situation and because I am keeping her in that condition. But even if I am responsible, and certainly if I am not responsible (e.g., I am just a passerby who sees a thirsty cow awaiting slaughter), I do not directly or even indirectly support the institutionalized exploitation of the animal by alleviating her suffering in that case. I am not trading away her interests in the hope that I may obtain rights for other animals at some point in the future. I am not neglecting her interest in not being treated as property. Indeed, to the extent that I regard the thirsty cow as a rightholder and regard her as a victim of institutionalized animal exploitation, I am acting consistently with her interests and her inherent value to provide her with water and to ease the suffering caused by the institutionalized exploitation. My act of aid does not affirm the institution of exploitation; indeed, it denies its legitimacy because, in giving the cow the water out of respect for her inherent value, I do not treat her exclusively as a means; I do not treat her as property. I regard her as closer to a person—to the person that I might encounter as a prison guard in a camp for innocents who have defied a corrupt regime.

If, however, as a step toward the abolition of all animal agriculture, I seek legislation to ensure that all cows have water, then I may be said to be acting in a manner inconsistent with the rights of those animals precisely because I am seeking to "reform" the institutionalized exploitation to make it more "humane" rather than abolish it. I am taking the position that it is all right to continue to violate the rights of these animals today in the hope that this change to the violation will lead to the recognition of legal rights for other animals at some point in the future. The means that I have selected to reach the long-term goal of abolition, means that condone the continued treatment of animals as *property,* are, at least arguably, inconsistent with the long-term goal, which is to remove animals from the category of property and lend them status closer to the category of personhood.

In sum, the new welfarist prescription for incremental change—that "any" measure that "minimizes" or "reduces" suffering should be supported by animal advocates (or at least not opposed) is simply not sensible if new welfarists desire to distinguish their position from that of the institutional exploiters of animals who agree that we ought to treat animals "humanely" and that they should not be subjected to "unnecessary" pain or suffering. It is precisely the failure of new welfarists to focus on this serious flaw in their approach that has led to a movement that seeks to distinguish itself from nineteenth-century welfarism paradoxically by using the very methods and reasoning that characterized those earlier efforts.

Animal Rights: The Possibility of Incremental Change

I now return to the issue left open earlier: assuming that the animal rights advocate wants to support incremental change other than solely through educating the public about the need for complete abolition, can she do so without compromising the principles of rights theory, which requires the abolition of institutionalized exploitation? In earlier work, I phrased this question as whether, short of abolishing the status of animals as property, we can have a "pluralistic system that characterizes animals as property but recognizes rights-type concepts on some level."[47]

I do not think that we can meaningfully speak of legal rights for animals as long as animals are regarded as property. To put the matter in the context of my earlier discussion of basic rights, as long as animals are property, their basic rights, or those rights that are a prerequisite for the enjoyment of other, nonbasic rights, can be sacrificed. As long as we can kill animals for food, or use them in experiments, or imprison them for their entire lives in cages so that we can be amused at zoos, or maim them for our amusement in rodeos, or shoot them for fun at yearly pigeon shoots, then to say that animals have rights is, as Shue observed, using "rights" "in some merely legalistic or otherwise abstract sense compatible with being unable to make any use of the substance of that right."[48] Basic rights are a prerequisite to the enjoyment of nonbasic rights, and the possession of nonbasic rights in the absence of basic rights is meaningless.

My critics will respond that every movement achieves rights incrementally. For example, Henry Spira "notes that in social movements, progress is made incrementally, through continual reform. 'If you push for all or nothing, what you get is nothing.' "[49] Spira attempts to compare incremental progress made in other social movements to incremental progress made toward the abolition of animal exploitation. This attempt must fail for the reason that no other situation—with the exception of slavery—is comparable with respect to the baseline protection afforded to animals. When we talk about incremental progress made in other social movements, we are talking about *rightholders* who seek greater rights protection. A "reform" in another area—improved labor conditions for factory workers, for example—operates in the context of actors who already have basic rights that they are seeking to extend. Put simply, we do not just arbitrarily kill and eat factory workers. Although interests may be balanced, some interests, such as the right of the worker not to be arbitrarily killed by the boss, cannot be traded away, because those interests simply are not on the table. But because animal interests are treated in a *completely* instrumental manner, that is, because all animal interests may be sacrificed if animal owners decide that there is a benefit in doing so, the animal will virtually always be on the short end of the stick.

To put the matter another way, once we have persons who are at least holders of basic rights, it makes sense to talk about making incremental reforms in rights; *but the basic right not be treated as property is a right that does not and cannot admit of degrees.* Indeed, the issue is not whether we achieve animal rights incrementally, but whether we can incrementally eradicate the property status of animals, because, in a sense, we are really only talking about *one* right—the right not to be treated as property.[50] A recognition of the validity of that one right would compel the conclusion that institutionalized animal exploitation violates principles of justice, a violation that could be tolerated only as long as animals were classified as property, which gave humans license to ignore the basic similarities between humans and nonhumans that are relevant for attribution of status as subject-of-a-life. But rights theory does not really concern the particular rights that animals have; rather, it asks whether, in the first instance, animals should be in the class of potential rightholders of those particular rights. Answering this question in the affirmative does not commit the rights advocate to particular animal rights beyond the right to respectful treatment, which precludes institutionalized exploitation but does not address much beyond that basic right not to be regarded as property, or, put in Regan's language, not to be treated *exclusively* as a means to an end.

The conceptual terrain here is very similar to an inquiry into the moral legitimacy of slavery. Institutionalized animal exploitation is structurally similar to American slavery. Slaves were regarded as the property of their masters, but for purposes of responsibility under criminal law, slaves were regarded as persons. Although there were supposedly laws that protected slaves from particular types of treatment, such as "excessive" beatings or "unnecessary" punishment, the law usually assumed that the master was the best judge of how slave property ought to be used and that the master would act in a self-interested way with respect to that property. Indeed, according to one state law, a master who killed a slave as part of disciplining the slave could not be said to have acted with malice (a prerequisite for a murder conviction), because the law presumed that the owner would not intentionally destroy the master's own property.[51] Whether slaves should have rights *at all* is an entirely different question from what rights slaves ought to have. To say that slavery should be abolished is nothing more or less than to maintain that slaves should be removed from the class of legal entities known as *things* and placed instead in the class of legal entities known as *persons*. To do so means that people who were formerly regarded as things that could not have nonbasic rights can now have these rights, but it does not specify the content of such rights beyond the basic right not to be treated as property. I may agree that slavery should be abolished, but I may disagree that former slaves should be given nonbasic rights such as a right to a certain level of material wealth.

As long as animals are regarded as property, we cannot really talk about their rights. That property cannot have rights follows from what it is to be property. The dualistic nature of our legal system recognizes that there are persons and property, and property is defined as that which cannot have relations with other property or with persons. We can be responsible *for* property, but not *to* property. In the former case, I may be responsible for the use to which my property is put, but my duties are owed to other persons and not to the property. As a matter of law, property is regarded as constituting means to ends selected by human owners and subject to some degree of state regulation. The law recognizes that animals have interests only to the extent that those interests facilitate the use of the animal as property. The status of animals as property accounts in part for why courts have struggled with the status of anticruelty laws, claiming that, for the most part, the duty not to be cruel is usually thought to be owed to other persons. Similarly, courts interpreted laws prohibiting certain types of slave punishment as protecting "public decency" and not any interests of the slave.

To be property *means* to possess no interests; to the extent that the law recognizes that property, a "thing," has interests, those interests may be sacrificed if the property owner thinks it to be in her interest, subject only to any legal regulation of the property, which generally protects the owner's interests and seeks to ensure that the value of property is not diminished. Any "rights" that we presently recognize do not constitute any concession that animals have interests that cannot be traded, as is the case when we are discussing human rights. As I indicated at the outset of the book, the whole idea of a right is to recognize an interest that cannot be sacrificed (at least not easily), even though such sacrifice might benefit others. But as long as animals are regarded exclusively as means to ends, then, by definition, they can have no interests that are protected in this way. They can have no relationship with persons that entitles them to protection from those persons at all costs, because, as property, animals exist as means to the ends of human owners—and nothing more.

These considerations indicate yet another reason why an advocate of animal rights cannot endorse the welfarist prescription for macro, or sociolegal, change—that we "minimize" or "reduce" suffering as a matter of social and legal policy and not merely on the level of individual moral action. Such laws or regulations or policies cannot, in light of the status of animals as property, lead to rights. Indeed, under present political and legal constraints, any protection that animals are accorded must take one of two general forms.

The first form is the requirement that animals be treated "humanely" and that they not be subjected to "unnecessary" suffering. This is the classical form of welfarist regulation, and, as I have tried to show, it is structurally defective because what is "necessary" is whatever conduct is needed to facilitate the exploitation of the animal in a manner that is least restrictive of the prerogatives of the property owner. Moreover, such laws do not create, for example, a "right" to humane treatment, as Rowan and others argue, because these laws merely require that animal interests, which are not protected by claims of right, be "balanced" against the interests of humans who have rights in general and, in particular, property rights in the animal whose interests are being "balanced."

The second form of animal protection law involves imposition of a particular standard. An example of such a law would be a government regulation requiring that animals used in experiments be provided with a minimum amount of wholesome food and water. Although it is tempting on first glance to regard such laws as providing a "right" to food and water, on further reflection this characterization proves problematic. As philosopher Neil MacCormick has observed, "Consider the oddity of saying that turkeys have a right to be well fed in order to be fat for the Christmas table."[52] To say that an animal that can be killed in a scientific experiment, or can be killed and eaten, has a right to be fed is to say that the animal has no basic right of physical security (the animal's interest in life can be traded away for consequential reasons) but has the nonbasic right to be fed. Animals have such "rights" to the extent that their recognition furthers the exploitation of the animals. Although the animal in the laboratory has an interest in being fed, and although a rule protects that interest, the protection provided by that rule can be ignored if, for example, the experimenter chooses to perform a hunger or a dehydration experiment, and the protection can always be ignored absolutely should the experimenter decide to kill the animal. So, there is no way in which the rights advocate can achieve the long-term goal of eradicating the property status of animals (or achieving the basic right of an animal not to be treated exclusively as a means to the end of others) by endorsing welfarist reform, because those reforms will have little or no effect (incrementally or otherwise) on eradication of the property status of animals. Indeed, in addition to being hopelessly vague, this supposed prescription for incremental change can only *reinforce* the property status of animals.

Under the welfarist approach, the animal's interest in being free from suffering is the only interest that is recognized; but an interest in being free from suffering is only *one* interest that an animal has. Just as humans have other interests, so too do nonhumans. And the basic interest for which Regan seeks to obtain rights status is the interest of an animal not to be treated exclusively as a means to an end of human property owners. It is the failure to respect this interest that causes the pain and suffering that the welfare advocate seeks to eradicate in the first place, and the institutionalized exploitation made possible by ignoring this interest also justifies virtually any pain and suffering as long as it produces some human "benefit."

In sum, to say that animals could have rights in a society in which they were still regarded as property would, in Shue's vocabulary, be tantamount to asserting that animals could have nonbasic rights in the absence of basic rights. But if animals can be killed and eaten at will

or used in experiments or used for entertainment, then their possession of nonbasic rights is meaningless because the prerequisite for their
enjoyment—the possession of basic rights, such as physical security—is
nonexistent. Moreover, because of the property status of animals, any
nonbasic rights would probably protect only those interests that were
necessary to facilitate the animal's use as property. Finally, *any* interest
so recognized (even if it were more generous) would virtually always be
subject to sacrifice if some relevant human interest in exploiting the
interest were identified.

Despite my view that it does not make sense to talk about animals'
having rights in a society in which they are regarded as property, my
reservation is related at least in part to the notion that any animal interests that are recognized under the animal welfare paradigm that currently regulates the human/animal relationship will almost always be
subject to sacrifice in the face of even trivial human interests. The only
way that this will change is if the characterization of animals as property changes and moves closer to personhood—which is another way of
saying that animals can only secure nonbasic rights after they have
secured the basic right of not being regarded exclusively as means to
human ends. The question becomes whether there is a way that this
right—the right not to be regarded property, the right *to be a holder of
other rights*—can be achieved incrementally in a manner that is consistent with animal rights theory. This question can be rephrased as
whether there is any way incrementally to change the legal status of
animals that is consistent with rights theory. I argued above that one
thing that the rights advocate *cannot* do and remain consistent with
rights theory is use welfare reforms to achieve her goal incrementally,
because such reforms, which necessarily assume the legitimacy of the
property status of animals, only reinforce the property characterization
and cannot create rights in animals.

The foundation of animal rights theory is the elimination of the
property status of animals. I argued that theory presents an argument
for the abolition of institutionalized animal exploitation. Regan argues
that it is wrong to treat animals exclusively as means to ends, by which
he means that it is wrong to treat animals in a completely instrumental
way, just as it is wrong to treat humans in a completely instrumental
way. And it is wrong because, at the least, animals that are subjects-of-
a-life have inherent value, and they have it because all subjects-of-a-life
are relevantly similar. There is simply no nonspeciesist way of differentiating human subjects-of-a-life from nonhuman ones, which have inherent value for precisely the same reason that the humans do: because
their life matters to them apart from whether it matters to anyone else.

The question remains whether it is possible to promote changes in the present structure, short of immediate abolition, that seek incremental eradication of the property status of nonhumans. Remember that education, protests, demonstrations, and boycotts that urge the abolition of this property status represent incremental change because the rights advocate, who recognizes that the immediate abolition of property status is wildly unlikely for many reasons and that "total victory" cannot be achieved in "one move," is trying to bring more and more people to the rights view. But can educational efforts or changes in laws and regulations aimed at an incremental eradication of the property status of animals (i.e., a prohibition on some but not all types of experiments involving animals) remain consistent with rights theory? If the answer to this is negative, that does not mean rights theory is "utopian" because it does not provide a practical macro strategy for the rights advocate to pursue. On the contrary, even if the rights advocate cannot urge incremental eradication of the property status, the rights advocate is still left with a weighty task that could occupy advocates for generations to come—to educate the public on the need, as a matter of personal morality, to stop exploiting nonhumans through diet and consumer choices and, as a political matter, to support the immediate abolition of the property status of nonhumans. Indeed, the rights advocate is left with a much more specific practical strategy than is the new welfarist, who, along with all of the vivisectors, factory farmers, furriers, and hunters, urges that we pursue sociolegal change that "minimizes" or "reduces" suffering.

It may be helpful to divide the question of an incremental strategy into three inquiries: (1) as a *conceptual* matter, is the incremental eradication of property status possible? (2) as a *theoretical* matter, is any possible incremental eradication of property status consistent with other relevant aspects of rights theory? and (3) as a *practical* matter, is incremental eradication of property status structurally possible?

Conceptual Matters: The trouble with property status for animals is that any interest that is recognized is subject to sacrifice and that, barring unusual and exceptional circumstances, these interests are always expendable as long as the requisite benefit is found. So, as a conceptual matter, it seems as though any incremental eradication of property status must involve interests that are not expendable *even if there is significant human benefit to be derived from ignoring the animal's interest.* As I have observed, although rights theorists differ as to what constitutes a right, there is general agreement that a right recognizes or protects an interest even when it would benefit society generally, or some group therein, to ignore that interest in favor of treating the being exclusively as a means to an end. Usually, however, we are discussing the interests of a being who is already a *person*, who is not a slave or a nonhuman piece of personal property. That is, we usually discuss whether a being who already has the basic right of physical security (i.e., has recognized and protected interests in not being treated exclusively as means to ends) has *other* interests that ought to be protected by nonbasic rights. This is what Spira means when he talks about incremental change in other social movements. But in the case of animal rights, incremental eradication of property status necessarily involves protecting interests that individually fall short of the minimal level of protection that is assumed in our normal discourse about these matters.

As a conceptual matter alone, however, it seems plausible that property status can be changed incrementally. This plausibility depends, at least to some degree, on the prohibition of individual practices of institutional exploitation—irrespective of the "benefit" that exploiters would derive from their continuation—an incremental abolition that would, at least arguably, result in eventual abolition of the institution altogether.

Theoretical Matters: Given that rights theory seeks as its long-term goal the abolition of institutionalized exploitation, can the individual, as a macro matter, advocate for incremental eradication of property status, or is the only legitimate incremental approach public education about the need to abolish immediately the use of animal products on the micro level and to demand complete and immediate abolition on the macro level? In the abstract, it would seem that pursuit of incremental steps toward eradicating property status would be acceptable. Upon closer examination, however, a central concern of rights theory militates against this conclusion. I have argued that using welfarist reform to achieve the eradication of property status cannot work as a structural matter because these reforms assume property status and reinforce it, and, by definition, property cannot have interests that are not expendable. Welfarist reform, however, is problematic for another reason. Regan's primary objection to animal welfare is that even if it did reduce animal suffering (an empirically dubious point in its finest moments), it would still be immoral because it fails to respect the inherent value of the animal. When animal advocates argue, for example, that laboratories ought to be required to provide psychological stimulation for laboratory primates, they accept the proprietary relationship between the laboratory and "its" primates, and that position is problematic particularly for those who claim to accept rights theory. The rights advocate believes that the primates have the moral right *today* to be liberated from property status and that the continued institutionalized exploitation of the primates violates those moral rights. For the rights advocate to regard as acceptable a reform that supposedly reduces suffering for primates used in experiments is tantamount to the advocate's ignoring the status of certain subjects-of-a-life *today* in the hope that the welfarist reform will lead to something better for *other* subjects-of-a-life *tomorrow.*

This situation is problematic for rights theory for all of the reasons that cause Regan to devote a major portion of *The Case for Animal Rights* to a critique of theories, such as utilitarianism, that are focused around precisely these sorts of trade-offs. For the welfarist, who may believe that humans have rights but certainly believes that animals do not, these sorts of trade-offs do not create a theoretical problem, because a central tenet of welfare thought is that animal interests can be traded away against a net gain for animals generally. For the rights advocate, however, whatever *other* nonbasic rights animals possess, they certainly possess the basic right not to be treated exclusively as means to ends, the right to have their inherent (as opposed to instrumental) value recognized and respected and protected under the law. And they possess this moral right whether or not the legal system recognizes it. This right is violated by the instrumental treatment of animals, notwithstanding the assumption underlying welfarist reforms that the status of animals as property is legitimate.[53]

So, although there seems to be no conceptual difficulty in maintaining that property status can be eradicated incrementally, it is important to ensure that animal interests in not being property are not bargained away in the process.

Practical Matters: Finally, there is the question whether it is "practical" to advocate incremental eradication of property status. Whether something is "practical" or not is sometimes difficult to determine even if everyone is agreed on what "practicality" entails. Moreover, this notion is often used rhetorically to short-circuit discussion; for example, new welfarists claim that rights theory is not "practical" even though it provides normative guidance that far exceeds that provided by welfare theory. In any event, for purposes of this discussion, I am concerned to discover whether there are any structural limitations, inherent in the relevant political or legal institutions, that would render the incremental eradication of property status implausible from the outset.

With respect to action such as education, protests, or demonstration, there seem to be no structural limitations that would render such advocacy of gradual elimination of property status an unrealistic endeavor. That is, there is nothing that would prevent the rights advocate from standing at the street corner and urging that the elimination of the property status of animals should be reduced gradually.

With respect to changes in laws or regulations, there are serious, although not necessarily insurmountable, structural obstacles to the gradual reduction or elimination of the property status of animals. As I hope is clear by now, the current legal structure of animal welfare is based upon the notion that animals are property and that property is an important value that is to be protected not necessarily at all costs, but at almost all costs, to the animals. This structure generally rejects even welfarist reforms if they impose regulations on property ownership that are not regarded as cost-justified by property owners. Campaigns that openly seek to threaten this property status through the recognition and respect of animal interests that cannot be traded away are likely to be met with a less-than-enthusiastic response by animal exploiters and the political process that has so effectively nurtured institutionalized animal exploitation, rejecting even modest regulations. In all likelihood, any such campaign would have to combine legal or legislative efforts with the public education necessary to create enough pressure to counterbalance the otherwise virtually inevitable protection of property interests by the legal system.

Moreover, the structural problems of animal welfare militate against effective enforcement by police and fair adjudication in courts. After all, American slaves supposedly enjoyed some "rights" guaranteed by law, but, as numerous historians have pointed out, these laws were never enforced, and courts routinely simply failed to punish those (usually the owners of the slave property) who violated these slave "rights." But several additional considerations are relevant here. Whatever notion of "practicality" is employed, welfarist reform, which has done little to help animals, is not "practical" in any significant way. However little we may gain by seeking incrementally to eliminate property status, we do not lose much in the process. As it presently stands, those who seek justice for nonhumans are being told to pursue a strategy that merely reinforces the very property paradigm that is responsible for the problem in the first place, and are told that continuing to reinforce the property status of animals through what are ineffective regulations on the use *of animal property* will lead to the abolition of institutionalized animal exploitation. That prescription provides—and *can* only provide—for the continuation of the property paradigm. Animal welfare cannot provide the normative guidance sought by someone who rejects the notion that animals are property; if animal rights theory can provide normative guidance, that is the most that can be asked for the present. It remains for those in the future to evaluate whether this normative guidance has been effective in eradicating property status.

In addition, campaigns that are designed to eradicate property status and are designated as such may have an indirect effect of raising public consciousness in situations in which welfarist reforms do not. As I discussed earlier, many new welfarists support welfarist reforms that they (mistakenly) believe will lead to the abolition of institutionalized exploitation, but they present these reforms not only as *not* threatening the property status of animals but, indeed, as *benefiting* animal exploiters. For example, advocates of legislation that supposedly makes the slaughter of animals for food more "humane" have argued that the public will consume more meat if they are assured that the process is "humane." Even if such tactics work, they have a serious drawback (in addition to providing exploiters with ammunition to argue that animal advocates hide their true goals): such a campaign does nothing to educate the public and in fact encourages the public to broaden conduct most animal advocates disagree with anyway.

Most people accept the moral view that we ought not to treat animals "inhumanely," although most people never bother to think through the implications of this moral view. In any event, when advocacy groups reveal that a slaughterhouse is allowing disabled animals to die slow and painful deaths, or researchers are cutting into the brains of unanesthetized animals when anesthesia would in no way interfere with the experiment, they are declaring that those particular actions should be prohibited. But these campaigns often do very little to raise public consciousness about the fundamental moral issues involved and, to some degree, may very well encourage people to continue to exploit animals because resulting welfarist regulation assures them that the animals are being used "properly."

Even if campaigns to eradicate property status are ultimately unsuccessful, these unsuccessful attempts may have enormous indirect success through their educational value. For example, a campaign that sought to outlaw completely the use of live animals in circuses and that was *explicitly* predicated on a rejection of the property status of animals, even if ultimately unsuccessful, could multiply manifold the number of people aware of the injustice of these animals' plight.

Finally, any assessment of the practicality of such measures must take into account that those who advocate for the rights of animals have never really tried an alternative approach. For the most part, animal advocates have always started with very moderate proposals for welfare reform. In my view, this is because most efforts to get changes in laws and regulations are undertaken by national animal advocacy organizations. But as I pointed out earlier, these groups, which are far more like bourgeois charities than revolutionary organizations, are not likely to have a go at the institution of private property. In any event, to approach this problem by calling for the incremental eradication of property status, rather than urging simply that we "minimize" animal suffering, has yet to be tried. It is clear, however, that to urge such changes as "insiders" is out of the question. But then, being an "insider" has not helped nonhuman animals very much at all.

Much of the disunity in the animal movement has resulted from continued focus by the new welfarists on the animal welfare paradigm that requires that we treat animals "humanely" and that we "minimize" suffering. It is no wonder that these terms engender so much controversy even within the animal movement: they are inherently vague, and within the structure of the law, they are virtually meaningless. A distinct advantage of the rights perspective is that, unlike welfarist or utilitarian thought, rights theory establishes clear normative guidance at least as far as the eradication of the property status of animals is concerned. As a result, there is a greater potential for normative unity, which is required to some degree by *any* social protest movement, than is afforded by animal welfare.[54]

Conclusion

Singer argues that as a general matter rights theory possesses weak normative force and is incapable (or more incapable than utilitarianism) of providing specific normative guidance in concrete situations. This is incorrect. For Regan, the ideal component of rights theory requires the abolition of institutionalized animal exploitation; in practical terms, this means that we should no longer eat animals or use them in experiments or clothing or for entertainment. Whether humans or other nonhumans would benefit from the institutionalized exploitation of animals is not relevant, because the respect principle simply rules such considerations out as a result of the equal inherent value possessed by all rightholders. For Singer, the question whether institutionalized exploitation would be abolished or modified—and, if the latter, in what ways—would be resolved on a case-by-case basis because Singer, as an act-utilitarian, is committed to applying the principle of utility on a case-by-case basis. Although his theory rejects speciesism and requires that equal interests be given equal consideration, such a principle provides very little normative guidance regarding the treatment of animals (or anyone else).

Moreover, rights theory provides concrete normative guidance on the level of individual moral choice concerning the abolition of institutionalized exploitation. And the macro component of rights theory allows for incremental change. Such change, however, should not be regarded as the incremental achievement of rights as a general matter. Part of the confusion that plagues the modern animal protection movement is connected to the failure to realize that rights theory has at its core the rejection of the property status of animals. In this light, the issue of incremental change is understood as the incremental eradication of this property status. I have argued that there are no conceptual, theoretical, or practical impediments to an animal rights advocate adopting an incremental approach. I have also argued that whatever the rights advocate does, it is not open to her to rely on welfarist reform to "reduce" or eliminate property status, because those reforms are incapable of leading to any rights and assume the legitimacy of the property status of animals. Animal welfare reforms continually reinforce the property paradigm in many ways, and it is a mystery why *anyone* thinks that welfarist reform will lead to the abolition of exploitation.

CHAPTER Seven

Rights Theory

An Incremental Approach

In the preceding chapter, I argued that, as far as conceptual, theoretical, and practical matters are concerned, there is nothing in rights theory that prohibits the advocate of animal rights from urging incremental change on a sociolegal level (changes in law, regulations, policy) as long as these incremental changes do not compromise the status of nonhumans as moral rightholders. I argued that what the animal rights advocate *cannot* do while remaining consistent with rights theory is urge that welfarist reform be pursued as a short-term means to achieve the abolition of institutionalized exploitation.

Here I propose some criteria that may be used to identify those measures short of abolition that would be consistent with animal rights theory. In presenting these criteria, I emphasize four points:

First, I rely on only two central aspects of rights theory and make no claims to consider the subsidiary aspects. My purpose is to keep my criteria as uncomplicated and uncontroversial as possible. The first aspect of animal rights theory on which I focus is its aim to abolish the institutionalized exploitation of animal subjects-of-a-life, the treatment of animals exclusively as means to ends. Put in legal language, rights theory seeks the eradication of the property status of nonhumans. This aspect of rights theory acknowledges that animals have interests other than mere protection from pain and suffering. The second aspect is that, in seeking this long-term goal, the rights advocate cannot endorse the sacrifice of fundamental interests of some animals today in the hope that other animals tomorrow will no longer be treated as the property of human owners. All subjects-of-a-life have equal inherent value, and it violates the respect principle to ignore the inherent value of any such being because some other beings would thereby "benefit."

These aspects of rights theory are central because they incorporate key notions of rights theory, but I have obviously omitted many more notions, including many of the more complicated ones. My point is to see what criteria can be derived from these basic notions. Further scholarship will, I hope, seek to develop further the relationship between animal rights theory and practice. In addition, I think that these aspects of rights theory are relatively uncontroversial—not, of course, in any absolute sense, but rather in that anyone who identified herself as an advocate of animal rights would probably agree both that these are key aspects of rights theory and with the content of these assertions. That is, if a person considers herself an animal rights advocate, she probably agrees with the statement of the long-term goal and the limitation placed on getting to that goal—by whatever means.

Second, I offer these criteria to *begin* and not to end discussion. Thus far, the modern animal movement has ignored the connection between theory and practice in favor of a sort of pragmatism that defeats itself. Animal advocates, understandably frustrated, have wanted to "take action" and have avoided ideological discussion, fearing it to be a waste of time. Although this sort of unity would be marvelous if it were helping to eliminate animal exploitation, the quality of animal life is getting worse, and the numbers of animals exploited are rising. It is crucial that animal advocates recognize that whether my views are right or wrong, the animal movement is, and has been for many years, drifting on a sea of uncertainty. The movement has thus far been unable to channel the energies of the hundreds of thousands—perhaps millions— of people who are deeply concerned about the staggering injustice that is, as a matter of our social institutions, visited upon animals every second of every minute of every hour of every day. This inability is owing partly to the absence of any conceptual rallying position that the movement might have conveyed to its members—other than the view that humans ought to "reduce suffering," which, as I have argued, is how the movement got into the predicament in which it currently finds itself.

Nevertheless, the animal welfare movement is as strong as it has ever been, especially in light of the support for welfare reform that has been offered by the new welfarists. If the animal *rights* movement is going to survive, it will need to begin an internal dialogue about the meaning of the movement, its goals, and its means for achieving those goals.

Third, I recognize that these criteria are somewhat imprecise. I apologize for this infelicity, but I stress that social protest movements cannot strive for the certainty in complicated ethical matters that we have in mathematics. Complicated ethical issues cannot be resolved with calculators or computers. All that can be done is to approximate some moral idea in a sensible way. Indeed, the primary problem that I have identified with new welfarism is that it fails to approximate any moral ideal other than that embodied in animal welfare, and that new welfarism, like animal welfare theory generally, is not very sensible, because the process of animal welfare applied by legal and political institutions will almost always resolve any human/animal conflict in favor of the human property owner. Moreover, since the animal rights movement has only just begun to discuss these issues, any efforts to connect theory with practice will have first to pave a road over which others will travel. The following is an attempt to start the foundation for that road, and initial attempts are always awkward.

Fourth, I want to stress that the rights advocate may reasonably conclude that *all* attempts to eradicate the institutionalized exploitation of animals through incremental legislation and regulation do not, at this point in the history of the human/nonhuman relationship, represent the most efficacious use of temporal and financial resources. Any attempt to dislodge animals from their status as property will, at the very least, meet with fierce resistance from animal exploiters, who have the support of the political and legislative establishment. But this does not mean that the rights advocate is left without an incremental program of practical change. On the contrary, the rights advocate is left with a most important and time-consuming project: education of the public through traditional educational means—protest, demonstrations, economic boycotts, and the like—about the *need* for the abolition of institutionalized exploitation on a social and personal level. This sort of advocacy, which in various manifestations is currently out of favor with a movement that emphasizes centralized control from national offices and elite "summits" of leaders who pronounce policy, is nevertheless some of the most important for a true social protest movement. Moreover, in light of the structural defects of animal welfare, *any* legislative or judicial campaign will need to be accompanied by a vigorous educational campaign.

Criterion 1: An Incremental Change Must Constitute a Prohibition

One of the key aspects of a right is that it constitutes a *claim*. A right involves other notions as well, but one very important component of a right is that it constitutes a claim that has a correlative duty.[1] For example, to say that Mary has a right to have people stay off her property means that she has a claim against everyone (unless she chooses to limit who is affected) to stay off her land and that everyone has a correlative duty not to enter upon Mary's land.[2] Central to a claim right, then, is a *prohibition* imposed on other people not to interfere with the right-holder's interest protected by the right. I argued earlier that laws that require that people treat animals "humanely" cannot, as Rowan and others have argued, create "rights" for animals precisely because *nothing* is prohibited by such laws except for the completely gratuitous waste of animals. The animal (or the representative of the animal) can claim nothing, because no one is under any obligation to refrain from any particular action. Some laws prohibit the "unnecessary" infliction of suffering, but such laws are useless if, as is the case, no one is under a duty not to do any particular act; and indeed, virtually all acts involving animals are considered "necessary" as long as there is some identifiable human benefit. Without such duties, there can be no rights of any kind.

Even when it appears as though there are prohibitions, oftentimes these do not prohibit behavior except in a very narrow sense. For example, in a 1982 Rhode Island case, *State v. Tweedie*, the defendant, who claimed he was curious what would happen, was convicted of killing a cat by placing it in microwave oven at his workplace cafeteria.[3] We cannot conclude, however, that in Rhode Island putting cats in microwave ovens is *prohibited*. Tweedie's crime was not in *what* he did, but in his doing it outside of recognized institutionalized exploitation. That is, had Tweedie been a research scientist curious about such matters, he would have been exonerated because such use would have been deemed "necessary." And there are many instances of such animal use in experimentation.[4] This reflects, and supports, the notion that animal use that occurs outside institutionalized exploitation is just about the only animal exploitation that is prohibited. But we cannot say that such narrow prohibitions are prohibitions in the sense that we use that notion in the context of claim rights. The interest that the animal has in not being killed in a microwave oven is the same whether the person turning on the switch has a doctoral degree or is a laborer. The fact that the interest can be sacrificed in one instance but not in another means that the protection accorded that interest is not the same as the protection accorded a right.

Although prohibitions are, in this sense, central to all claim rights, they are particularly central in the case of animal rights. As I have argued throughout this book, the theory of animal rights says nothing about what particular rights animals have other than the right not to be treated as the property of humans, which is what makes their institutionalized exploitation possible in the first place. To the extent that we cast animal rights theory in terms of claims, the animal claim will not be a claim *to do something*, as are most human claim rights, but will be a claim *against instrumental treatment*. In this sense, the claim right involves a prohibition not only in the sense that others are prohibited from interfering with the protected interest but also in the sense that others are prohibited from treating animals *exclusively* as a means to an end. This is not a claim involving contracts (which create other legal interests) or the relationship of animals as rightholders to other property.

So, the first criterion for any incremental change other than education of the public about the need for the abolition of institutionalized animal exploitation is that it *prohibit* some reasonably identifiable behavior. This prohibition must also be correlative with the ability of the animal to claim (through a representative) the protection of the right. (I discuss this notion later in the chapter.)

The requirement that there be a prohibition, and not merely a regulation that requires "humane" treatment, is sometimes phrased as a requirement that there be the "abolition" of a particular practice. Although this is a correct description of the matter, it can cause confusion by equating the abolition of institutionalized animal exploitation with incremental measures that, it is hoped, will lead to that abolition. According to moral theory's ideal, animal rights is clearly "abolitionist" in that its long-term goal is the complete eradication of institutionalized animal exploitation. To say that the incremental means must themselves be "abolitionist" is correct if what is meant is that there must be a prohibition of some reasonably identifiable conduct and that engagement in that conduct would constitute a failure to respect a particular animal interest. But these incremental means are by definition not "abolitionist" in the sense that no one incremental prohibition will effect the long-term goal of ending animal slavery. In order to avoid confusion, I think it is better to reserve "abolition" for the long-term goal of rights theory and to use "prohibition" as one criterion of incremental measures that seek to realize that long-term goal.

The requirement of a prohibition is a start, but it is only a start because, standing alone, the requirement is arguably incomplete. For example, there are legal regulations that require that animals used in experiments be provided with water regularly. This law would not have the same problem as one that required that animals be treated "humanely," because the latter does not really require any particular human conduct at all; therefore, we cannot say that the latter law prohibits anything. But a law that requires specifically that animals be watered is different because it does prescribe a standard: it prescribes that a particular interest of the animal must be observed. The property owner has a duty to give water to the animals. And precisely because the standard is correlative with a duty, such a law could be called a prohibition in that it prohibits withholding water from animals used in experiments. Although water may be withheld if the animal is used in a dehydration experiment, that limitation is sufficiently definite to delimit a very clear class of instances to which the duty would apply, so that it would be permissible to say that a prohibition is involved in all those cases in which the animal was not being used for purposes that specifically required water deprivation for some other purpose.

The requirement of a prohibition has the advantage of ruling out from the class of incremental measures any rule that does not establish a standard of behavior with a correlative duty that has behavioral content, that is, a standard of behavior that prohibits the property owner from engaging in—or places the property owner under a duty not to engage in—some conduct. This exclusion would involve all welfarist laws and regulations that require only that the property owner treat the animal property "humanely." The disadvantage of the prohibition requirement as a single criterion for identifying incremental measures is that any law or regulation that does establish a standard with a correlative duty could be regarded as a prohibition even though the standard was agreed to be (even by welfarists) nothing more than a welfarist reform. So, although the requirement of a prohibition is useful and excludes *some* welfarist reform (the rules that prescribe "humane" treatment and proscribe "unnecessary" suffering), it is not yet sufficient.

Standing alone, however, the prohibition requirement is problematic in another sense. Laws that prohibit only "inhumane" behavior do not constitute true prohibitions, and I have argued that as a matter of legal process these laws are interpreted only to require that level of animal care that will facilitate the exploitation of the animal property without allowing the property owner to inflict gratuitous harm on the animal, which will only decrease overall social wealth. So, although these laws do not prohibit any *particular* behavior, they may be interpreted, for example, as placing the owner under a duty, unless the owner has a good objection, to provide the animal with water in order to keep the animal alive.

This argument suggests that *all* welfarist laws, including those that require that animals be treated "humanely" or not be used in "unnecessary" ways and do not prescribe duties that proscribe certain conduct, nevertheless constitute prohibitions. Even if the standard that requires water would have been adopted in the absence of a specific requirement and would, at least in theory, be adopted even in the absence of a rule requiring "humane" treatment, there are important differences between the general and the specific standard. The costs associated with interpreting the general standard may result in uncertainty that would be ameliorated by the specific standard.

There are many reasons why property owners act in ostensibly irrational ways and do not maximize the value of their property; ignorance of relevant information is one important reason in the context of animal property, where relatively little is known about animal "welfare" (understood as that which makes animals good "producers" for their human owners). Although the indefinite standard may, in theory, lead to the same result (a definite standard), that process of evolution is fraught with many uncertainties that, at least on the level of practical reasoning, distinguish such a standard from what I am describing as a prohibition. Moreover, there may be cases in which welfarists propose a reform that provides a standard that is not cost-justified.[5] (I have more to say about this, however, and will continue the discussion below.)

Criterion 2: The Prohibited Activity Must Be Constitutive of the Exploitative Institution

Consider the following proposals:

Proposal 1: to reduce the number of hens confined in a battery cage (floor space usually is a twelve-inch square) from four hens to three hens.

Proposal 2: to illegalize the use of animals in drug addiction experiments.

These proposals cannot be distinguished using the first criterion alone, because, for the reasons stated above, both of these can be considered to involve prohibitions. Although proposal 2 accords more with the notion of a prohibition, proposal 1 can be conceptualized as a prohibition on keeping four chickens in a cage.

This is not to say, however, that there are no distinctions between proposal 1 and proposal 2. With respect to the illegalization of the use of animals in a certain type of experiment, a particular activity that is constitutive of the general practice of vivisection has been stopped. At any given time, vivisection as an institution for the exploitation of nonhumans involves the use of animals for a number of discrete and identifiable purposes, such as experiments, or testing, or education. This is, however, not the only way in which the institution of vivisection may be understood in terms of its constitutive activities. For example, vivisection may also be understood from the standpoint of the animals used; that is, vivisection may be considered as the use of nonhuman primates for *all* research, testing, and educational purposes, the use of dogs for *all* such purposes, and so forth. Or it may be understood as the use of all animals of a particular species for particular purposes.

The problem is that at some point the description of the constitutive activities of vivisection will become so detailed that the concept of constitutive activity will cease to have any usefulness apart from providing a list that contains a statement of every animal used in every procedure for all research, testing, or educational purposes. For example, were I to argue that one of the constitutive parts of the general practice of vivisection was the use of *this* particular rabbit in *this* particular experiment, I would, of course, be correct, strictly speaking, but then the very same experiment done with five different rabbits would constitute five different "activities." In this context (as in most others), words like "activity" pertain more generally to a class of actions. This is not to say that the usage of the concept is governed in some determinate way; there will, of course, be close cases. But just because there are close cases does not mean that there is no difference between using "constitutive activity" to apply to the use of all animals in a particular type of research (proposal 2) and using that concept to describe the use of a particular animal in a particular experiment. For example, our description of events collectively as an "activity" must be based on relevant similarities shared by those events. As an initial matter at least, the activity described in proposal 2 qualifies as a constitutive activity because it describes a significant group of events and collects them together based on the *character and purpose* of the use (i.e., drug addiction experiments).

The question now becomes whether, based on this analysis, there is a difference between proposal 1 and proposal 2. Assuming that the institution of exploitation at issue is animal agriculture (the analogue of vivisection as a general matter), the question is whether changing the number of hens in the cage from four to three constitutes a prohibition of a constituent activity of the overall practice. This question asks whether we can regard having four hens in the cage a *different activity* from having three hens in the cage. At some point, the constitutive activities of animal agriculture may become so specific as to be nothing more (or less) than a list of every animal that has been used in animal agriculture, so that, in a given year, there are eight billion different constitutive activities in the United States alone. The hen example is not yet at that end of the spectrum, but it also seems to use a notion of constitutive activity that differs from that used in proposal 2. If proposal

1 read instead that we would keep the four hens in the cage but would make some other environmental adjustment, such as giving "treats" to the hens,[6] I do not think that anyone would say that we had effected a prohibition of a constitutive activity because keeping four hens in a cage with cookies is a different activity from keeping four hens in a cage without cookies. That does not mean that the two situations are the same; it means only that it tugs at our notions of what "constitutive activity" means when we try to apply it in the cookie example.

Applying this analysis, and recognizing that we are often dealing with matters of degree, it appears that although proposal 1 can be said to contain a prohibition, it does not rise to the level of eradicating an activity that is constitutive of animal agriculture. It *does* represent a change in the character of the exploitation, but I think that it stretches the concept of "constitutive activity" to say that every such change (or this change) is anything more than just that—a *change*, but not the cessation of something that might be called an activity. On the other hand, if "constitutive activity" has any meaning, it would appear as though proposal 2, which classifies a group of events together based on the nature of the experiments (viz., *all* drug addiction experiments) and prohibits that class of events, does involve an "activity" that is "constitutive" of the overall offending institution.

This discussion indicates that whether something is a "constitutive activity" or not may depend on degree. For example, if proposal 1 required that we take all four hens out of the battery cage entirely and place them in a small hen house that afforded more movement, we might be inclined to say that the proposal involved abolishing an activity that was constitutive of animal agriculture, namely, the battery cage. Again, the fact that the difference between what is and what is not regarded as a "constitutive activity" may frequently be a matter of degree rather than of category does not obviate the usefulness of the concept as a tool to distinguish between certain states of affairs. It only means that sometimes it is difficult to apply the concept.

In sum, the second criterion—that the prohibition end a salient part of the institution of exploitation—can help to distinguish further incremental change that reflects the rights philosophy, but the combination of these two criteria cannot do the job completely. Many cases fall into a gray area in which it is difficult to be certain whether a prohibition really does involve a significant activity that is part of the exploitation, and there may very well be cases in which the prohibition may be said to affect a constitutive activity but the incremental change nevertheless violates salient aspects of rights theory.

Criterion 3: The Prohibition Must Recognize and Respect a Noninstitutional Animal Interest

Although some question whether animals can be said to have "interests,"[7] most people, including those who exploit animals, regard animals as having a wide range of interests. Animal interests play a central role in the moral theories of both Regan and Singer. Indeed, the difference between their views can be understood in terms of the animal interests on which they focus. For Singer, although animals may have many interests, their primary interest is in not suffering; for Regan, animals have more interests, including the interest in not being treated exclusively as a means to an end.

The law supposedly protects animal interests; but for the most part these are the interests that facilitate the exploitation of the animals for the particular property use. So, for example, the law protects the interests of animals used in experiments to the extent necessary to ensure that the animals produce data acceptable to research scientists. Indeed, those who support the use of animals in experiments assure the public that "only those animals that are cared for properly will be good research subjects"[8] and that the federal Animal Welfare Act and other sources of regulation provide for the requisite care. In this sense, each form of institutionalized exploitation of animals has rules about "humane" care that are tailored to that particular use of animal property and that reflect the particular concerns of that exploitative activity.

To the extent that we seek the incremental eradication of the property status of animals, it is necessary that there be a corresponding recognition of the interests of animals in not being regarded as property, or, as Regan would say, in not being treated exclusively as a means to human ends. This follows from one of the two primary aspects of rights theory: that the goal of rights theory is to eradicate the property status of animals so that animals are no longer treated exclusively as means to ends. To the extent that the only interests recognized by a proposed incremental measure are those that are necessary in order to exploit animal property, such interests do not represent any movement (incremental or otherwise) toward eradication of property status and, instead, reinforce that exploitation. For example, Temple Grandin's animal-handling guidelines, which have been adopted by the American Meat Institute and endorsed by McDonald's, are based on the notion that animal welfare is important *because* failure to observe certain standards will result in carcass damage and worker injuries. Grandin writes, "Once livestock arrive at packing plants, proper handling procedures are not only important for the animals' well-being, but can also mean the difference between profits and losses due to meat quality or worker safety. . . . Healthy animals, properly handled, keep the meat industry running safely, efficiently and profitably."[9] Grandin's "humane" slaughter reforms are supported by animal advocates such as Henry Spira and Kenneth Shapiro, and, indeed, this support very neatly fits Singer's exhortation that animal advocates support *any* measure that "reduces the suffering of animals or enables them to meet their needs more fully."[10] So, although Grandin's proposals, if implemented, will supposedly reduce animal suffering, her recommendations are explicitly presented as measures that will be of benefit to the meat industry. *She urges these measures as something that will help the meat industry to remain profitable.*

As Garner has observed about animal slaughter in Great Britain, there are laws and regulations whose ostensible purpose is to ensure that the "suffering of farm animals in the last moments of their life should be minimal." But, according to Garner, "animal welfare often takes second place to cost-cutting."[11] Grandin's recommendations, like the rule that requires that an animal used in experiments be given drinking water, reduce animal suffering only to enhance the value of the animal property. —An animal who dies unintentionally of dehydration is not likely to produce "good" data, or, indeed, any data at all. Similarly, if a cow at the slaughterhouse panics and injures a worker involved in her slaughter or bruises her "meat" when she regains consciousness and finds herself hanging upside down from one leg and flails around from the pain in her broken pelvis, the meat packer will lose money. If the meat packer observes Grandin's stunning rules, the animal will supposedly remain unconscious throughout the process, which is better for the animal and better for the meat packer.

In an important sense, then, proposals such as Grandin's place animal welfarists in the role of providing information to animal exploiters to ensure that they act rationally with respect to their animal property. A rational property owner who wants to use an animal in an experiment will give the animal food and water sufficient to ensure that the animal remains alive for the necessary period. Moreover, a rational property owner should recognize this whether the law specifically requires the watering of animals or merely requires that animals be treated "humanely" or does not address the matter at all. Imposing a specific legal requirement on property owners to treat animal property in a particular way (e.g., to water animals every three hours) reduces the likelihood that some property owners may behave irrationally out of ignorance of empirical facts (e.g., how often animals need water) and thereby reduces the moral hazard that animal property will be wasted and overall social wealth diminished. What Grandin is proposing is what a rational property owner would do anyway if the owner possessed Grandin's supposed expertise as an animal scientist. But these rules have nothing to do with recognizing the interests of the animals— *except instrumentally as means to human ends.*

Any incremental eradication of the property status of animals will entail recognition of animal interests that are noninstitutional, recognition that does not simply ensure that the animal is used "wisely" in whatever context of exploitation is involved. Recognition of institutional interests, such as the interest of a turkey destined for slaughter in being fed, merely *reinforces and supports* the property status of animals. The test for such an interest is simple, but, like the second criterion, necessarily admits of degrees: if the interest imposes a significant cost or tax on the ownership of animal property under circumstances in which the cost is clearly not justified in light of the "benefit" to the property owner, then the interest recognized is extra- or noninstitutional. The test is simple to apply because, at least in theory, it requires merely that we identify what costs are imposed by the regulation on property ownership and whether those costs will significantly exceed any benefit that animal property owners derive. In most cases, the property owners will be more than pleased to identify such regulations through their opposition to the proposals.

Of course, animal property owners tend to object that virtually any proposed regulation imposes such costs. For example, although those involved in the use of animals in experiments often concede that the federal Animal Welfare Act ensures what the scientists themselves want—economical producers of reliable data—they routinely oppose amendments to the act. In the case of vivisection, this opposition may be attributable to concerns about academic freedom and the regulation of science. In the context of "humane" slaughter regulation, which does not involve such values, the affected industries often support welfarist reform. Nevertheless, exploiter opposition to a proposal may be attributable to many causes, and although it may be used as an indicator that a regulation satisfies this criterion, it is not by any means a guarantee, and animal advocates will need to make their own assessments of the costs and benefits involved. When the costs significantly exceed the benefits, that is an indication the proposal is seeking to protect an interest that the animal has beyond those interests that a rational property owner would observe to ensure the efficient exploitation of the animal property.[12]

This criterion admits of degrees insofar as the "significance" of the difference between the costs imposed on property ownership and the benefits reaped by property owners will vary. Many proposed reforms will add costs to property ownership, costs that represent recognition of a noninstitutional interest, but many of these costs may be trivial. For example, in proposal 1 of the preceding discussion of constitutive activities, the removal of one bird from the battery cage may be proposed for "moral" and not economic reasons (i.e., the property owners, if completely rational but left to their own devices, would not institute such a change), but it is still questionable whether the proposed change is "significant" or is so trivial that its acceptance might constitute cost-effective appeasement offered by property owners to placate moral sentiment in favor of animals.

In any event, what is clear is that a great many welfarist reforms would be disqualified by application of this criterion alone; Grandin's meat reforms and similar proposals, which seek the recognition of those interests that any rational property owner would recognize in the absence of such rules, are seen as part of the problem and not part of the incremental eradication of the problem. So in that sense, the criterion is useful in further differentiating acceptable incremental measures from unacceptable ones.

Alternatively, one could think about this criterion as targeting those interests the animal would have *were the animal no longer regarded as property*. This parallels the preceding section's identification of activities that are constitutive of exploiting institutions. If, for example, laying hens were removed completely from the battery cage and placed in an environment where the treatment they received was consistent with that which these animals should receive were they no longer regarded as human property—that is, in a way that respected *completely* their interest in bodily movement—then that change would qualify as a prohibition of an activity that is constitutive of the exploiting institution. Similarly, this prohibition would respect a noninstitutional interest in a way that is more certain in some respects.

Thinking about animal interests in this way may also help us to determine when there is a prohibition on a constitutive activity. If the prohibition achieves a state of affairs that is consistent with the status of animals as subjects-of-a-life, then that prohibition abolishes a constitutive activity of exploitation. For example, if egg batteries are abolished but hens, still regarded as property, are kept under circumstances that would be appropriate were their property status abolished entirely (i.e., they have freedom of movement and are otherwise kept as they would be were they no longer regarded as property), then, although the hens will continue to be exploited as property, the prohibition of battery cages recognizes an interest that the animal would have were the animal no longer regarded as property, and the prohibition may be said to prohibit a constitutive activity of exploitation.

Criterion 4: Animal Interests Cannot Be Tradable

I argued earlier that within the current structure of animal welfare theory embodied in the law—a set of doctrines that I call legal welfarism—the *only* interest of animals that cannot be sacrificed is the animal's interest in not being "wasted," or being exploited in a manner that produces no socially recognized "benefit." I also argued that where any other interests are recognized, these are recognized only to the extent that they do not conflict with human property rights; once there is a conflict, the animal's interest is systematically and, in light of the normative assumptions of the system, *necessarily* ignored. But this sort of sacrifice of interests is, as I have noted, completely inconsistent with the notion of a right as something that protects an interest from sacrifice.

This is not to say that a right cannot be overridden by another right that we judge to be more important. For example, although the law guarantees my right of free speech, it also provides for a right of physical security through a number of criminal and civil laws. If I wish to yell "fire" in a crowded theater when there is no fire and where there is no purpose served by my act other than my amusement at watching a stampede of frightened people, your right to be free of the physical harm of being trampled will trump my right of free speech. But this judgment is not based on the "benefit" to any of the parties. The judgment would not change even if it could be shown that I would benefit far more by being able to yell "fire." Assume the following: (1) a rich friend tells me that she will pay me $5 million if I yell "fire" in the theater; and (2) I reasonably believe that even if anyone is injured as a result of my joke and sues me, their injuries, quantified by what they would get if they sued for their injuries, would only amount to $1 million under a worst-case scenario. I might be tempted to proceed with the prank if only civil liability were involved; if my only concern was that I might get sued for civil damages, I might very well go ahead, pay the maximum of $1 million, and pocket the remaining $4 million. But I would still be liable under the criminal law for causing these injuries and would be subject to criminal punishment. And the reason for this is clear: the criminal law recognizes that people have some interests that should not be sacrificed even though someone else will benefit. When we evaluate rights for purposes of deciding conflicts between rights, we do not look at consequences solely or even primarily. Rather, we look to the interests protected by rights and the competing values involved. In the above example, free speech is recognized as important in part because we value diverse contributions to the marketplace of ideas. But yelling "fire" in a crowded theater when there is no fire does little to add valuable input to our common pool of ideas. As a result, it is relatively easy to rank the rights in this case, but no ranking has been done by reference to the aggregation of consequences.

In light of the status of animals as property, the law recognizes that animals have interests that exceed institutional interests only insofar it recognizes no social benefit to be gained from the exploitation of those interests. Once such benefit is identified, the interest is traded way to secure the human benefit. For example, for some years various humane societies have prosecuted people involved in animal "sacrifices," or the use of animals in religious ceremonies. Most of these sacrifices involve Caribbean religions such as Santeria. Although these same state agencies would do nothing about the conditions of commercial slaughterhouses, they are eager to protect the interests that animals have to be free from use in these religious ceremonies. The reason for the disparate treatment is clear, though often unstated: meat eating is an accepted use of animals, and ceremonial sacrifices are practiced by unpopular religions whose adherents are generally people of color or economically disadvantaged classes.[13] One use of animals was considered "necessary" and therefore not violative of anticruelty laws; and one use was regarded—by those empowered persons who enforce laws—as "unnecessary" and violative of the anticruelty laws. In 1993, the Supreme Court held that it violated the constitutional guarantee of freedom of religion to regard the religious killings as "unnecessary" without demonstrating how the legal and the allegedly illegal killings differed.[14] The Court held that the humane societies that were prosecuting the Santeria practitioners simply did not understand that for the practitioners the animal sacrifices provided a spiritual "benefit." Once that benefit was identified, any "balancing" was over with just as soon as it began: the animal interest was ignored.

If the property status of animals is to be incrementally eradicated, then the noninstitutional interests recognized under criterion 3, following the second salient assumption of animal rights theory, cannot be tradable just because the aggregation of consequences indicates that the trade is justified to secure the human "benefit." Indeed, animals are property precisely because they have no interests (beyond those that must be observed if the animals are to serve their "purpose" as our property) that are safe from being "balanced" away to serve some human "benefit."

In one sense, this criterion seeks to ensure that the incremental eradication of property status is indeed an incremental "assembly" of personhood status for nonhumans through the recognition of their inherent value. At present, we do not recognize animals as having any value except for their value *to us*. For example, philosopher Joseph Raz claims that although animals may have some value apart from their instrumental use to people, animals cannot have inherent value, because any value of the animal ultimately derives from the animal's contribution to the happiness and well-being of some human or humans, who do have inherent value. Raz's view is, I think, representative of the views held by many people.

In one sense, this fourth criterion could be said to address the enforceability of protection for recognized interests. By way of analogy, consider slavery as practiced in the United States. Some laws seemed to recognize that slaves had interests other than ones directly related to keeping them alive and fit for whatever purpose they were intended. For the most part, however, these interests were ignored whenever they conflicted with the interests of the master, whose property rights were held to outweigh the slave's interests. If animal interests are to be taken seriously, then, to the extent that the law regulates the use of animal property beyond what is necessary to exploit the animal property, that regulation must be held as *eliminating the property right to the extent necessary to protect the interest*. Otherwise, the victory for animals will be illusory: as soon as the rights of human property owners are triggered, the animal interest will be ignored. Accordingly, the interest of the animal must be seen explicitly as an interest that is to be protected as would a true "right" within the legal system. The interest would not be a "right" in the full sense, in that animals would not yet possess the basic right not to be regarded as property (they would still be used for food and in experiments), but animals would have something approximating nonbasic rights, something that could be said to be building blocks of the basic right not to be property. These nonbasic "rights" must, however, be treated as though they *were* rights, in the sense that they must be regarded as protecting interests from any interest balancing.

To protect animal interests in this manner would require a deliberate recognition of a type of legal norm that our legal system does not yet recognize: a norm that functions *like* a true right—in that it recognizes an interest that cannot be balanced away—but is held by a being who has not yet achieved status as a holder of the basic right not to be regarded exclusively as a means to an end. Indeed, every time we recognize such a right, we move away from treating the being *exclusively* as a means to human ends; the problem is that the being's most fundamental interests in not being eaten or used in experiments or kept in a zoo have not yet been recognized. These incremental measures may be seen, however, as recognizing pieces of the basic right not to be regarded as property. So, although these interests represent nonbasic rights in one sense, the interests are more properly regarded as "parts" of the basic right of animals not to be treated exclusively as means to human ends. Tom Regan calls my normative notion a "protoright" because it functions like a right but runs to the benefit of a nonrightholder, properly speaking.[15] I adopt Regan's terminology here because it requires that we focus on the notion that this sort of norm is something different from a right and something very different from what now exists under legal welfarism.

In order to recognize that animals have such interests, it is necessary that these interests be understood as trumping the interests of property owners. And in order to be effective, it would be necessary for the legal system to recognize that it is animals who hold this interest, and not their owners or government agencies, such as the USDA, which protects only those animal interests that make animals property in the first place. It would be necessary to recognize that animals (or, more properly speaking, the guardians of animals) have *standing* to articulate these interests *against* property owners, which would functionally require that some sort of guardian be recognized.[16]

Because animals are regarded as property, and because property is, by definition and several hundred years of accepted understanding, that which *cannot* have legal relations with persons or other property, courts have developed doctrines that preclude animals or their surrogates from articulating their interests in courts of law and before regulatory agencies. This exclusion is based on the supposed *inability* (in terms of the power of the court) to adjudicate claims made by *property* or those who purport to represent that property. So, if the extra- or noninstitutional interests of animals are to be nontradable, then those interests, which must be seen as "minitrumps" of the property rights of animal owners, must be protected by the legal system, and this will require that animal interests have legal standing and that some human actor have standing to articulate those claims before the appropriate body. This is, of course, not a new idea. In "Should Trees Have Standing? Toward

Legal Rights for Natural Objects," Christopher Stone argued the inherent value of nonhumans could be recognized and protected by guardians just as are the rights (basic and nonbasic) of children or the mentally disabled.[17]

Criterion 5: The Prohibition Shall Not Substitute an Alternative, and Supposedly More "Humane," Form of Exploitation

The fifth criterion follows from both aspects of rights theory that I identified at the outset of this chapter: that the long-term goal is the eradication of the property status of animals and that the right of animals not to be regarded as property cannot be compromised for consequential reasons. In many respects, this fifth criterion is the most significant of the group because it is this criterion that will often be the most helpful in determining whether a proposed incremental measure is consistent with rights theory, although, like the other criteria, this one is not exact and will not provide an easy answer in all cases, or even in most. But then, the idea is to *try* to make a morally informed decision.

To put the matter simply, the fifth criterion holds that it is inconsistent with rights theory to treat some animals exclusively as means to the ends of others, or as property, in order to secure some benefit that is hoped will eventually secure a higher moral status for other animals. Indeed, this is a serious problem for the new welfarist who purports to endorse the long-term goal of animal rights by using short-term welfarist reforms to achieve the abolition of institutionalized exploitation. The new welfarist, who purports to believe in the rights of animals, disregards the inherent value of some animals in order to secure a benefit for other animals. For example, the federal Animal Welfare Act provides that animals be used in biomedical experiments as long as their use is "humane" and they are not forced to suffer "unnecessarily." The new welfarists who supported the 1985 amendments to the act believe that the act will itself reduce animal suffering and, more important, that laws like the 1985 act are "stepping stones" to the future recognition of animals' interests that are now ignored. I argued earlier that there is simply no way to determine whether laws like the 1985 act actually reduce animal suffering and that such laws, given the structural defects of welfare theory generally, will generally be held to require only that conduct which facilitates the use of the animal as property—and nothing more. Apart from the rather puzzling logic of getting to a non-property status of animals by persistent reinforcement of the property paradigm, there is something theoretically objectionable when a rights advocate *explicitly endorses* the property status of animals as a way of eradicating that status on an incremental basis.

The present point can be made in the context of the tradability of interests that I discussed in the preceding section. The third criterion specifies that in order to effect an incremental eradication of the property status of animals, recognized interests must be extra- or noninstitutional. The fourth criterion requires that these incremental protorights, which will, by definition, fall short of the basic right in not being property, nevertheless be respected as providing protection that cannot be compromised for consequential reasons alone. The fifth criterion requires that in securing protorights for animals, we cannot trade away or disavow the present moral status of animals as rightholders in the sense of ignoring the fact that their continued status as property is violative of their moral rights.

This fifth criterion is also related to, but distinct from, the second criterion, that the prohibition serve to eradicate an activity that is constitutive of the overall institutionalized exploitation. As I argued at that point, there are different ways of understanding the "parts" that make up the "whole" of vivisection; one can look at experiments as a group, species of animals used as a group, and so forth. An "activity" could be defined based on the use of particular animals, or the purpose of experiments, or the kinds of procedures used. But the fifth criterion serves to place even further limits on the second in that *even if* the prohibition stops a constitutive part of the institutionalized exploitation, it cannot do so at the expense of substituting alternative forms of exploitation. So, for example, a complete prohibition on the use of chimpanzees in certain procedures can reasonably be said to constitute the prohibition of a constitutive activity, but to the extent that the advocate urges or accepts that *other* animals, such as dogs, should be used instead, there is a conflict with rights theory because such a rule would secure the benefit by treating subjects-of-a-life who have *equal inherent value* differentially by using species to determine membership in the protected class. To put the matter another way, such a rule would violate the fundamental proscription against *speciesism*.

In order to understand more fully the point of this fifth criterion, consider the following example: Animal advocates propose to lobby for a law whose preamble explicitly recognizes that animals have moral interests that are flouted by the current configuration of battery cages. The body of the law provides that in recognition of the interests that hens have, no more than two shall be placed in battery cages, and that these cages shall be enlarged to provide 196 inches of floor space rather than 144 inches. The egg industry objects to this arrangement vehemently because it is not "necessary" to the maximization of the animal property's value and will, in fact, impose a significant cost on the owners. The law provides that this animal interest must be protected irrespective of the economic consequences.

The traditional welfarist will undoubtedly support this measure because it will, in the welfarists's view, reduce animal suffering. The new welfarist, who seeks as a long-term goal the abolition of animal exploitation, will also undoubtedly support this, not only because it will supposedly reduce suffering but because it is a "stepping stone" or "springboard" into abolition at some future time.[18] The new welfarist and the traditional welfarist have the same view—that the measure will reduce suffering—but the new welfarist, unlike the traditional welfarist, believes that *because* the measure will reduce suffering, it will act as an incremental measure on the road to the long-term goal.

The animal rights advocate first dismisses the view that avoiding pain and suffering are the only interests that animals (human or nonhuman) have. If pain and suffering were the only relevant moral interests, then what would prevent us from using small numbers of "undesirable" humans to eradicate large amounts of human pain and suffering? Obviously, although we all have strong interests in avoiding pain and suffering, we do limit the ways in which pain and suffering can be alleviated, so as to respect other interests. Second, the rights advocate dismisses the new-welfarist view that a measure that reduces pain and suffering will lead to incremental achievement of the long-term goal of equal consideration for equal interests (Singer) or the abolition of all institutionalized exploitation (Regan) simply because it reduces pain and suffering. The rights advocate knows that some measures that reduce pain and suffering will generally do nothing more than assure that animals receive protection that is consistent with their status as property and that facilitates their use as particular types of property.

The rights advocate begins by asking whether the proposal contains a prohibition or a regulation and concludes that the proposal prohibits keeping more than two hens in the cage. She is unclear whether, even if the proposal is a prohibition, it constitutes a prohibition of an activity that is constitutive of the overall form of exploitation. She errs in favor of regarding the measure as prohibiting a constitutive activity. She is clear, however, that the proposal recognizes an interest that is extra-institutional in that it is not tied to the property status of the hens. The proposal recognizes that the hens have inherent value beyond their status as property, which status would justify only that level of regulation that facilitated animal use. Moreover, the proposal provides that these interests cannot be traded away and therefore constitute protorights.

The problem with the proposal is that it endorses the status of animals as property without inherent value and trades away the basic right of the hens not to be property in favor of a recognition of moral status that falls short of recognition of the basic right, or the complete protection of some interest that the animal has, for example, in bodily movement. By agreeing to the two-hen arrangement, animal advocates are trying to achieve protorights while at the same time endorsing an alternative form of exploitation—two hens in a cage—that is supposedly more "humane."

In the present case, it seems reasonable to say that the interest involved is the interest that the hens have—all of them—in not being in the battery cage in the first place and in having freedom of movement that is appropriate to the species. To the extent that the proposal recognizes and respects that interest, the prohibition arguably does not substitute another form of exploitation and is acceptable. That is, assume that a prohibition abolishes the battery cage *entirely* and replaces it with a rearing system that accommodates *all* of the hen's interests in freedom of movement and thereby fully recognizes the interest of the hen in bodily integrity. Such a prohibition *ends* a particular form of exploitation that has violated a particular noninstitutional interest that we have now decided to respect. But this sort of substitution differs considerably from that in which two hens are merely removed from the cage: although we have not yet abolished the institutionalized exploitation, the substitution eliminates the exploitation involved in the confinement system through a *full* recognition of the interest of the hens in their freedom of movement.

In any event, *any* substitution of exploitation raises serious questions for the rights advocate. If the incremental eradication of the property status of animals is to be consistent with rights theory, it is important that proposed measures not substitute one form of exploitation for another, supposedly more "humane" form of exploitation. Oftentimes the alternative form of exploitation will provide for "humane" treatment, which then feeds the whole matter right back through the mechanisms of legal welfarism, which, as I have argued before, are structurally defective and systematically devalue animal interests. But even if the substitute form of exploitation is more definite (e.g., there shall be no more than two birds per cage), and even if the proposal recognizes that the animals have *some* inherent value that justifies the recognition of a noninstitutional, nontradable interest, that recognition comes at the expense of endorsing another form of exploitation that rests on the legitimacy of the status of animals as property. This sacrifices the moral right of the animal not to be property for a protoright that is designed to effect the incremental eradication of property status. The substitution of exploitation raises issues of moral conflict with rights theory.

This discussion, however, demonstrates that as a practical matter certain campaigns will be difficult for animal rights advocates to pursue if they agree with this fifth criterion. It seems that the rights advocate really has no choice but to condemn *any* form of substitute exploitation with the *possible* exception of an alternative arrangement that completely eradicates an activity constitutive of institutional animal exploitation through the *full* recognition of relevant animal interests. The animal advocate must not herself suggest an alternative and must not agree to any alternative offered by the exploiter. To do either would involve the rights advocate in sacrificing the basic right of animals not to be property in order to secure a less-than-basic protoright that, while it does recognize and respect that animals have personlike interests that transcend their status as property, is achieved by supporting the notion that "bettering" the system of animal slavery can render it acceptable, which is to reinforce the notion that animal slavery itself is acceptable. These considerations militate in favor of conducting the sort of educational campaign that may not succeed (at least initially) in overturning any particular exploitative practice but may have a powerful effect on the public. And such education, whether sought directly in the classroom or as part of a militant campaign, is in any event probably the best thing that the animal rights advocate can do at this stage of history. After all, we live in a society that tolerates the slaughter of eight thousand live pigeons on Labor Day every year at Hegins, Pennsylvania, just for the "fun" of the activity. Animals truly are treated *exclusively* as means to human ends, and *anything* that challenges this status is more likely to effect the long-term goal than reinforcing that property status through continued emphasis on avoiding pain and suffering—as if that were the *only* value involved here.

Some Examples

The best way to illustrate the five criteria is to apply them in concrete circumstances. A wide range of welfarist reforms will be automatically disqualified if we adopt these criteria. Welfarist reforms such as those requiring that animals be treated "humanely" or that animals not be subjected to "unnecessary" suffering do not prohibit anything and, in the best case, respect only those institutional interests that facilitate animal exploitation. The "pain scale" formulated by Kenneth Shapiro and Peter Field would be excluded immediately by application of the criteria above. The scale itself represents a normative judgment about the relative moral status of the various rated activities and an implicit judgment that some forms and amounts of pain are acceptable, depending on scientific "necessity." Once we exclude those types of welfarist reforms and focus instead on more definite standards, this exercise can become more difficult.

Some proposals that easily conform to the criteria are absolute bans on leghold traps to catch fur-bearing animals. The rule consists of a prohibition of an activity that is a constitutive part of the overall exploitation of animals for clothing or fur purposes. The interest recognized is extra-institutional and nontradable, and proposal does not substitute another form of exploitation, such as the padded trap.

Similarly, the absolute prohibition of animal use, or of the use of particular sorts of animals, for particular types of experiments, would also qualify. For example, a number of animal advocates, including Tom Regan and me and, paradoxically, Peter Singer, are supporting efforts, known as the Great Ape Project, to remove chimpanzees, orangutans, and gorillas from all exploitation *through a declaration that they are no longer the property of humans and that they are rightholders.*[19] Such a measure clearly constitutes a prohibition that ends a particular and reasonably identifiable activity that is constitutive of vivisection and other institutionalized animal exploitation, and recognizes that certain animals have the basic right not to be property. In a sense, the proposal is *absolute* for the animals involved and incremental with regard to other animals. That is, the proposal eliminates completely the property status of some animals as an incremental step toward the complete eradication of that status. And the Great Ape Project is careful not to advocate that *other* animals be used instead; that would merely be a substitution of one form of exploitation for another. Singer's participation in the Great Ape Project is ironic because Singer explicitly denies that animals have rights; yet, in connection with his efforts to save the great apes, he states, "We want chimps to cease to be items of property, and to be seen as persons with rights."[20] This assertion is consistent with rights theory but blatantly conflicts with Singer's utilitarianism and his rejection of animal rights.

Other (relatively) easy cases would be the absolute prohibition of animal use for product testing or in experiments involving drug addiction. In many respects, the efforts in the United States and Great Britain in the early 1980s to move in the direction of prohibiting particular forms of experimentation were efforts to eradicate the property status of animals incrementally. There is a tendency to think that although the notion of rights-oriented prohibitions are sensible when talking about vivisection and testing, or hunting and trapping, an incremental rights approach has nothing to offer the advocate who seeks incremental change in the context of the use of animals in agriculture. For example, Garner discusses whether the rights advocate can pursue an incremental program, and concludes that although this might work in the context of vivisection through, for example, the complete elimination of toxicity tests, "this position does not regard reforms to animal agriculture as acceptable because, whatever the methods used, killing animals for food continues."[21]

Garner's concerns are legitimate, but he concludes incorrectly that the incremental approach is more difficult to apply in the agricultural context than in the experimentation context because the animals used in agriculture will be killed anyway. Unless a proposed reform states, for example, that certain uses of animals in laboratories will be prohibited and that all of the animals that were going to be used for that purpose have been identified and will be used for no other laboratory purpose, the reform is qualitatively no different from those Garner identifies in the agricultural context. That is, even an *absolute prohibition* against using animals for *some* purposes does not mean that they will not be exploited for some other purpose. Even in the so-called easy cases there is this danger. For example, an absolute ban against trapping animals does not mean that those same animals will not be shot by hunters.

What this demonstrates, however, is not that the incremental approach cannot work but rather that it is essential to understand, in analyzing a proposed prohibition on particular animal use, that the rights advocate cannot fairly be made to account for what others do to effect other types of exploitation. For example, if I abolish the forced labor of children who work sixteen hours a day in Indian carpet mills, I have prohibited a particular activity that is constitutive of child slavery. If someone comes along and forces these children into an alternative form of servitude, such as child prostitution, that does not mean that my efforts have not resulted in an increment in the total eradication of the status of children as the property of their parents. I may know with some certainty that, people being who and what they are, the exploitation of children will continue in various forms. That recognition, it seems, does not relieve me of the obligation to seek the eradication of those forms of exploitation that I can eliminate. And to the extent that consequences are important, this whole matter is far more vexing for Singer and the animal welfarists than it is for Regan or rights advocates. After all, the utilitarian needs a fairly detailed theory that serves to distinguish her *acts* from the *consequences of her acts*. The reason for this is that utilitarian theory requires that we judge *acts* in light of *consequences*. But this is a theoretical and not an empirical matter. As philosopher Jonathan Bennett argues, a description of what someone *did* will include certain upshots of certain bodily movements, but certain upshots will not be included in a description of what the person *did*, but rather, as the *consequences* of what the person has done. "There are various criteria for drawing the line between what someone did and the consequences of what he did; and there can be several proper ways of drawing it in a given case," and "there are wrong ways of dividing a set of happenings into action and consequences."[22] We can be grateful that we do not need to develop a theory to distinguish actions from consequences in the sense that is required by the new welfarist or the utilitarian, who need a fully developed theory of consequences in order to evaluate the morality of actions. The rights theorist, who lacks the crystal ball that would be required in such a case, can rely on the principle of moral agency.

Once this becomes clear, there are incremental measures that may be taken in the agricultural context that at least arguably comply with the five criteria. For example, a proposal to eliminate *entirely* the dehorning or castration of animals used for food or to eliminate the battery cage completely arguably does what the prohibition on the use of all animals in drug-addiction experiment does: it recognizes that animals have inherent value and interests that go beyond those necessary to ensure that animals are fit for the type of exploitation at issue and its prohibition is not accompanied by a substitution of other forms of exploitation. Moreover, to the extent that the animal has an interest in not being subjected to a procedure *at all*, then the prohibition of the procedure altogether effects a recognition of the identified interest. The prohibition on dehorning would be analogous to a prohibition on some procedure used widely in vivisection, such as footpad injections in mice and rodents. Animals will continue to be used for the overall exploitative purpose of the institution (vivisection, food), but a "piece" of the exploitative industry has been eliminated as the result of the recognition that animals have interests in not having these procedures done even though the owners of the animals have concluded otherwise. Both prohibitions are based on the inherent value of the animals, which is the only consideration, in the absence of animal use that yields no socially recognizable benefit, that could serve to overcome the presumption that property owners are the best parties to decide the value of their animal property. Moreover, rights theory objects to the use of the animal exclusively as a means to an end. In both examples above, the prohibitions recognize interests that would be recognized were the animals not property at all, and therefore treats the animals as more than means to human ends. In addition, since the prohibition is nontradable and is recognized as respecting the inherent value of property, the covered interest will be recognized as a limit on the treatment of future generations of animals who are exploited within the institution exclusively as means to human ends.

It is not enough to say that animals raised in veal crates ought to be raised instead in more "humane" ways, or, worse yet, to support a particular form of substitute exploitation. This would be like saying that we should prohibit the use of animals in drug-addiction experiments but that we approve of the use of animals in other, more "humane" experiments—or, as actually did happen several years ago, to argue for the complete prohibition of the steel-jaw leghold trap while proposing the substitution of a padded trap. The position that is consistent with rights theory, it seems, is that the veal crate should be prohibited or that the battery cage ought to be prohibited. The only time that a rights advocate should explicitly endorse an alternative arrangement is possibly, as I argued earlier, when that alternative *fully respects some relevant animal interest.* In such a case, the alternative removes some form of exploitation and grants a protoright, which requires treatment of the animal that, at least with respect to the relevant interest, would be required were the animal no longer regarded as property at all.

If animal exploiters accommodate animal interests and eliminate the battery cage in favor of some other form of hen enclosure that continues their status as property and does not fully respect their interest in, for example, bodily integrity, that does not necessarily undermine the incremental eradication of property status. This effect on property status has been accomplished by forcing the property owner to recognize, albeit in a limited way, that the animals have inherent value that must be respected whether or not the property owner thinks that such respect is cost-justified in light of the status of the animal as property. The battery hens will in all likelihood be placed in an alternative form of confinement. What the exploiter does in addition to this cannot fairly be said to be a consequence of the rights advocate's action, unless, of course, it is the rights advocate who actively urges this substitute exploitation. But in the absence of such support for alternative forms of exploitation (unless the alternative form of confinement fully recognizes the animals' interests in freedom of movement), the rights advocate who obtains a ban on trapping (even though the animals may still be hunted) or a prohibition of certain forms of experiments (even though the animals may still be used in other experiments) or a prohibition on various practices that are constitutive of factory farming has nevertheless achieved one incremental step in the general eradication of the property status of the animal through the recognition of a noninstitutional, nontradable interest that is based on the inherent value of the animal.[23]

Similarly, a complete prohibition on the selling of nonambulatory, or "downed," animals, a prohibition that would completely eradicate the market for these animals, may satisfy the five criteria as long as the supposed "prohibition" does not substitute another form of exploitation. If, however, the supposed "prohibition" merely requires that the downed animal be treated in a more "humane" manner but nevertheless allows the animal still to be sold under some conditions, as California law now provides, then it fails to move away from the property status of animals and, indeed, reinforces that status.

What is essential in seeking any incremental change is that rights advocates recognize that their efforts must be accompanied by a continuing and unrelenting political demand for the complete eradication of the property status of animals. Too often, animal advocates propose laws or regulations that they argue will "help" the industry. A case in point involves support by animal advocates for "improvements" in "humane" slaughtering practices that will help the meat industry to achieve greater profitability. Such strategies fail to take into account that incremental measures are designed, at least in part, to help educate and to mobilize public support for change. In many respects, *all* incremental measures are directed toward education in a very broad sense. When an animal advocate uses such a strategy, the pedagogical force of the effort is lost, and the property paradigm is reinforced. This concern may even represent another criterion: in all cases of incremental change, the change should be accompanied by a clear statement that it *is* only an increment in a larger scheme and that the ultimate goal of the rights advocate is the abolition of all institutionalized exploitation.

Some Observations

It is clear that animal welfare has not worked and, as a structural matter, cannot work. Moreover, animal welfare reforms often conflict directly with the fundamental values of rights theory. In proposing these five criteria, however, I am mindful that this is just a beginning— and an untidy one at that. In acknowledgment of that untidiness, I make the following observations.

First, incremental measures that are acceptable to welfarists and to rights advocates may very well overlap. It is easy to imagine animal advocates of both varieties supporting, for example, a true prohibition on the marketing of downed animals that would eliminate that part of the "meat" market entirely. Welfarists—and perhaps the new welfarists—would probably support this change by urging that it would make agricultural practices more "humane." That has been the favored strategy of animal advocates up to this point. The rights advocate should never engage in the normative charade of labeling any institutionalized exploitation "humane"; instead, the rights advocate should accompany any demand for prohibition of particular practices with a continuing objection to the institutionalized exploitation altogether. It does not help the overall cause for animal advocates to secure prohibitory legislation by telling people that they will feel better about eating meat if they do not have to contemplate the agony of disabled animals.

So, although the actual proposals made may overlap, the rights advocate must do all that is possible to ensure that each incremental measure is *understood* for what it is, and is not characterized in politically convenient ways that may have a detrimental effect on the long-term goal of eradication of property status. For example, in Great Britain, animal protesters demanded a prohibition on the shipping of live animals across the English Channel.[24] These protesters held daily demonstrations throughout much of 1994 and 1995, and many advocates accompanied their demonstrations and demands to stop the shipping with a further demand for the end of animal agriculture altogether. This campaign seems to satisfy the five criteria that I have discussed in this chapter. But I do think that the difference between those who protested and explicitly endorsed eating more "humanely" slaughtered meat and those who protested and accompanied their protests with demands for abolition of meat eating altogether is very significant.

Second, as I stated at the outset, these criteria are not precise; they involve concerns and ideas that cross over various categories, and it is not difficult to think of examples that constitute hard cases. The point is not to provide criteria that will be clear-cut. Unfortunately, the resolution of difficult moral problems does not often work in such a convenient fashion. The point is to help identify values that are central to the gradual reduction of the property status of animals. Moreover, proposed incremental changes may be judged by how close they come to satisfying all the criteria, and these criteria can be used to focus discussion on possible difficulties with various proposals.

Those who disagree with my overall approach and critique of welfarism may be tempted to urge rejection of these criteria by pointing out hypotheticals that cannot be made to fit easily in the framework that I have established. All I can say in reply is that I am already aware of the imperfections of my approach. But on one level, *any* attempt to eradicate incrementally the property status of nonhumans will *necessarily* have to confront the fact that all incremental measures are imperfect because none will succeed in securing the basic right of animals not to be regarded as property.[25] The goal in this chapter was not to establish some airtight set of categories but to introduce a system of rights-oriented values into the consideration of what incremental measures ought to be favored by those who claim to accept rights theory and who, unlike the new welfarists, regard rights theory as qualitatively different from animal welfare.

Third, I have not even attempted to provide any sort of "ranking" of which incremental measures ought to be pursued over others. That task transcends the scope of this work, and in any event, I doubt that such criteria could be developed. In a sense, this state of affairs is desirable because it means that, contrary to the myths of the new welfarists, rights theory offers myriad possibilities for positive concrete action. The rights advocate may decide to remain an "outsider" altogether and not try to achieve incremental change in the form of legal or regulatory measures, and may instead confine her activities to educating the public about the need to abolish all institutionalized exploitation and to eschew animal exploitation on the micro level of personal behavior.

Fourth, there are other problems I have not even discussed, but these problems would attend *any* significant effort to affect people's property rights in animals. For example, under some circumstances, regulation of animal property may be considered to be a "taking" that requires compensation to the owners. As a preliminary matter, it seems that in most cases the regulation of animal property could fairly be characterized as the sort of regulation that has traditionally been part of state police power. Nevertheless, this is a shifting area of law, especially in light of the resurgence of property concerns among those who, for example, regard environmental laws as effecting compensable "takings" of property.

Fifth, I stress that any attempt to effect legal or administrative regulation will invariably involve the animal advocate's seeking *some* sort of "insider" status. Indeed, even if the advocate stresses that she is an "outsider" who regards institutionalized exploitation as completely il-legitimate, involvement in legislative or administrative processes al-ways entails risks. Any animal advocate who seeks to effect incremental eradication of the property status of animals in these ways is well ad-vised to proceed with caution.

Conclusion

Despite claims by new welfarists that rights theory is "utopian," it is clear that rights theory provides a strategy on a macro, or socio-legal, level for incremental eradication of the property status of animals, which is the long-term goal of the animal rights ideal. These incremen-tal measures may be indirect; they may consist primarily in educating the public about the need to eliminate the property status of animals. Or they may be direct; they may consist in changing the institutions of exploitation through legislation and administrative regulation.

At the center of any of these efforts is a recognition that although animals have an interest in avoiding pain and suffering, this interest, if it is ever to realized, requires that we incrementally recognize the many interests that collectively constitute the basic right of the animal not to be property, not to be treated as a means to the ends of human property owners. The rights advocate who seeks legal and regulatory change pursues prohibitions that stop particular activities constitutive of in-stitutionalized exploitation through the recognition and protection of extra- and noninstitutional interests that are not tradable. And the rights advocate cannot, consistent with animal rights theory, urge the substitu-tion of some other, supposedly more "humane" form of exploitation.

And above all, the rights advocate makes one thing very clear: that animal rights is a position of the *outsider* who ultimately seeks a para-digm shift in the way that law and social policy regard the status of animals, as well as in the human / animal relationship.

Conclusion

Scholars who have studied the modern animal movement have argued that a number of differences separate the animal *rights* position from the animal *welfare* position. The most important difference, however, is that animal rights theory recognizes that animals have inherent value that cannot be sacrificed to achieve "benefit" for humans. Animal welfare, unlike animal rights, rests on the notion that animals are *property* and that virtually *every* animal interest can be sacrificed in order to obtain "benefits" for people. It is accepted in the academic literature and by the media as well that the animal rights movement "contemptuously attacked the 'welfarist' approach as favouring 'longer chains for the slaves.' "[1] The problem, however, is that the organized national animal movement in the United States has rejected its own mythology.

Certain segments of the modern animal "rights" movement use the notion of rights in a rhetorical, not a philosophical, sense. That is, although the movement depicts itself and is depicted by scholars as rejecting the instrumentalist view of animals in favor of the notion that at least some animals can be regarded as rightholders, these animal advocates accept the status of animals as rightholders only as a long-term goal of the movement. In the meantime, these advocates support welfarist reforms that are no different from those advocated in the nineteenth century, except that the animal advocates in the nineteenth century were often more progressive than their modern counterparts. These modern advocates, whom I have called new welfarists, defend the use of nonrights means to achieve a rights end, on the ground that ideological distinctions are meaningless or, alternatively, that welfarist reforms will somehow lead someday to the abolition of animal exploitation. They support these welfarist means because they believe that rights theory, although proposing a laudable moral ideal, is "utopian" and incapable of providing concrete normative guidance.

I have argued that animal welfare is a theory that was born to feed on itself forever. Under the law, animals are regarded as property, and as such, animals may be used exclusively as means to the ends of their human owners. Although society can regulate the use of animal property, just as it regulates the use of any property, strong natural-right notions of property ownership militate in favor of deference to the property owner, and the laws that have evolved seek to ensure only that animal property is used "efficiently." We do not want animal property owners to waste their animal resources any more than we want other property owners to waste their property and diminish overall social wealth. But as long as the animal use produces a recognizable human "benefit," then any pain, suffering, or death is invariably regarded as "necessary" to the use. The desire to use animal welfare reforms as a "springboard into animal rights" has the new welfarist chasing her tail to decrease pain and suffering that are permitted in virtually unlimited amounts and in virtually unlimited ways as long as there is an identifiable human "benefit." This is what "institutionalized animal exploitation" *means*; any animal interest, however fundamental, may be sacrificed in order to serve human interest, however trivial.

Moreover, the new welfarist errs in characterizing animal rights theory as "utopian." Ironically, an analysis of the competing theories of animal rights and animal welfare indicates that all three components of rights theory provide clear normative guidance and that all three components of welfare theory are hopelessly muddled—both conceptually and morally. Moreover, the macro component of animal rights theory, which involves legal, regulatory, or social change, contains nothing that prohibits the advocate from seeking incremental change. The rights advocate, however, recognizes that what is at issue is not merely the incremental eradication of pain and suffering; indeed, the structure of legal welfarism makes it clear that pain and suffering will be permitted in virtually any circumstance in which they will facilitate the intended use of the animal. What will be considered "unnecessary" suffering may change from time to time, but the substantive content of the standard remains the same and is useful only in cases where animal use is truly gratuitous. Indeed, as one welfarist put it, the goal of animal welfare is to eliminate "the *gratuitous* harm done to animals by humans."[2]

The rights advocate recognizes that not all incremental measures are created equal and does not seek the incremental reduction of pain and suffering, but rather seeks the incremental eradication of the *property* status of animals. That is, the rights advocate seeks to eliminate the status of animals exclusively as means to the ends of human property owners and thus recognizes that the personhood of nonhumans requires that we respect more than just an interest in avoiding pain and suffering. This does not, of course, mean that the rights advocate is *unconcerned* about animal pain and suffering. Quite the contrary, the human avoids pain and suffering, and thankfully, for most of us, pain and suffering is the *exception* and not the *rule* of life. For nonhumans involved in the various institutionalized forms of exploitation, pain and suffering is the rule—the constant—and efforts to alleviate the intense and unrelenting pain and suffering will never make much of a dent until the institution itself is limited by something other than rules that deliberately seek to protect the property status of nonhumans.

I have offered several criteria that are intended to ensure that incremental measures erode the property paradigm, not support it. Although I hope that my criteria are useful, they are secondary to the need for an incremental eradication of the property status that *causes* the pain and suffering in the first instance. However this is achieved, its means should differ qualitatively from welfarist means, which expressly fortify the notion that animals are "things" whose fundamental interests may be traded away to satisfy trivial human interests.

I have noted that many new welfarists use examples, such as the thirsty-cow parable, and argue that our natural desire to alleviate the suffering of the thirsty cow on the way to slaughter militates in favor of our seeking—on a legal, regulatory, or social level—a rule that cows ought to receive water on the way to slaughter. But that is like saying that if I am obligated to give a dying human slave a drink of water, then I should seek rules that require that slaves be given water so as to treat them humanely. If I am absolutely opposed to slavery as an institution, however, it is difficult to understand how my seeking rules about water furthers my aim to *eradicate the institution*. My desire to reduce slave suffering is laudable, but the system of institutionalized slavery permits pain, suffering, and death *whenever* it is in the interests of property owners. There is no threshold below which the deprivation of interests cannot sink; everything is "fair game" for the interests of property owners. If there is someday to be an end to this, that end *cannot* come simply by trying to reduce suffering, but can only come by eradicating the institutionalized exploitation of animals. Any measure that threatens the property status in animals out of the recognition that animals possess inherent value accomplishes that result, but the supposed alleviation of pain and suffering—even when it is successful, and that is very,

very rare—will only be replaced by *other* pain and suffering that result from the systematic deprivation of the interests that are constitutive of a minimal notion of personhood.

Consider the following example: We have a rule that says that *everything* can be manufactured in various shades of blue as long as it is considered "beneficial" by the public, who will indicate the level of benefit by their purchasing choices. A group of people opposed to this situation and who wish to see the rule change so that there will be *no* blue objects relentlessly challenges whether the blueness of a particular object is "beneficial" in particular circumstances. Sometimes, the "blue opponents" win; most of the time they do not. But their winning bears no relationship to the ultimate change of the standard. The opponents merely argue that particular instances of blue things are not beneficial; but the overall premise—that everything ought to be blue unless it can be shown that there is no benefit—remains firmly intact. Similarly, a challenge to pain and suffering does *nothing* to challenge the underlying normative notion that the institution that causes that pain and suffering, as well as the deprivation of other interests, is unjust and should be eradicated.

In any event, it is clear that even if I am obligated to give a thirsty cow water on the way to slaughter, it does not follow that I should pursue that obligation as a legal or social policy, for the practical reason that it will never and can never succeed on an institutional level, and for the theoretical reason that it conflicts directly with the notion that animals have rights.

I recognize that some will claim that my focus on the distinction between rights and welfare is itself too confined in light of *other* moral theories such as ecofeminism, sentientism, or whatever. Such claims would, however, misconstrue a central thesis of this book. Rights theory, at least as I have discussed it here, comprises the *minimal conditions for personhood* within a social or legal system that has two primary normative entities: persons and property. The conflict between the rights theorist and the welfarist is, on this level, a conflict over the acceptability of compromise: whether the property status of a being can be permitted under certain circumstances or whether it must be absolutely prohibited. For example, an ecofeminist needs some concept of the individual, a being who possesses at least *some* interests that cannot, under any circumstances, be traded away; otherwise the ecofeminist may find herself having to accept sexism and its ugly attributes were these justified in light of consequential considerations. And in light of the fact that sexism (as well as racism and other such doctrines) has in the past

sought justification precisely by reference to consequential considerations, my concern does not seem unrealistic.

Similarly, sentientism, or painism, a doctrine developed by Richard
Ryder, purports to combine rights- and utility-type considerations by
combining "Singer's emphasis upon pain and Regan's concern for the
individual."[3] But Ryder recognizes that even if consequential considerations play a role in a theory, that theory must provide for protecting
interests *beyond* the interest in avoiding pain and suffering and must
respect those interests that are constitutive of an "individual." So, despite the theory favored by the animal advocate, *any* theorist must decide fundamental questions about the tradability of interests. The rights
advocate maintains that some interests—constitutive of a minimal notion of personhood—cannot be traded; the welfarist maintains that all
interests are, at least in theory, tradable in pursuit of a greater "gain."

Finally, I emphasize again that my analysis is not concerned with,
and should not be read as, criticizing in any way the motivations of any
particular people or groups. I assume that everyone is well motivated
and that these are simply difficult issues that have not been subjected to
a great deal of intramovement discussion, perhaps in part because animal advocates are so overwhelmed with the day-to-day struggles that
theory has been regarded as an irrelevant "luxury."

Even if that were true in the past—and I doubt that it was—we can
no longer regard theory as a "luxury" when the positions adopted by
institutional animal exploiters and by many animal welfare advocates
have merged and become indistinguishable. As I was writing this conclusion, an article appeared in the *New York Times* that perfectly cap-
tures the problem. The article described the Laboratory for Experimental Medicine and Surgery in Primates (LEMSIP) in upstate New York.
According to the article, the "routine [at LEMSIP] varies from fun and
games to medical tests"; "while five diaper-clad baby chimps tumbled
or napped amid a collection of stuffed toys and a pair of 3-year-olds
watched 'The Wizard of Oz' on television," adult chimpanzees in other
buildings were infected "with the AIDS virus or hepatitis or were taking part in vaccine studies."[4] What occasioned the article was a proposal, approved several days later, to transfer ownership of LEMSIP
from New York University to the Coulston Foundation, a primate center in New Mexico that has been found in violation of the federal Animal Welfare Act in connection with its own primate housing.

According to the article, LEMSIP's director, Jan Moor-Jankowski,
who was terminated by the university, claims that the sale occurred in
order to punish him for criticizing other animal research occurring at

New York University. An organization that considers itself an animal rights organization, In Defense of Animals, immediately issued a press release condemning the transfer of LEMSIP to the Coulston Foundation. Rather than emphasize that a bad situation will now be made worse, the press release was filled with praise for Moor-Jankowski as a "humane" researcher open to the concerns of the animal rights community. This echoed PETA's Alex Pacheco, who has praised Moor-Jankowski in the past, asking, "Why can't they all be like Moor-Jankowski?"[5]

This is somewhat confusing because it suggests that Moor-Jankowski, who infects healthy primates with AIDS and hepatitis and supports cross-species organ transplantation, is different from and better than the animal "exploiters" because Moor-Jankowski's animals are clad in diapers, play with stuffed toys, and watch television, though they are occasionally "participants" in deadly research that is no different from that performed by animal "exploiters." This is like saying that Moor-Jankowski is better than the others because he pats his animals on the head before subjecting them to unspeakable iniquities; surely this is a "distinction without a difference."

If the difference between the animal rights movement and its predecessors is that the former requires stuffed toys and television in the sterile metal cages that imprison the victims of institutionalized exploitation, then there is some reason to fear for the status of the animal rights movement as a social protest movement. In another context, legal scholar Richard Delgado argues that whenever a social movement portends a paradigm shift, there is a rejection of any solution that pushes thought too far forward and threatens stability. The result is an embrace of "doomed, moderate approaches."[6] It is such an embrace that animal *rights* advocates must reject if they are to achieve justice for nonhumans.

Postscript
Marching Backwards

I n Chapter Two, I stated that certain more conservative animal advocates, led by the National Alliance for Animals (NAA), planned a June 23, 1996, march for animals in Washington, D.C. The promotional materials for the march did not initially mention "rights" at all; instead, they used expressions like "animal protection" and the "humane movement." I contrasted the 1996 march with the 1990 march for animals, which had an explicitly rights-oriented theme. Certain events that have occurred since I completed the manuscript for this book deserve further attention.

The 1996 march is being sponsored by a number of organizations that have explicitly rejected the rights approach. For example, the arch-conservative Humane Society of the United States (HSUS), which, as I discussed in the text, eschews "animal rights" in favor of "animal protection," explicitly endorses the "humane" use of animals in experiments, supports eating animals raised in accordance with the principles of "humane sustainable agriculture," and approves of killing wild animals when "the welfare and responsible management of animals . . . necessitate[s] the killing of wildlife."[1]

The 1996 march is also being supported by the American Humane Association, which endorses the "humane" use of animals in motion pictures and television; Psychologists for the Ethical Treatment of Animals, which seeks "to balance the value of experimentation and other animal use against the suffering of animals";[2] the American Anti-Vivisection Society (AAVS), which promotes animal welfare as "something good and positive";[3] Farm Sanctuary, whose downed-animal legislation in California was *praised* by the meat industry as "codifying [meat] industry practice and philosophy";[4] and Don Barnes of the National Anti-Vivisection Society, which endorses "minimal and responsible animal use"[5] through its funding of the International Foundation for Ethical Research. Other 1996 march supporters include the American Society for the Prevention of Cruelty to Animals and the Massachusetts Society for the Prevention of Cruelty to Animals, both of which condone the killing of healthy animals in shelters.

People for the Ethical Treatment of Animals (PETA) is also a principal sponsor of the 1996 march. Although it was once considered the "radical" U.S. animal rights group, PETA has endorsed sharpshooting as a "humane" alternative to the snaring of boar in Hawaii as well as the killing of healthy animals at its Aspen Hill "no-kill" shelter.[6] Moreover, PETA has continued to foster the use of sexist imagery and messages in its anti-fur and anti-transplant campaigns to promote animal rights.[7] Also listed as a supporter of the 1996 march is Frederick's of Hollywood, which sells clothing that is rightly characterized as sexist, some of it made from leather.[8]

Scheduled speakers at the march include astronomer Carl Sagan, who has endorsed experiments with animals in light of his own illness;[9] anthropologist Jane Goodall, who has endorsed efforts to "improve" vivisection, refused to condemn outright even the use of chimpanzees in experiments,[10] and supported xenografts, or cross-species transplantation;[11] and primate behaviorist Roger Fouts, who keeps chimpanzees in captivity for non-invasive research and advocates the use of bigger cages to house chimpanzees used in experiments.[12]

The "International Advisory Board" for the march includes Cleveland Amory, who is not a vegetarian and whose group, the Fund for Animals, does not promote vegetarianism.[13] As I discussed in Chapter Four, the *Village Voice* reported that Amory knew about and permitted the involvement of the Fund's Black Beauty Ranch in raising hogs and cattle for slaughter.[14] Also on the Advisory Board is Gretchen Wyler, director of the Ark Trust, which promotes the "humane" use of animals in entertainment and which presented a 1996 award to "Babe," a film that used live animals who were ultimately relegated to the intensive confinement of a breeding farm.[15] Wyler and the Ark Trust have also very visibly supported other films in which live animals were exploited, such as "Project X."[16] Peter Singer, who, as a utilitarian, explicitly denies that animals have rights and admits to using rights only as "a convenient political shorthand,"[17] is also a member of the Advisory Board.

The Steering Committee for the march includes HSUS Vice-President Wayne Pacelle, who claims that the rights / welfare debate involves a "distinction without a difference";[18] Ken Shapiro, co-editor of the *Journal of Applied Animal Welfare Science* and an advocate of the use of pain scales to rate the invasiveness of vivisection;[19] Kim Stallwood, editor of *Animals' Agenda*, who maintains that those who distinguish between rights and welfare are "divisive";[20] and AAVS education director Zoe Weil, who argues in favor of animal welfare.[21]

In the face of criticism and the threat of a boycott by many animal rights advocates, *some* of the NAA promotional materials for the march were changed to include the term "animal rights," but the overtly welfarist sponsors and speakers remain the sponsors and speakers.[22] It was clear that in making this change, the NAA's use of "rights" did not reflect the notion of the term as implying—logically and morally—the rejection of *all* institutionalized animal exploitation. As a number of other scholars and commenters have already observed, much of the confusion between rights and welfare can be traced to Singer's "rhetorical" use of "rights" as a political slogan to describe *any* vaguely "pro-animal" position.

The level of confusion about the rights/welfare issue is so profound that the completely cosmetic adoption of the rhetorical use of "rights" by NAA apparently sufficed for some advocates. For example, rights advocate Tom Regan initially called for a boycott of the march on October 21, 1995, at a speech given in Ann Arbor, Michigan. Shortly thereafter, Regan circulated a paper entitled "Why We Will Not Be Marching," in which he claimed that the march could not "possibly be an animal rights march" and that it "will increase rather than lessen the confusion over what animal rights means and how this differs from animal welfare." Regan strongly urged animal advocates to boycott the march, maintaining that "there are better things we can do with our limited time, money and energy than to help lend credibility to something that misrepresents the truth and is morally offensive in the bargain." Regan derided the choice of Peter Singer as a keynote speaker at the march, claiming that "Singer denies that animals have rights." Regan's essay also pointed out that Pacelle, Shapiro, Barnes, and NAA administrator Peter Gerard had all endorsed overtly welfarist positions. The essay stated that "what will be served-up at the March will be a mish-mash of conflicting ideologies," and it cautioned that the march would merely perpetuate the myth that welfare and rights are related and consistent.[23]

After Regan announced the boycott and spoke and wrote in support of the boycott, he was invited by the NAA to give the keynote address at an event that will precede the march.[24] Regan initially declined the offer and continued his call to boycott, but in March 1996 he changed his position, indicating that he would attend and support the march. Regan stated that he continues to believe that the march will not be an animal rights event. He noted that "not all the March sponsors advocate vegetarianism, for example, nor do they all object to vivisection." He also alluded to the sexist campaigns promoted by PETA and agreed that some march sponsors conduct campaigns that seek to advance animal interests by exploiting "members of the extended human family." Nevertheless, Regan concluded that although the march was a welfarist event, welfarist organizations "do some good," and he announced his intention to participate in the march.[25]

Whether welfarist organizations "do some good" is, of course, not the point. The point is whether there is a logical and moral inconsistency between the rights and welfare positions and whether this march will further confuse the issue by encouraging the public to believe that animal rights and the "humane ethic" are one and the same. The point is also whether animal rights, as a *political* ideology, is consistent with the overt sexism that has tainted—and trivialized—certain movement campaigns. When Regan originally called for the boycott, he criticized the march because it fostered the view that there could be some sort of movement "unity" based on the notion that *all* participants—rights advocates and welfarists alike—"care" about animals. He noted—correctly in my view—that "the fact is, everybody 'cares' about animals." He cautioned against "perpetuating the myth" that there is such a thing as a movement "compris[ing] everyone 'who cares about animals.' "[26] It is difficult to understand why Regan changed his views and how he can reconcile his current position with his earlier position.

Some supporters of the march have argued that welfarist groups also supported the 1990 march. But that was 1990, and a great deal has happened since then to help clarify the qualitative difference between animal rights and animal welfare as solutions to the problem of animal exploitation. Moreover, the overall theme of the 1990 march was animal rights as a radical and preferable alternative to welfarism, and many of the speakers at the 1990 march explicitly disavowed animal welfare.

Other supporters claim that the public cannot draw a distinction between the rights and welfare positions. But that is just to restate the problem and not to propose a solution. The public does not understand the distinction because the movement has thus far failed in its goal to educate the public about the need to abolish—and not merely regulate—institutionalized animal exploitation.

More animals are being exploited in 1996, and in more horrific ways, than in 1990. Perhaps it is time to recognize that welfarist reforms lead to more animal exploitation, not to abolition. As long as the animal movement perpetuates the confusion that permits even well-meaning animal advocates to believe that animal rights and animal welfare are substantially similar concepts and that "animal rights" is merely a "rhetorical" term to be used only as a political slogan, the animal protection movement will continue to march in one direction—backwards.

April 8, 1996

Notes

Introduction
    1. James M. Jasper and Dorothy Nelkin, *The Animal Rights Crusade* (New York: Free Press, 1992), 5.
    2. Bernard E. Rollin, "The Legal and Moral Bases of Animal Rights," in *Ethics and Animals,* ed. Harlan B. Miller and William H. Williams (Clifton, N.J.: Humana Press, 1983), 106.
    3. Kenneth J. Shapiro and Peter B. Field, "A New Invasiveness Scale: Its Role in Reducing Animal Distress," 2 *Humane Innovations and Alternatives in Animal Experimentation* 43 (1988). Shapiro is president of the board of the *Animals' Agenda* and has chaired the Summit for the Animals.
    4. Shapiro is editor of the *Journal of Applied Animal Welfare Science;* the quoted language is from the publisher's promotion for the journal.
    5. Robert Garner, *Animals, Politics, and Morality* (Manchester: Manchester University Press, 1993), 51.
    6. Don Barnes, "The Dangers of Elitism," *Animals' Agenda,* vol. 15, no. 2 (1995), at 45.
    7. *See* Marti Kheel, "Nature and Feminist Sensitivity," in *Animal Rights and Human Obligations,* 2d ed., ed. Tom Regan and Peter Singer (Englewood Cliffs, N.J.: Prentice Hall, 1990), 256–65; Patrice Greanville, "The Search for a New Global Ethic," *Animals' Agenda,* December 1986, at 40 (quoting Tom Regan).

Chapter One
    1. For a general discussion of the law as it relates to animals, including anticruelty laws, see Gary L. Francione, *Animals, Property, and the Law* (Philadelphia: Temple University Press, 1995); "Animals, Property and Legal Welfarism: 'Unnecessary' Suffering and the 'Humane' Treatment of Animals" 46 *Rutgers Law Review* 721 (1994). For a more descriptive approach, see David S. Favre and Murray Loring, *Animal Law* (Westport, Conn.: Quorum Books, 1983); Animal Welfare Institute, ed., *Animals and Their Legal Rights,* 4th ed. (Washington, D.C.: Animal Welfare Institute, 1990).
    2. Lawrence Finsen and Susan Finsen, *The Animal Rights Movement in America: From Compassion to Respect* (New York: Twayne Publishers, 1994), 53.
    3. For a general description of various animal protection laws, including historical context, see Animal Welfare Institute, *Animals and Their Legal Rights;* for a general analysis of animal welfare laws, see Francione, *Animals, Property, and the Law.*
    4. Peter Singer, *Animal Liberation,* 2d ed. (New York: New York Review of Books, 1990), 97.

5. *See, e.g.*, Richard D. Ryder, *Victims of Science*, rev. ed. (London: National Anti-Vivisection Society, 1983).

6. *See generally* Francione, *Animals, Property, and the Law*.

7. For a general discussion of legal welfarism, see *id.* at 3–33.

8. *See* Animal Welfare Institute, *Animals and Their Legal Rights*, at 269.

9. Robert Garner, *Animals, Politics, and Morality* (Manchester: Manchester University Press, 1993), 1–2.

10. Finsen and Finsen, *The Animal Rights Movement in America*, at 4.

11. Other philosophers, of course, have made important contributions to the discussion about animals and moral theory. *See, e.g.*, Ted Benton, *Natural Relations* (London: Verso, 1993); Stephen R. L. Clark, *The Moral Status of Animals* (Oxford: Clarendon Press, 1977); Mary Midgley, *Animals and Why They Matter* (Athens: University of Georgia Press, 1984); Bernard E. Rollin, *Animal Rights and Human Morality*, rev. ed. (Buffalo, N.Y.: Prometheus Books, 1992); S. F. Sapontzis, *Morals, Reason, and Animals* (Philadelphia: Temple University Press, 1987). These scholars rely on diverse arguments, but as others have noted, it is Regan's and Singer's work that has "rightly or wrongly . . . been subject[ed] to most scrutiny by their academic peers." Garner, *Animals, Politics, and Morality*, at 11.

12. For a general discussion and critique of the foundational principles of utilitarian philosophy, see Samuel Scheffler, *The Rejection of Consequentialism*, rev. ed. (Oxford: Oxford University Press, 1994); Samuel Scheffler, ed., *Consequentialism and Its Critics* (Oxford: Oxford University Press, 1988); J.J.C. Smart and Bernard Williams, eds., *Utilitarianism: For and Against* (Cambridge: Cambridge University Press, 1973). For a discussion of Singer's utilitarian theory, see Tom Regan, *The Case for Animal Rights* (Berkeley and Los Angeles: University of California Press, 1983), 206–26. *See also* Garner, *Animals, Politics, and Morality*, at 12–35.

13. J.J.C. Smart, "An Outline of a System of Utilitarian Ethics," in *Utilitarianism*, ed. Smart and Williams, at 9.

14. Peter Singer, *Practical Ethics* (Cambridge: Cambridge University Press, 1979), 12–13.

15. "Speciesism" was originally coined by British psychologist Richard D. Ryder.

16. Peter Singer, "Ethics and Animals," 13 *Behavioral and Brain Sciences* 45 (1990).

17. The purpose of the present discussion is limited to describing Regan's theory in sufficient detail to enable the reader to assess the various claims made about that theory by new welfarists. In particular, I do not survey the enormous literature that has developed around Regan's theory, some of which advances it, some of which is supportive of it, and some of which is critical of it. For criticisms of Regan's views, see Peter Carruthers, *The Animals Issue* (Cambridge: Cambridge University Press, 1992). *See also* Michael P. T. Leahy, *Against Liberation* (London: Routledge, 1991). This is not to say that I agree in all respects with Regan's views. For example, I disagree with his notion that death for a human is *always* a comparably worse harm than death for a nonhuman (or any number of nonhumans). *See* Gary L. Francione, "Comparable Harm and Equal Inherent Value: The Problem of the Dog in the Lifeboat," *Between the Species* (forthcoming, 1996). In addition, I reject what I regard as Regan's differential treatment of rights claims held by nonhumans. *See* Chapter Two, note 36, below. I also hold views different from those of Regan concerning the larger political context into which the animal rights issue fits. *See* Anna E. Charlton, Sue Coe, and Gary L. Francione, "The American Left Should Support Animal Rights: A Manifesto," *Animals' Agenda*, January / February 1993, at 28.

Another interesting rights theory may be found in Evelyn Pluhar, *Beyond Prejudice: The*

Moral Significance of Human and Nonhuman Animals (Durham, N.C.: Duke University Press, 1995).

18. A 1991 article in the *Economist* noted that although Singer argues in favor of recognizing animal interests and weighing them equally with equal human interests, he "never actually grants rights to animals," and that "it was left to Tom Regan, a philosopher from North Carolina, to build the [rights] arguments into a book, 'The case for animal rights,' that was published in 1984." "Animal Rights," *The Economist*, November 16, 1991, at 22.

19. One version of deontological theory is found in the "categorical imperative" of Immanuel Kant, which may be formulated as "Act so that the maxim [reasons or intentions of actions] of our action can be willed to be a universal law." It is important to understand that the inability to will the maxim of action to be a universal law is not related to the consequences involved. *See* Immanuel Kant, *The Groundwork of the Metaphysic of Morals*, trans. H. J. Paton (New York: Harper & Row, 1964). For example, if I make a promise to you that I intend from the outset not to honor, I could not will the maxim of my act to be adopted by everyone, because if everyone dishonored promises, no one would believe promises anymore, and the very institution of promising would be completely undermined. An alternative deontological approach is the rights view, which holds that certain individuals have rights that are independent of consequences.

20. This view is, of course, not new; indeed, philosopher Immanuel Kant articulated a very similar position, which Regan acknowledges. What Regan does, however, is extend the notion of inherent value to moral patients (including nonhuman animals), something that Kant explicitly rejected.

21. Regan, *The Case for Animal Rights*, at 82.

22. When Regan talks of animal "welfare" in the context of his discussion of animal awareness and the fact that individual animals have interests, he is not referring to "welfare" in the sense that I use the word throughout this book. Rather, Regan simply means that what happens to animals matters to them apart from the consequences for others.

23. This alternative theory of value avoids some of the more problematic aspects involved in the interaction between the principle of utility and the equality principle relied on by utilitarians. As long as the value of individuals is understood only in terms of intrinsic value, aggregations of consequences—and nothing else—will determine right action. This leads to many unacceptable results, such as the secret killing of innocent moral agents on the assumption that the killing will bring about the best aggregate consequences.

24. The respect principle is a sort of Kantian "transcendental" principle that Kant himself regarded as unifying moral judgments.

25. Regan, *The Case for Animal Rights*, at 267.

26. *See* John Stuart Mill, *Utilitarianism* (New York: Liberal Arts Press, 1957).

27. *See* Joel Feinberg, *Rights, Justice, and the Bounds of Liberty* (Princeton, N.J.: Princeton University Press, 1980), chap. 2.

28. Regan calls this the "miniride" principle.

29. Regan calls this the "worse-off" principle. These "special considerations" include the presence of acquired duties or rights, certain voluntary acts (e.g., risky activity), and the past perpetration of injustice on moral agents or patients. These "special considerations," of course, simply serve to clarify Regan's notions of what sort of harm matters for his theory. For example, a slave owner is not "harmed" when a slave is liberated against the master's will. The master is guilty of behavior that violates the right to respectful treatment and the prima facie right not to be harmed. The master cannot, then, be the

beneficiary of the miniride or worse-off principles, both of which pertain to the justifiable infliction of harm on moral innocents.

30. Regan examines in detail several controversial issues in light of his rights theory. First, he observes that preference for, say, family members is a considered moral judgment but potentially incompatible with the miniride and worse-off principles. He argues that moral bonds between and among family members may serve as a special consideration that would limit the application of the miniride or worse-off principles. Second, he argues that although infants and fetuses of mature gestation do not qualify as subjects-of-a-life, lines are difficult to draw, and it is probably prudent to err on the side of generosity with respect to rights. He is careful, however, to note that we do not owe any duties of justice to fetuses in early stages of development.

31. Although Regan certainly is explicit in his condemnation of institutional exploitation, it is not clear that he recognized that his theory really did not specify the scope of rights that animals would have were they no longer regarded solely as means to human ends. In addition, if the right of animals not to be treated instrumentally were respected, it would result in our no longer breeding animals for food, research, or entertainment. Once those animals now in existence died, human-animal conflict would be restricted primarily to issues involving wild animals.

32. Regan argues that acceptable moral principles must exhibit the following characteristics: (1) consistency (no moral principle should imply that the exact same act can be wrong and right simultaneously); (2) adequacy of scope (a moral principle should be applicable in a variety of circumstances in which moral decisionmaking is called for); (3) precision (a moral principle should provide determinate direction); (4) conformity with intuitions (a moral principle should be in "reflective equilibrium" with our moral beliefs either by "matching" our considered intuitions or by unifying these intuitions on a common moral ground); and (5) simplicity (all other things being equal, the simpler principle is to be preferred).

The most controversial of these criteria concerns conformity of moral principles with intuitions. By "intuition," Regan makes clear that he is *not* talking about G. E. Moore's ethical propositions, which are (according to Moore) "incapable of proof," or W. D. Ross's "self-evident" moral truths. *See* G. E. Moore, *Principia Ethica* (Cambridge: Cambridge University Press, 1903), and W. D. Ross, *The Right and the Good* (Oxford: Clarendon Press, 1930). Rather, Regan uses "intuition" to refer to our considered moral judgments. These are moral views that exhibit the characteristics of (1) conceptual clarity (concepts used to express the judgment should be clearly understood); (2) adequate informational and empirical basis; (3) rationality (the judgment should observe basic laws of logic); (4) impartiality (the judgment should respect the principle of formal justice that requires the similar treatment of similar individuals); and (5) emotional calm. So Regan's methodology requires that we strive to achieve what John Rawls has called a "reflective equilibrium" between our reflective, or considered, moral judgments and moral principles that also satisfies other criteria of acceptability. *See generally* John Rawls, *A Theory of Justice* (Cambridge: Harvard University Press, 1971).

33. Finsen and Finsen, *The Animal Rights Movement in America*, at 62. Most of this section's material on Henry Spira was obtained from Henry Spira, "Fighting to Win," in *In Defense of Animals*, ed. Peter Singer (Oxford: Basil Blackwell, 1985), 194. Additional material came from Finsen and Finsen, *The Animal Rights Movement in America*, and James M. Jasper and Dorothy Nelkin, *The Animal Rights Crusade* (New York: Free Press, 1992).

34. Spira, "Fighting to Win," at 198.

35. The NIH funds only a small portion of experiments for which funding is sought. In order to distinguish the supposedly worthy from the supposedly unworthy experiments, NIH and other federal agencies, using a peer review process, ask experts in the field to assess the merits of the particular proposal. The proposals are then ranked, and those at the top of the ranking process are funded. A group of prestigious researchers, acting under the auspices of the nation's premiere research institution, NIH, found the museum studies to be scientifically meritorious and worthy of hundreds of thousands of tax dollars over other experiments that were denied funding. Spira's opposition to the experiments was not based on the museum's failure to observe the minimal conditions of animal husbandry mandated by the federal Animal Welfare Act; rather, he claimed that the studies themselves—even if conducted in perfect conformity with all animal welfare regulations—were worthless and cruel.

36. Caroline Fraser, "The Raid at Silver Spring," *New Yorker*, April 19, 1993, at 66.

37. Jasper and Nelkin, *The Animal Rights Crusade*, at 30.

38. Deborah Blum, *The Monkey Wars* (New York: Oxford University Press, 1994), 106.

39. Finsen and Finsen, *The Animal Rights Movement in America*, at 62.

40. Andrew N. Rowan, *Of Mice, Models, and Men* (Albany: State University of New York Press, 1984), 63.

41. Most of the material contained in this section is drawn from Kathy S. Guillermo, *Monkey Business* (Washington, D.C.: National Press Books, 1993), and Alex Pacheco and Anna Francione, "The Silver Spring Monkeys," in *In Defense of Animals*, ed. Singer, 135. *See also* Jasper and Nelkin, *The Animal Rights Crusade*; Finsen and Finsen, *The Animal Rights Movement in America*; Fraser, "The Raid at Silver Spring." The author was counsel to PETA during various stages of the Silver Spring Monkey case in later civil proceedings.

42. There is a tremendous amount of confusion concerning this aspect of the Taub case. The Maryland Court of Appeals did *not* hold that because of their federal funding Taub's experiments could not be regulated under state law. The court held only that at the time the Maryland legislature drafted the state anticruelty law, its intent was that the law not apply to scientific experiments per se, irrespective of the source of funding.

43. Blum, *The Monkey Wars*, at 117.

44. The title "Unnecessary Fuss" was taken from a newspaper quote from Thomas Gennarelli in which he declined to discuss the specifics of the experimentation, because it would cause an "unnecessary fuss" on the part of those concerned about the animals.

45. Garner, *Animals, Politics, and Morality*, at 51.

46. *Id.* at 52 (quoting Alex Pacheco and Anna Francione, "The Silver Spring Monkeys," at 135).

47. Garner, *Animals, Politics, and Morality*, at 18.

48. Jeremy Waldron, *The Right to Private Property* (Oxford: Clarendon Press, 1988), 27.

49. C. Reinold Noyes, *The Institution of Property* (New York: Longmans, Green & Co., 1936), 290 n. 13 (quoting *Restatement of the Law of Property* [St. Paul, Minn.: American Law Institute, 1936]).

50. Jasper and Nelkin, *The Animal Rights Crusade*, at 5.

51. *Id.* at 9.

52. *Id.* at 5.

53. Susan Sperling, *Animal Liberators* (Berkeley and Los Angeles: University of California Press, 1988), 2.

54. Garner, *Animals, Politics, and Morality*, at 49.

55. Finsen and Finsen, *The Animal Rights Movement in America*, at 3.

56. "People and Animals," *The Economist*, August 19–25, 1995, at 19 (emphasis added).

57. For a discussion about the opposition of the biomedical establishment to animal welfare legislation, see Francione, *Animals, Property, and the Law*, at 185–200.

58. Letter from Susan Paris to Dean Lewis Kerman, April 7, 1994. This letter was part of a mailing from Americans for Medical Progress Educational Fund.

59. *Id.* (emphasis in original). Apparently, AMP is concerned about the human right to own and use animals, but is not concerned about other important human rights. For example, the AMP letter warns about the teaching of a "dangerous philosophy" of animal rights, as opposed to the "legitimate" philosophy of animal welfare. It is, however, impossible to make such judgments about speech without discriminating on the basis of content, which discrimination would be prohibited by the First Amendment to the Bill of Rights of the United States Constitution were a state institution or actor to try to define protected speech in that way. Indeed, the AMP letter is a warning to educators to *keep particular ideas from being taught, because they are "wrong" or "dangerous."* That, of course, is censorship, and smacks of precisely the sort of dogmatism that scientists claim to reject.

60. *Id.* Again, AMP seems to forget about the United States Constitution, which has been interpreted as requiring that people accused of crimes be presumed innocent until proven guilty and which, in the Sixth Amendment to the Bill of Rights, guarantees the right to counsel in criminal cases. So, when a person is *accused* of "destroy[ing] research facilities," we assume that the person is innocent until proven guilty and that she is *entitled* to a defense. AMP, however, seems upset about this arrangement, and apparently believes that people *accused* of these crimes are not entitled to a presumption of innocence or to counsel in criminal cases. This rather selective approach to constitutional rights is also reflected in the blanket accusations by AMP and other similar groups that all people who believe that animal rights make sense are "terrorists" who, it seems, do not deserve to be treated as well as others.

In addition, "extremists" do not "cripple biomedical research with excessive regulation." "Extremists" cannot impose *any* sort of regulation—only legislators and administrative agencies can. So, if AMP is concerned that "extremists" will hire lawyers to lobby for legal and regulatory changes, then again they ought to take their fight up with the Constitution, which guarantees the right to free speech and to petition government.

61. Letter from John M. Clymer to the editor, *Philadelphia Inquirer*, July 21, 1995, at A18.

62. Frederick K. Goodwin, "Animal Welfare vs. Animal Rights," a narrative manuscript accompanying Goodwin's slide show.

63. Letter from Frederick K. Goodwin to Dante B. Fascell, February 10, 1992 (copy on file with the author).

64. Lorenz O. Lutherer and Margaret S. Simon, *Targeted: The Anatomy of an Animal Rights Attack* (Norman: University of Oklahoma Press, 1992), 10, 11.

65. *Id.* at 10. This position is, of course, incorrect insofar as it claims that merely by using illegally obtained information, the user condones the illegality of the acquisition. Indeed, many prominent conservatives likewise insist on the incorrectness of this position when they argue against the exclusionary rule, which prohibits the use of evidence in court when the evidence has been obtained in violation of the constitutional prohibition against unreasonable searches and seizures. These conservatives argue that use of the illegally obtained information against the criminal defendants does not suggest approbation of the illegal seizure.

66. Ronald M. McLaughlin, "Animal Rights vs. Animal Welfare: Can Animal Use Meet the Needs of Science and Society?" in *Animal Research, Animal Rights, Animal Legislation,*

ed. Patrick W. Concannon (Champaign, Ill.: Society for the Study of Reproduction, 1990), at 12–13 (emphasis in original).

67. Foundation for Biomedical Research, *Animal Research and Human Health* (Washington, D.C.: Foundation for Biomedical Research, 1992), 8.

68. *Id.* at 1.

69. *See, e.g.*, Rod Preece and Lorna Chamberlain, *Animal Welfare and Human Values* (Waterloo, Ont.: Wilfred Laurier University Press, 1993) (arguing that animal rights and animal protection are different and inconsistent approaches to the human-nonhuman relationship); Rod Strand and Patti Strand, *The Hijacking of the Humane Movement* (Wilsonville, Ore.: Doral Publishing, 1993) (arguing that animal rights represent "extremism" that threatens the "humane" movement).

Chapter Two

1. Don Barnes, "The Dangers of Elitism," *Animals' Agenda*, vol. 15, no. 2 (1995), 44.

2. Kim W. Stallwood, "Utopian Visions and Pragmatic Politics: The Challenges of the Animal Rights Movement" (paper presented at the National Alliance for Animals conference, June 24, 1995). Stallwood has apparently changed his views; in the 1980s he took precisely the "divisive" posture that he now argues against. For example, Stallwood, who in 1983 was employed by the British Union for the Abolition of Vivisection (BUAV), declined to support the Scientific Procedures Act of 1986 as it was endorsed by welfarists, because it did not contain prohibitions on particular types of experiments. *See* Robert Garner, *Animals, Politics, and Morality* (Manchester: Manchester University Press, 1993), 206–7.

3. Zoe Weil, Book Review, *AV Magazine*, September/October 1995, at 20 (emphasis in original).

4. *See AV Magazine*, September/October 1995, at 18.

5. *See* Carol Adams and Josephine Donovan, *Beyond Animal Rights: A Feminist Caring Ethic for the Treatment of Animals* (New York: Continuum, 1995) (quotation from the publisher's prepublication description).

6. Ingrid Newkirk, "Total Victory, Like Checkmate, Cannot Be Achieved in One Move," *Animals' Agenda*, January/February 1992, at 43–45.

7. Lawrence Finsen and Susan Finsen, *The Animal Rights Movement in America: From Compassion to Respect* (New York: Twayne Publishers, 1994), 81 (quoting Alex Pacheco).

8. Letter from John Hoyt to Clayton Yeutter, September 13, 1990 (quoted in Gary L. Francione, "A Common Bond," *Animals' Voice*, vol. 4, no. 2 [1991], at 54 [emphasis added]).

9. Wayne Pacelle, "Wayne Pacelle, Unplugged," *Animals' Agenda*, vol. 14, no. 6 (1994), at 28.

10. Mark Harris, "The Threat from Within," *Vegetarian Times*, February 1995, at 70 (quoting Henry Spira).

11. Finsen and Finsen, *The Animal Rights Movement in America*, at 259. Finsen and Finsen make these statements as part of a discussion about the views expressed elsewhere by the author and Tom Regan. Finsen and Finsen do not necessarily agree with the position advocated by the author and Regan, although they do appear to agree that the long-term goals of the animal rights advocate are different from those of the welfare advocate, and that rights advocates often use reformist means in their attempts to achieve those long-term ends.

12. Harris, "The Threat from Within," at 70 (quoting Henry Spira).

13. Newkirk, "Total Victory," at 44.

14. Letter from Kenneth Shapiro to Gary L. Francione, April 12, 1995 (copy on file with the author).

15. Barnes, "The Dangers of Elitism," at 44.

16. Harris, "The Threat from Within," at 69 (quoting Don Barnes).

17. Kim W. Stallwood, "The Editor's Agenda," *Animals' Agenda*, vol. 15, no. 3 (1995), at 2.

18. Andrew N. Rowan, "Laboratory Animal Numbers: Good News or Bad?" *Animal People*, December 1994, at 5.

19. The position now articulated by Barnes and NAVS is markedly different from the one adopted in 1990. On June 10, 1990, Peter Linck (who has since changed his name to Peter Gerard), of the National Alliance for Animal Legislation (whose name has since been changed to the National Alliance for Animals), and Tom Regan organized a "march for animal rights" in Washington, D.C. Barnes introduced the speakers, and the highlight of the march—and a truly significant moment in the history of our relationship with nonhumans—was the presentation of the Declaration of the Rights of Animals by Kenneth Shapiro, executive director of Psychologists for the Ethical Treatment of Animals (PSYeta), and Mary Margaret Cunniff, executive director of NAVS. The declaration was endorsed by more than forty national organizations, representing the vast majority of those who then considered themselves part of the animal rights movement. The declaration stated that nonhumans "have the right to live free from human exploitation, whether in the name of science or sport, exhibition or service, food or fashion." Moreover, the declaration recognized that animals have the "right to live in harmony with their nature rather than according to human desires" and a "right to live on a healthy planet." Barnes and Cunniff issued a separate public statement on behalf of NAVS proclaiming a belief that "all species are entitled to fundamental rights." These rights, according to Barnes and Cunniff, included "the right to be treated with respect, compassion, and justice" and "the right to live free from acts of cruelty and exploitation, and under conditions suited to their nature and biological needs." *See* Declaration of the Rights of Animals, June 10, 1990.

20. Andrew N. Rowan, "Animal Rights Versus Animal Welfare: A False Dichotomy?" 7 *Animal Policy Report* 1–2 (1993).

21. Kim Bartlett, "A New Fundamentalism," *Animals' Agenda*, November 1991, at 2. At least one academic commentator has also used this expression in connection with those animal rights advocates who reject animal welfare. *See* Garner, *Animals, Politics, and Morality*, at 248. Garner takes the expression from the editorial in the *Animals' Agenda*.

22. Stallwood, "Utopian Visions and Pragmatic Politics."

23. Merritt Clifton, "Listen, Talk, Dicker," *Animal People*, January / February 1994, at 2. The use of "fundamentalism" by animal advocates—especially ones who claim to be animal rights advocates—to describe the position that excludes animal welfare is, of course, somewhat bizarre. Both the AMA and the NIH announced in the late 1980s that their strategy for combating the growing influence of the animal rights movement was to distinguish animal rights from animal welfare, promote animal welfare as the theory accepted by both a majority of the public and those who used animals in experiments, and isolate rights advocates as "extremists." Ironically, the AMA and the NIH have been aided in this endeavor by prominent animal advocates who have sought to isolate as "fundamentalists" those rights advocates who reject welfarism.

Also interesting is the fact that the expression "fundamentalist" has been used in scholarly comment in a way that would encompass many of the new welfarists as well. For example, Jasper and Nelkin claim that animal advocates who subscribe to the view that animals have "inherent, inviolable rights" are "animal rights *fundamentalists* [who] believe that people should never use animals for their own pleasures or interests, regardless of the benefits." James M. Jasper and Dorothy Nelkin, *The Animal Rights Crusade* (New York: Free Press, 1992), at 9 (emphasis in original). PETA's mission statement provides that "animals have an intrinsic worth of their own apart from their utility to humans and should not be reduced to human commodities." Irrespective of benefit, animals "are not ours to eat, wear, experiment on, or use for entertainment." This surely qualifies as a "fundamentalist" position as Jasper and Nelkin use that term.

24. Jasper and Nelkin, *The Animal Rights Crusade*, at 8–9.

25. Jasper and Nelkin also argue that the "critique of instrumentalism also gained from the popularity of the so-called New Age philosophies." *See id.* at 22.

26. *Id.* at 142.

27. Garner, *Animals, Politics, and Morality*, at 17.

28. *Id.* at 18.

29. *Id.* at 52.

30. *Id.* at 50.

31. *Id.* at 51.

32. *Id.* at 50.

33. Pacelle, "Unplugged," at 28.

34. Brian Klug, "Animal Rights: The Slogan and the Movement," *Animals' Agenda*, vol. 4, no. 2 (1984), at 25 (quoting Tom Regan).

35. Barnes, "The Dangers of Elitism," at 44–45.

36. Interestingly—and ironically—even some animal rights stalwarts have fallen into this trap. For example, Tom Regan has cautioned against adopting a "purist" or absolutist attitude about the animal rights position. *See* Tom Regan, "The Best People" (paper delivered at Ann Arbor, Michigan, October 21, 1995; copy on file with the author). But if rights theory holds that the eating of animal food violates the respect principle, then strict adherence to that view—and insistence that others conform—is no more "purist" than condemnation of murder and the requirement that others conform on pain of criminal sanction (or other legal or moral sanction). "Yes, I am a 'purist' with respect to murder" is logically no different from "Yes, I am a 'purist' with respect to the eating of animal food."

Regan's objection to strict adherence to the rights view seems to follow from his observation that since most animal rights advocates were once animal exploiters who ate meat and wore leather, they cannot legitimately criticize others. But this does not follow. If that argument is valid, then given that almost everyone was an overt racist thirty years ago, we should not insist on rigid adherence to nonracist norms today. The problem is that we do insist on an absolutist approach concerning fundamental *human* rights, and in some cases the law actually imposes such an approach. For example, the law *prohibits* rape and murder, and does not permit "gentle" rape or "gentle" murder pending our "evolution" to more progressive positions. To say that we should not insist that others adhere to similarly strict norms concerning the fundamental rights of nonhumans is merely to reject the application of the human approach to rights to the nonhuman context. It is certainly not an argument for that differential treatment. Indeed, it appears as though treating the animal context differently raises a prima facie problem of species bias.

In addition, Regan objects to "purity" on the grounds that alternatives to animal products also involve exploitation. For example, he argues that if one wears vinyl shoes instead of leather shoes, one is still harming nonhumans through the processing of petroleum. But surely Regan sees the difference between a lamp shade made of human skin and a lamp shade made from petroleum products, the production of which often causes some harm to humans and nonhumans alike.

37. Barnes, "The Dangers of Elitism," at 45.

38. Letter from Helen Jones to the *Animals' Agenda*, vol. 4, no. 4 (1984), at 3.

39. Helen Jones, "Animal Rights: A View and Commentary," *Society for Animal Rights Report*, October 1981, at 3. Jones praises Singer's *Animal Liberation* as a book about animal rights, but it is clear that her focus is primarily Singer's discussion of speciesism. In any event, Jones obviously does not endorse Singer's utilitarian views, since she expressly adopts abolition as a matter of formal justice.

Chapter Three

1. I say that it would "probably" maximize overall utility to give the money to John, because there are conceivable circumstances that would point in the other direction. Assume that John is a mass murderer; if we alleviate his starvation by giving him the money, we can be reasonably sure that he will kill more innocent people. In such a case, saving John's life generates desirable consequences, which will certainly be lost if he is not given the money, and undesirable consequences, specifically, the possibility (however great, but not a certainty) that others will be killed if we do give John the money. This example also illustrates the difficulty of "micromanaging" morality through a theory like Singer's, which must rest on assessments that an insurance actuary would find daunting.

2. Peter Singer, *Animal Liberation*, 2d ed. (New York: New York Review of Books, 1990), 8.

3. James M. Jasper and Dorothy Nelkin, *The Animal Rights Crusade* (New York: Free Press, 1993), 8.

4. Peter Singer, "Ethics and Animals," 13 *Behavioral and Brain Sciences* 45, 46 (1990) (emphasis in original).

5. Robert Garner, *Animals, Politics, and Morality* (Manchester: Manchester University Press, 1993), 27.

6. Singer, *Animal Liberation*, at 228.

7. *Id.* at 229.

8. *Id.* The context of Singer's comments is an examination of the argument that meat eaters actually do animals a favor by causing them (directly or through consumption demand) to come into existence in the first place. Singer acknowledges that although in the first edition of *Animal Liberation* he rejected this view as "nonsense" (*id.* at 228), he is now uncertain about its validity and concludes that it is difficult to deny that bringing a being into the world confers a benefit on that being as long as the being has a pleasant life. This leads him to the view that it may be morally permissible to eat animals who have been raised and slaughtered humanely.

9. *Id.* at 229–30.

10. *Id.* at 230. It should be noted that Singer argues that if a being does have desires for the future or a continuous mental existence, then killing that being would be wrong even if the killing were painless. Unfortunately, this view is inconsistent with Singer's utilitarian theory. The fact that X may have future desires counts against killing X, because the frustration of X's future desires is a negative consequence for a preference utilitarian like Singer. But Singer cannot maintain that there is any absolute rule against killing such a being, because the aggregation of consequences may militate in favor of such killing.

11. Tom Regan, *The Case for Animal Rights* (Berkeley and Los Angeles: University of California Press, 1983), 221.

12. *See* R. G. Frey, *Rights, Killing, and Suffering* (Oxford: Basil Blackwell, 1983), 197–203.

13. Regan, *The Case for Animal Rights*, at 222.

14. Jasper and Nelkin claim that Regan's rights argument has come "to dominate the

rhetoric of the animal rights agenda." Jasper and Nelkin, *The Animal Rights Crusade*, at 96. And that is precisely the difficulty: in most discussions of animal "rights," the notion of rights is used *rhetorically* to describe *any* measure that is thought to minimize suffering, whether or not the measure embodies the position that animals have "inherent" and "inviolable" rights. The substance of Regan's moral and political theory of animal rights has largely been ignored by the movement. Moreover, it is clear from their analysis that Jasper and Nelkin believe that the pragmatists, represented by Singer, Henry Spira, and others, have played the most significant roles in shaping the modern movement.

15. Deborah Blum, *The Monkey Wars* (New York: Oxford University Press, 1994), 115.

16. Susan Sperling, *Animal Liberators* (Berkeley and Los Angeles: University of California Press, 1988), 82.

17. Lawrence Finsen and Susan Finsen, *The Animal Rights Movement in America: From Compassion to Respect* (New York: Twayne Publishers, 1994), 23, 55.

18. *Id*. at 74.

19. Jasper and Nelkin, *The Animal Rights Crusade*, at 90.

20. Merritt Clifton, "Listen, Talk, Dicker," *Animal People*, April 1993, at 2.

21. Jasper and Nelkin, *The Animal Rights Crusade*, at 26.

22. Finsen and Finsen, *The Animal Rights Movement in America*, at 58. *See also* Garner, *Animals, Politics, and Morality*, at 64 ("Henry Spira, a leading American activist, enrolled in a course run by Singer at New York University").

23. Jasper and Nelkin, *The Animal Rights Crusade*, at 28.

24. Garner, *Animals, Politics, and Morality*, at 45.

25. Finsen and Finsen, *The Animal Rights Movement in America*, at 76.

26. Caroline Fraser, "The Raid at Silver Spring," *New Yorker*, April 19, 1993, at 69.

27. Jasper and Nelkin, *The Animal Rights Crusade*, at 30.

28. *Id*. at 80.

29. PETA, "Catalog for Cruelty-Free Living," *PETA News*, Spring 1994, 16.

30. Garner, *Animals, Politics, and Morality*, at 27.

31. Singer, *Animal Liberation*, 2d ed., at 245. The article that Singer quotes from is found in *Newsweek*, May 23, 1988.

32. Peter Singer, ed., *In Defense of Animals* (Oxford: Basil Blackwell, 1985).

33. Peter Singer, *How Are We to Live?* (Amherst, N.Y.: Prometheus Books, 1995). Interestingly, the copyright page of the book states that "Peter Singer asserts the moral right to be identified as the author of this work." It is difficult to understand the context of this assertion in light of Singer's preference utilitarianism. For example, if the aggregation of consequences affecting the interests of all concerned weighed in favor of allowing others to plagiarize Singer's work, his assertion of a "moral right" would be odd, to say the least.

34. Scott Allen, "Apes on Edge; Air Force Pioneers' Future Unclear," *Boston Globe*, November 7, 1994, at 1.

35. Garner, *Animals, Politics, and Morality*, at 27.

36. Andrew N. Rowan, "Animal Rights Versus Animal Welfare: A False Dichotomy?" 7 *Animal Policy Report* 1, 2 (1993). There appears to be a three-way paternity suit emerging concerning exactly *who* should be credited with the fatherhood of the animal *rights* movement. Singer claims the title, although he expressly rejects rights. Regan also claims the title, for having developed a theory of animal rights. But now, Andrew Linzey, an Anglican minister, claims that his book *Animal Rights* (London: SCM Press, 1976) "heralded the modern animal movement." *See* press announcement for Andrew Linzey, *Animal Theology* (London: SCM Press, 1995).

37. Garner, *Animals, Politics, and Morality*, at 27.

38. Jasper and Nelkin, *The Animal Rights Crusade*, at 9.

39. *Id*. at 5.

40. Lawrence Finsen and Susan Finsen argue that although much of Singer's theory is based on utilitarianism, Singer's demand that we avoid speciesism is more absolute, and "not based on a utilitarian calculation." Finsen and Finsen, *The Animal Rights Movement in America*, at 186. Although Finsen and Finsen may very well be correct here, it is difficult to understand *how* this can be the case in light of Singer's endorsement of utilitarianism as the relevant moral principle. Simply put, if utilitarianism dictates result X, and avoidance of speciesism dictates that we do Y, and, in fact, we do Y, then we have violated the principle of act utility. Moreover, to regard Singer's demand that we avoid speciesism as a principle separate from the principle of utility would contradict Singer's claim that he is not a "moral absolutist."

41. Peter Singer, *Practical Ethics* (Cambridge: Cambridge University Press, 1979), 2.

42. *Id*. at 3.

43. *Id*.

44. Garner, *Animals, Politics, and Morality*, at 112.

45. Singer, *Animal Liberation*, at 20–21.

46. *See* Garner, *Animals, Politics, and Morality*, at 31.

47. *See* statement of Peter Singer, contained in the Declaration of the Rights of Animals.

48. Kim W. Stallwood, "A Conversation with Peter Singer," *Animals' Agenda*, vol. 14, no. 2 (1994), at 25.

49. Singer, *Animal Liberation*, at 233.

50. Singer's statement is contained in the Declaration of the Rights of Animals, June 10, 1990.

51. *See* Jasper and Nelkin, *The Animal Rights Crusade*, at 9.

52. Henry Spira, "Fighting to Win," in *In Defense of Animals*, ed. Peter Singer (Oxford: Basil Blackwell, 1985), at 200.

53. One of Spira's patrons, Pegeen Fitzgerald, also a member of the board of directors of HSUS, paid for a full-page advertisement in the *New York Times* to condemn Revlon's killing of rabbits for the sake of human vanity.

54. Spira, "Fighting to Win," 203.

55. *Id*. at 204.

56. In 1995, Spira criticized the animal rights movement for failing to praise Procter & Gamble's claimed reduction in animal use. *See* Merritt Clifton, "In League with the Devil," *Animal People*, June 1995, at 1.

57. Barnaby J. Feder, "Pressuring Perdue," *New York Times Magazine*, November 26, 1989, at 72.

58. *Id*. at 60 (quoting Henry Spira).

59. *Id*.

60. *Id*. (quoting Ingrid Newkirk).

61. *Id*. (quoting Peter Singer).

62. *Id*. (quoting Ingrid Newkirk).

63. Andrew N. Rowan, *Of Mice, Models, and Men* (Albany: State University of New York Press, 1984), 274.

64. In media interviews, Pacheco clearly condemned "most experimentation" explicitly on moral grounds. PETA also used the Taub case to articulate its long-term abolitionist goal before Congress. For example, in the 1981 congressional hearings, Pacheco testified about what he observed in Taub's lab and stated as a general matter that the "ethical cost" of animal use was too high, that he was opposed to "a great deal of" research that involved animals, and that for moral purposes he saw no distinction between experimen-

tation on a monkey and experimentation on a frog. *The Use of Animals in Medical Research and Testing: Hearings Before the Subcommittee on Science, Research, and Technology of the House Committee on Science and Technology,* 97th Cong., 1st Sess. 54 (1981) [hereinafter *Hearings*] (statements of Alex Pacheco). Pacheco also stated that he was not aware of any animal use that had benefited human beings.

65. *Id.* at 57 (statements of Alex Pacheco).

66. Blum, *The Monkey Wars,* at 108 (quoting Alex Pacheco).

67. *See Hearings,* at 199 (statement of Christine Stevens).

68. *Id.* at 224, 248 (statement of Michael A. Giannelli). It is interesting to note that Giannelli has taken to defending the use of animals in entertainment, which involves a completely gratuitous use of animals. *See* note 28 to Chapter Five.

69. *Hearings,* at 193–94 (statements of Michael Fox). The bill Fox spoke in favor of was H.R. 4406 (1981). H.R. 4406 provided for ethical merit review of research by the animal care committee. That is, the bill provided that the committee could make substantive decisions about the merits of various research. That provision was vehemently opposed by researchers, who claimed that this would result in governmental control of science. The animal-care-committee requirement that was ultimately included as part of the 1985 amendments to the federal Animal Welfare Act ensured that the committee would have no authority to conduct merit reviews of research, which the U.S. Department of Agriculture (USDA) has confirmed in its various pronouncements on the subject.

70. *Id.* at 189 (statement of Michael Fox).

71. Garner, *Animals, Politics, and Morality,* at 208.

72. Certain aspects of the Taub case involved a very instrumentalist treatment of animals. For example, when the monkeys were first removed from Taub's lab by the police, they were housed temporarily in the home of a PETA employee. Taub sued to regain possession of the monkeys, and the court granted the motion, but the monkeys disappeared before Taub could get them. After the prosecution insisted that the monkeys be returned before prosecuting Taub, animal advocates returned the animals to the police, who, despite assurances to the contrary, returned them to Taub. Although the motivation of the animal advocates involved was undoubtedly laudable, a decision was made to treat the monkeys as a means to an end. The end—to expose the abuse of animals used in research—was consistent with the notion that animals are rightholders who should not be used in experiments. But the means—the offering up of animals that had already been "freed"—was the very instrumentalism that is supposedly rejected by the animal rights movement.

73. Blum, *The Monkey Wars,* at 106, 109.

74. *Id.* at 109.

75. *Id.* at 119.

76. Rowan, "Animal Rights Versus Animal Welfare," at 1, 2.

77. *Id..*

78. Mark Harris, "The Threat from Within," *Vegetarian Times,* February 1995, at 70 (quoting Henry Spira).

79. Jasper and Nelkin, *The Animal Rights Crusade,* at 9.

80. *Hearings on H.R. 3424 Before a Subcommittee of the Senate Committee on Appropriations,* 99th Cong., 1st Sess. 691 (1985) (statement of Christine Stevens).

81. On a number of occasions, the Animal Liberation Front raided facilities, such as the University of California at Riverside and the City of Hope Hospital in Los Angeles, and then anonymously supplied the information to PETA. In virtually all of these cases, PETA and other advocacy organizations focused more on violations of federal and state law and regulations, and did not use the events to facilitate social discussion about

vivisection per se. This was done, at least in part, to enable the formation of coalitions that included more conservative animal welfare groups, and to ensure that scientific experts who were not amenable to supporting an abolitionist position would provide assistance.

82. Finsen and Finsen, *The Animal Rights Movement in America*, at 80. Interestingly, it was Kim Stallwood, who joined PETA in 1987, who helped to implement PETA's closure of its chapters. Garner argues that Stallwood played a role in developing grassroots organizations in England. *See* Garner, *Animals, Politics, and Morality*, at 52. Garner makes other observations indicating that Stallwood has changed his views since the early 1980s. For example, Stallwood claims credit for organizing, and praises the efficacy of, a British campaign called Putting Animals into Politics, which "was directed by the General Election Coordinating Committee for Animal Protection (GECCAP)." Kim Stallwood, "The Editor's Agenda," *Animals' Agenda*, vol. 15, no. 3 (1995), at 2. What Stallwood fails to disclose, however, is that he was employed by, and was a very visible leader of, the British Union for the Abolition of Vivisection (BUAV), which, according to Garner and other sources, broke from GECCAP in 1983 to form the Animal Protection Alliance because GECCAP was not radical enough for BUAV. *See* Garner, *Animals, Politics, and Morality*, at 206. Similarly, Garner states that BUAV joined with other groups to oppose certain welfarist legislation and the animal welfare groups that supported the legislation. *Id.* at 207. This would seem to conflict with Stallwood's more recent call for movement "unity" and his characterization of any intramovement disagreement as "divisive."

83. *See, e.g.*, Marsh Gravitz, "Animal Rights in the Community," *Animals' Agenda*, vol. 4, no. 1 (1984), at 26 (discussing PETA's Florida chapter, which was "committed to the rights of all animals" and to encouraging commitment to animal rights "in the community").

84. Finsen and Finsen, *The Animal Rights Movement in America*, at 80.

85. *Id*. at 80–81 (statements of Alex Pacheco).

86. *See, e.g., PETA's Animal Times*, July / August 1995.

87. Harris, "The Threat from Within," at 65.

88. *Id*. at 66.

89. Interview of Angi Metler, director of NJARA, by the author, June 28, 1995.

90. Finsen and Finsen, *The Animal Rights Movement in America*, at 82.

91. *See* Don Barnes, "The Dangers of Elitism," *Animals' Agenda*, vol. 15, no. 2 (1995), at 44–45.

92. *Id*. at 45. Barnes claimed that NAVS had a "Small Grants Program, which has provided funds, materials, and expertise to scores of grassroots activists." *Id*. I wrote to, and personally spoke with, Mary Margaret Cunniff, executive director of NAVS, to obtain information and supporting documentation about NAVS financial support of grassroots activism. Cunniff responded that it was impossible to determine the dollar amount allocated to the program.

93. For a discussion of this relationship, see Anna E. Charlton, Sue Coe, and Gary L. Francione, "The American Left Should Support Animal Rights: A Manifesto," *Animals' Agenda*, January / February 1993, at 28.

94. Other conservative legislators who have played a major role in the modern animal movement include Robert Dornan of California and Robert Smith of New Hampshire, both of whom played leading roles in support of PETA's efforts in the Taub matter. PETA has also been open in its embrace of right-wing extremists, such as G. Gordon Liddy and Paul Harvey.

95. At some of these events, men too are naked, which is supposed to "erase" any sexism. It is difficult to argue, however, in light of differential treatment of men as a group

and women as a group, that the sexist portrayal of women is somehow balanced by an ostensibly sexist portrayal of men. The depiction of males, especially white males, may be sexist, but it does not reinforce social notions about the property status of men; such is not the case with women, who are viewed as "commodities" in an overwhelming amount of social imagery and cultural belief.

96. For a discussion of the moral issues pertaining to xenografts, see Gary L. Francione, "Xenografts and Animal Rights," 22 *Proceedings of the International Society for Transplantation* 1044 (1990).

97. *The Ottawa Citizen*, August 12, 1995, at B5.

98. Finsen and Finsen, *The Animal Rights Crusade in America*, at 80 (quoting Alex Pacheco).

99. *See* "PETA and Pornographic Culture," *Feminists for Animal Rights*, vol. 8, nos. 3–4 (1994–95). FAR originally planned to publish a dialogue involving Newkirk and feminists, but declined because of certain comments that Newkirk made during the recorded session.

100. *See* Kenneth White and Kenneth Shapiro, "The Culture of Violence," *Animals' Agenda*, vol. 14, no. 2 (1994).

101. The *Agenda* cover was one of several similar advertisements sponsored by the Washington Humane Society and used on billboards in the Washington, D.C., area. Only one of the advertisements used the photo of the African-American child. The demonstration was directed specifically against the billboard.

102. Interview of Shelton Walden by the author, July 10, 1995.

Chapter Four

1. Singer's statement is contained in the Declaration of the Rights of Animals, June 10, 1990.

2. *See* Jack Rosenberger, "Wolves in Sheep's Clothing," *Vegetarian Times*, February 1995, at 70.

3. *Id.* (quoting American Animal Welfare Foundation).

4. *Id.* (quoting American Animal Welfare Foundation).

5. Margaret E. Wallace, "Meeting the Needs of Captive Mice and Their Caretakers," 8 *Humane Innovations and Alternatives* 565 (1994).

6. Viktor Reinhardt, "Arguments for Single-Caging of Rhesus Macaques: Are They Justified?" 6 *Animal Welfare Information Center Newsletter* 1 (1995).

7. Committee on Pain and Distress in Laboratory Animals, "Synopsis: Recognition and Alleviation of Pain and Distress in Laboratory Animals," 33 *ILAR News* 71 (1991).

8. U.S. Department of Health and Human Services, Public Health Service, National Institutes of Health, *Guide for the Care and Use of Laboratory Animals* (Bethesda, Md.: National Institutes of Health, 1985). The Public Health Service Policy is contained as appendix D to the *Guide*.

9. Andrew Petto et al., "Promoting Psychological Well-Being in a Biomedical Research Facility: Sheep in Wolves' Clothing," 6 *Humane Innovations and Alternatives* 366 (1992).

10. David L. Oden, "A Minimum Stress Procedure for Repeated Measurements of Nociceptive Thresholds and Analgesia," 1 *Humane Innovations and Alternatives in Animal Experimentation* 11 (1987).

11. Kenneth J. Shapiro and Peter B. Field, "A New Invasiveness Scale: Its Role in Reducing Animal Distress," 2 *Humane Innovations and Alternatives in Animal Experimentation* 43 (1988).

12. This policy statement is found on the inside cover page of *Humane Innovations and Alternatives*.

13. This policy statement is contained in a preface to each issue of *Humane Innovations and Alternatives*. *See, e.g.*, vol. 8 (1994).

14. *See* Viktor Reinhardt and Helga Tacreiter, "Conversations with Authors: Exploring the World of Cows and Cattle," 8 *Humane Innovations and Alternatives* 533 (1994).

15. *See* the editor's note on page 617 of Temple Grandin's article, "The Two Major Animal Welfare Problems of the Dairy Industry: Treatment of Newborn Calves and Handling of Downed Cows," 8 *Humane Innovations and Alternatives* 616 (1994).

16. *See* 4 *Humane Innovations and Alternatives* (inside cover) 1990.

17. This language is quoted from the announcement of the *Journal of Applied Animal Welfare Science*.

18. Shapiro and Field, "A New Invasiveness Scale," at 43.

19. *See, e.g.*, Mark Solomon and Peter C. Lovenheim, "Reporting Requirements Under the Animal Welfare Act: Their Inadequacies and the Public's Right to Know," 3 *International Journal of Studies in Animal Problems* 210 (1982); Animal Welfare Institute, ed., *Beyond the Laboratory Door* (Washington, D.C.: Animal Welfare Institute, 1985). *See also* Gary L. Francione, *Animals, Property, and the Law* (Philadelphia: Temple University Press, 1995), 218–24.

20. *See Improved Standards for Laboratory Animals Act; and Enforcement of the Animal Welfare Act by the Animal and Plant Health Inspection Service: Hearing on H.R. 5725 Before the Subcommittee on Department Operations, Research, and Foreign Agriculture of the House Committee on Agriculture*, 98th Cong., 2d Sess. 24 (1984) (statement of Bert Hawkins); *Improved Standards for Laboratory Animals: Hearing on S. 657 Before the Senate Committee on Agriculture, Nutrition, and Forestry*, 98th Cong., 1st Sess. 178 (1983) (statement of John Block). *See also* Francione, *Animals, Property, and the Law*, at 219–20.

21. Animal Welfare Institute, *Beyond the Laboratory Door*.

22. Shapiro and Field, "A New Invasiveness Scale," at 43.

23. Letter from Kenneth J. Shapiro to Gary L. Francione, April 12, 1995 (copy on file with the author).

24. Shapiro was also copresenter of the Declaration of the Rights of Animals at the 1990 march on Washington.

25. FBR "publicizes the medical results of animal research," and NABR "lobbies state and federal legislatures" in support of vivisection. James M. Jasper and Dorothy Nelkin, *The Animal Rights Crusade* (New York: Free Press, 1992), 133. FBR has produced such provivisection propaganda as "Will I Be All Right Doctor?"—a video featuring children whose lives have supposedly been saved as a result of animal experiments—and ads that contain a picture of animal rights protesters together with a caption reading, "Thanks to animal research, they'll be able to protest 20.8 years longer." *Id.* at 133–34. Organizations like FBR and NABR are classic examples of support for the institutionalized exploitation of animals in laboratories.

26. Foundation for Biomedical Research, *Animal Research and Human Health: Caring for Laboratory Animals* (Washington, D.C.: Foundation for Biomedical Research, 1992), 1 (emphasis added).

27. Foundation for Biomedical Research, *Animal Research and Human Health: Understanding the Use of Animals in Biomedical Research* (Washington, D.C.: Foundation for Biomedical Research, 1992), 17.

28. Interview with Henry Spira, *Foundation for Biomedical Research Newsletter*, January / February 1993, at 5–6.

29. PSYeta, another organization that supposedly supports animal rights, also explicitly endorses the "three Rs."

30. For a general discussion of pre-1966 efforts to regulate animal use in experiments, see Francione, *Animals, Property, and the Law*, 187–90.

31. For a general discussion of the federal Animal Welfare Act and its various amendments, see *id.* at 190–207.

32. 116 Cong. Rec. 40,461 (1970) (statement of Sen. Dole).

33. *Regulate the Transportation, Sale, and Handling of Dogs and Cats Used for Research and Experimentation: Hearings on H.R. 9743 et al. Before the Subcommittee on Livestock and Feed Grains of the House Committee on Agriculture*, 89th Cong., 2d Sess. 4 (1965) (statement of Rep. Poage).

34. *Id.*

35. In 1990, the AWA was amended again, and again the amendments were supported by both animal rights and animal welfare organizations. *See* Food, Agriculture, Conservation, and Trade Act of 1990, § 2403, Pub. L. No. 101-624, 104 Stat. 3359, 4066–68. This law is codified at 7 U.S.C. § 2158 (Supp. 1991). Although the legislation originated in concern about the treatment of animals at auctions, the law as passed omitted all reference to auctions. Instead, the amendment requires that shelters and pounds hold random-source (i.e., not purpose-bred) dogs or cats for at least five days before selling them to a USDA-licensed dealer; the delay is intended to give people an opportunity to recover stolen or stray pets who otherwise may end up in the facility of a USDA dealer. The law also requires that the dealer provide certain documentation to the research facility that purchases the animal, including information about the dealer, the animal, the place from which the animal was obtained, and assurances that the waiting periods have been observed and that the pound or shelter (but not the person giving up the animal to the shelter) was informed that the animal might be used for research or educational purposes. In many respects, the 1990 amendment represents a return to the 1966 origins of the AWA—to protect the *property* of people.

36. Laboratory Animal Welfare Act, Pub. L. No. 89–544, 80 Stat. 350 (1966), §§ 13, 18.

37. House Committee on Agriculture, *Report on the Animal Welfare Act of 1970*, H.R. Rep. No. 1651, 91st Cong., 2d Sess. 1 (1970), *reprinted in* 1970 U.S.C.C.A.N. 5103, at 5104.

38. Animal Welfare Act of 1970, Pub. L. No. 91–579, 84 Stat. 1560, § 3.

39. *Id.* § 14.

40. The 1976 amendment for the most part pertained to the class of animal suppliers subject to regulation rather than those who used animals in experiments. The 1976 act did prohibit animal fighting involving animals transported in interstate commerce. Pub. L. No. 94–279, 90 Stat. 417.

41. *The Use of Animals in Medical Research and Testing: Hearings Before the Subcomittee on Science, Research, and Technology of the Committee on Science and Technology*, 97th Cong., 1st Sess., 277 (1981) (statement of Henry Spira).

42. *See, e.g.*, Friends of Animals, Inc., Committee for Humane Legislation, "A Review of the Animal Welfare Act, the Proposed Amendments, and the Proposed Policy of Friends of Animals," September 8, 1985. FoA's New England director (and now president), Priscilla Feral, also publicly opposed attempts to amend the AWA. Letter from Priscilla Feral to the editor, *The Hour*, August 25, 1983.

43. Interestingly, in the early 1980s, the animal movement in Britain began efforts to overhaul the 1876 British law concerning the use of animals in experiments. Although the 1876 law was stronger than the federal Animal Welfare Act has ever been (including *after* the 1985 amendments), campaigners in Britain sought more extensive changes. The rights contingent of the British movement, like Jones and Herrington in the United States,

favored the complete prohibition of the use of animals for particular purposes, such as cosmetics and weapons testing. *See* Robert Garner, *Animals, Politics, and Morality* (Manchester: Manchester University Press, 1993), 146–47, 207. The "welfarist" contingent of the British movement agreed to the government's proposals for moderate regulation that did not prohibit any particular animal use. The welfarist contingent prevailed.

44. *See* H.R. 556, 87th Cong., 1st Sess. (1981).

45. Andrew Rowan writes that the alternatives bill "was gutted by Congress because the legislators could not accept its radical demands." Andrew N. Rowan, *Of Mice, Models, and Men* (Albany: State University of New York Press, 1984), 3. For a discussion of this claim, see Chapter Six below.

46. Carol Grunewald, "Protection vs. Prevention—Which (If Any) of Two Proposed Laws Would Help Lab Animals Now?" *Animals' Agenda*, vol. 5, no. 3 (1985), at 12, 13.

47. *See* 7 U.S.C. § 2143(a)(3)(A) (directing the secretary of agriculture to develop standards "for animal care, treatment, and practices in experimental procedures to ensure that animal pain and distress are minimized, including adequate veterinary care with the appropriate use of anesthetic, analgesic, tranquilizing drugs, or euthanasia"). For discussions that take the view that the 1985 amendment significantly changed the AWA structure, see, e.g., Esther F. Dukes, "The Improved Standards for Laboratory Animals Act: Will It Ensure That the Policy of the Act Becomes a Reality?" 31 *St. Louis University Law Journal* 519 (1987); Rebecca Dresser, "Assessing Harm and Justification in Animal Research: Federal Policy Opens the Laboratory Door," 40 *Rutgers Law Review* 723 (1988).

48. 7 U.S.C. § 2143(a)(6)(A)(i) (1988).

49. The animal care committee must have at least three members; at least one member must be a veterinarian, and one member must (1) not be affiliated with the facility, (2) not be a member of the immediate family of anyone affiliated with the a facility, and (3) represent "general community interests in the proper care and treatment of animals." 7 U.S.C. § 2143(b)(1)(A), (B)(i–iii). According to the statute, a quorum of the committee is required to approve all animal use at the facility, although the USDA permits delegation of protocol review to one member of the committee. Any committee member can request full-committee review of any particular project, but in the absence of a request for such plenary review, one member of the committee has authority to approve an experiment involving pain and distress. 9 C.F.R. § 2.31(d)(2). In addition, the committee is required to conduct regular inspections of facilities in which animals are used. Although many facilities had some sort of animal use committee as the result of certain NIH guidelines, this committee process was given full legal status only in 1985.

50. 54 Fed. Reg. 36,142 (1989).

51. U.S. Department of Agriculture, Office of the Inspector General, *Enforcement of the Animal Welfare Act*, Audit Report No. 33600-1-Ch (Washington, D.C.: U.S. Department of Agriculture, 1995).

52. 7 U.S.C. § 2143(a)(3)(D)(i–ii).

53. *Id*. § 2143(a)(2).

54. 7 U.S.C. § 2157(a).

55. For example, the State University of New York has argued that the 1985 amendments made confidential virtually *all* information about animal use at the facility. *See* Francione, *Animals, Property, and the Law*, at 243–49.

56. Mark Harris, "The Threat from Within," *Vegetarian Times*, February 1995, at 69.

57. *Id*. at 69–70 (quoting Wayne Pacelle).

58. 1991 APHIS Report.

59. 1992 APHIS Report.

60. 1993 APHIS Report.

61. 1994 APHIS Report.

62. I make no causal claims regarding these apparent increases.

63. For a discussion and critique of USDA / APHIS reporting requirements, see Francione, *Animals, Property, and the Law*, at 218–24.

64. Foundation for Biomedical Research, *Animal Research and Human Health: Understanding the Use of Animals in Biomedical Research*, at 14.

65. In many respects, discussion about the use of animals in experiments is framed by various laws and regulations that govern the activity. This is not to say that this discourse is *necessarily* constrained, but as a *structural* matter, it is so constrained. That is, once the movement accepted the 1985 amendments to the AWA—or even the initial act of 1966—it became inevitable that further progress and development would have to occur within the parameters established by the act and its amendments. As a result, most animal advocacy groups who seek to use the legal or political processes to ameliorate the suffering and distress of animals take as their starting point the AWA and its amendments, which they attempt to "tighten" through further amendment. But this process means that, as a practical matter, animal advocates often urge changes that are, in a relative sense, quite minor. The area of disagreement between animal exploiters and animal defenders is often quite narrow. For example, in one case, animal advocates urged that rats, mice, and birds, which are excluded under the Animal Welfare Act, be included as covered "animals." *See Animal Legal Defense Fund v. Madigan*, 781 F. Supp. 797 (D.D.C. 1992), *vacated sub nom. Animal Legal Defense Fund, Inc. v. Espy*, 23 F.3d 496 (D.C. Cir. 1994). In another case, animal advocates argued that Congress had intended that the U.S. Department of Agriculture, not research facilities, should establish standards for canine exercise and primate psychological well-being. *See Animal Legal Defense Fund v. Secretary of Agriculture*, 813 F. Supp. 882 (D.D.C. 1993), *vacated sub nom. Animal Legal Defense Fund, Inc. v. Espy*, 29 F.3d 720 (D.C. Cir. 1994). For an extended discussion of these cases, see Francione, *Animals, Property, and the Law*, at 78–86, 236–40.

Nothing about the positions taken in *either* suit was any different from positions taken by the most conservative welfarists *before* the emergence of the animal rights movement. Moreover, because the range of dispute between animal advocates and animal exploiters was determined by the structure of the AWA, which reinforces the property status of animals and allows virtually any use of animals that is determined by the experimenters to be scientifically "necessary," the positions taken by the advocates and the exploiters did not differ all that much.

66. *Humane Slaughtering of Livestock: Hearings on S.1213, S. 1497, and H.R. 8308 Before the Committee on Agriculture and Forestry*, 85th Cong., 2d Sess. 132 (1958) (statement of William Eshbaugh, representing the American Meat Institute).

67. *Id.* at 309 (statement of Christine Stevens).

68. *Id.*

69. *Humane Methods of Slaughter Act of 1977: Hearing on H.R. 1464 Before the Subcommittee on Livestock and Grains of the Committee on Agriculture*, 95th Cong., 2d Sess. 24 (1978) (statement of Robert Welborn).

70. *Id.* at 35 (statement of Emily Gleockler).

71. *Id.* at 46 (statement of Ann Cottrell Free).

72. *Humane Methods of Livestock Slaughter: Hearing on S. 3092 Before the Subcommittee on Agricultural Research and General Legislation of the Committee on Agriculture, Nutrition, and Forestry*, 95th Cong., 2d Sess. 11 (1978) (statement of Christine Stevens).

73. "McDonald's Agrees to Adopt Humane Code," *Animal People*, April 1994, at 1, 3.

74. *Id.* at 3.

75. For example, in *Humane Innovations and Alternatives*, the journal of PSYeta, Grandin is described as an "effective and talented hero . . . with a mission" for designing "humane" slaughterhouse facilities. *See* note 15 above.

76. Temple Grandin, *Recommended Animal Handling Guidelines for Meat Packers* (American Meat Institute, 1991), 1.

77. *See* Temple Grandin, "Behavioral Principles of Livestock Handling," *Professional Animal Scientist*, December 1989.

78. Oliver Sacks, *An Anthropologist on Mars* (New York: Knopf, 1995), 268 (quoting Temple Grandin).

79. Grandin, "The Two Major Animal Welfare Problems of the Dairy Industry," at 616.

80. There is an interesting parallel in the coverage extended by federal laws involving both animal experimentation and animal slaughter. Although rats and mice are the most commonly used animals in laboratories, they are excluded by the USDA from coverage under the AWA.

81. Veganism is a diet that excludes all animal products, including eggs and dairy products. Many vegetarians are not vegans and justify this on the ground that animals used in the production of dairy and egg products are not killed, as are animals used for meat. This is both true and false. An animal used in the egg industry may not be killed in order to make a particular egg; but ultimately, once she is "spent," that hen will be slaughtered in the same way as her "broiler" counterpart. That is, animals used for eggs end up at the same slaughterhouse as do broilers. Similarly, cows used for milk end up being slaughtered just as do their "beef" counterparts. Moreover, animals used for dairy and egg products are often kept alive longer, and their lives often involve far more suffering than do the lives of animals used in meat production. For a general discussion of the conditions of intensive agriculture concerning both meat and dairy products, see Jim Mason and Peter Singer, *Animal Factories*, rev. ed. (New York: Harmony Books, 1990).

82. *See* "Interview with Karen Davis," *VivaVine*, May / June 1995, at 3.

83. *Id.* at 6.

84. *The Downed Animal Protection Act; Humane Methods of Poultry Slaughter Act; the Meat and Poultry Products Inspection Amendments of 1993: Hearing on H.R. 559, H.R. 649, H.R. 3646 Before the Subcommittee on Livestock of the Committee on Agriculture*, 103d Cong., 2d Sess. 192, 202 (1994) (statement of Christine Stevens).

85. *Id.* at 68 (statement of Karen Davis).

86. *Id.* at 49, 50 (statement of Alice Johnson).

87. "Downed Animal Legislation in 1995," *Humane Farming Action Fund*, May 1995.

88. *Hearing on H.R. 559, H.R. 649, H.R. 3646*, 75 (statement of Lowell L. Wilson on behalf of the Farm Animal Welfare Coalition).

89. Bauston was not involved in the decision not to print the HFA materials, but did not protest the censorship, at least publicly.

90. Don Barnes, "The Dangers of Elitism," *Animals' Agenda*, vol. 15, no. 2 (1995), at 44.

91. Jasper and Nelkin, *The Animal Rights Crusade*, at 66.

92. *Id.* at 67.

93. *Id.* at 68.

94. Tom Regan, *The Case for Animal Rights* (Berkeley and Los Angeles: University of California Press, 1983), 116.

95. Jasper and Nelkin, *The Animal Rights Crusade*, at 67.

96. Jack Rosenberger, "The Ugly Secret of the Black Beauty Ranch," *Village Voice*, December 18, 1990, at 39.

97. *Id*. (quoting Cleveland Amory).

98. *Id*. at 41.

99. *Id*.

100. As of July 1995, Amory is still a member of the *Agenda* board of advisers. *Agenda*'s editor in 1990 was Merritt Clifton, who has since become editor of *Animal People*. Clifton claims that he did not visit the ranch until 1991, and by that time, Amory had replaced Saxon with Chris Bryne. His reason for not writing the story in *Agenda* is that "by rural Texas standards" the conditions at the ranch "hadn't been bad." Clifton claimed that he "didn't see any point in making anything of any of the allegations of animal care. There was no substantiation of any abuse having taken place, none of any animals having been sold to slaughter." Letter from Merritt Clifton to Anna Charlton, dated July 13, 1995 (copy on file with the author).

Amory *admitted* that Saxon was intermingling a livestock business with his activities as ranch manager, and that he knew about this *before* he hired Saxon in 1984. Amory never denied saying that it was "unfortunate" that people could not accept that Saxon cared about animals even though he raised them for slaughter. Indeed, Pacelle admitted that Saxon had been operating a hog-and-cattle slaughter operation since 1984, and admitted knowing about the matter "for quite some time." Saxon never denied using Fund equipment, feed, and employees for his slaughtering operations, and "also admitted breeding The Fund's boars with his sows, then selling the offspring for slaughter." Vanessa Kelling and Laura A. Moretti, "The Not-So-OK Corral," *Animals' Voice*, vol. 4, no. 1 (1991), at 52. Clifton's explanation for *Agenda*'s failure to report the matter is explicitly and unequivocally refuted by all extant evidence—including the admissions of Amory, Pacelle, and Saxon.

101. Jasper and Nelkin, *The Animal Rights Crusade*, at 188 n. 14.

102. Kelling and Moretti, "The Not-So-OK Corral," at 54 (emphasis in original).

103. In a subsequent issue of the *Animals' Voice*, pictures were printed that purported to be of starving and dead burros at the Black Beauty Ranch. The editors included letters from readers responding to the story, and although some advocates commended the coverage, some complained that it was the "responsibility" of movement publications to report "information that propels the animal rights movement forward, not backward" (letter from Mark D. Boswell to the *Animals' Voice*, *Animals' Voice*, vol. 4, no. 2 [1991], at 56), and that the *Animals' Voice* had acted in an "unforgivable" way by harming "an effective group" and with "callous disregard for the animals who will be indirectly affected" (letter from Sharon Lawson to the *Animals' Voice*, *Animals' Voice*, vol. 4, no. 2 [1991], at 57). One letter reprimanded the *Animals' Voice* for being the "Geraldo Rivera" of the movement and stated, "You can leave professional journalism in the true interest of animals in the hands of the writers of *Animals' Agenda*." Letter from Elizabeth Stummer to the *Animals' Voice*, vol. 4, no. 2 (1991), at 56.

104. Wayne Pacelle, "Wayne Pacelle, Unplugged," *Animals' Agenda*, vol. 14, no. 6 (1994), at 28.

105. For an article by PETA on its sanctuary, see David J. Cantor, "Notes on the Care of Chickens, Sheep, Rabbits, and Turkeys at Aspen Hill," 4 *Humane Innovations and Alternatives in Animal Experimentation* 175 (1990).

106. Susan Okie and Veronica Jennings, " 'Rescued' Animals Killed: Animal-Rights Group Defends Euthanasia," *Washington Post*, April 13, 1991, at A1 (quoting Ingrid Newkirk).

107. Arlo Wagner, "Animals Put Down by PETA," *Washington Times*, April 13, 1991, at A1.

108. "Two Monkeys Put to Death After High Court Gives OK," *Los Angeles Times*, April 13, 1991, at A20.

109. Okie and Jennings, " 'Rescued' Animals Killed," at A1.

110. Ironically, at about the same time that PETA killed the rabbits and roosters, PETA was opposing the euthanasia of one of the Silver Spring monkeys, Billy, despite the fact that a veterinarian chosen by PETA had recommended Billy's euthanasia because the animal was suffering horribly. PETA rejected the veterinarian's recommendation. This irony was noted in virtually all print coverage of the Aspen Hill killings. In an interview with Deborah Blum, PETA's chairperson, Alex Pacheco, stated that although he "respected" the PETA veterinarian's position, " 'if [Billy] had a chance of recovering, then I couldn't just let him die. I couldn't treat a member of my family like that.' " Deborah Blum, *The Monkey Wars* (New York: Oxford University Press, 1994), 129 (quoting Alex Pacheco). However sick the rabbits at Aspen Hill were, no one has ever suggested that they were in worse condition than Billy, for whom PETA fought strenuously against euthanasia.

More recently, PETA has stirred controversy by supporting the killing of feral cats living in colonies, even when a human has spayed or neutered the animals and even when the cats are being fed and otherwise cared for adequately.

Chapter Five

1. Lawrence Finsen and Susan Finsen, *The Animal Rights Movement in America: From Compassion to Respect* (New York: Twayne Publishers, 1994), 259.

2. As I discussed earlier, Singer is not a conventional new welfarist, because he does not necessarily see the abolition of animal exploitation as a desirable long-term goal, although he indicates clearly that he opposes the overwhelming majority of animal exploitation. Singer is an act utilitarian, and as such, what he *must* want is that all animals— human and nonhuman—receive equal consideration for their equal interests and, beyond this, that preference satisfaction is maximized and that pain and suffering are minimized consistent with the principle of utility. This view does not preclude animal suffering or animal death, including the suffering or death of humans.

3. Peter Singer, *Animal Liberation*, 2d ed. (New York: New York Review of Books, 1990), 233.

4. In a sense, this view reflects a central doctrine of traditional welfarism. For example, many courts have expressed the view that anticruelty laws have a dual purpose: "to protect [the] animals [and] to conserve public morals." *See, e.g., Waters v. People*, 46 P. 112, 113 (Colo. 1896). The former purpose is often subordinated to the latter, and most courts agree that these statutes are intended to prevent humans from acting cruelly toward each other, and they regard the cruel treatment of animals as leading to the cruel treatment of humans by other humans. Indeed, in the *Model Penal Code*, which represented an attempt to rationalize the whole of substantive criminal law, the drafters reported that "the object of [anticruelty] statutes seems to have been to prevent outrage to the sensibilities of the community." *Model Penal Code* (Philadelphia: American Law Institute, 1980), § 250.11 cmt. 1. These statutes are thought to improve human character by requiring kind treatment of animals. Early cases concerned with the protection of children articulated a similar rationale.

5. Finsen and Finsen, *The Animal Rights Movement in America*, at 5.

6. Robert Garner, *Animals, Politics, and Morality* (Manchester: Manchester University Press, 1993), 234.

7. *Id*. at 103.
8. *Id*. at 211.
9. *Id*. at 119.
10. *Id*. at 125.
11. *Id*. at 126.
12. *Id*. at 127. Part of the difficulty involved in trying to assess the impact of animal advocates on institutionalized animal exploitation is that people often react based on considerations other than animal concerns. For example, many people for health reasons do not eat animal products, and many oppose experiments involving animals on the ground that such experiments are unsound from a scientific point of view.
13. Garner, *Animals, Politics, and Morality*, at 122.
14. *See, e.g.,* Jeremy Rifkin, *Beyond Beef* (New York: Dutton Books, 1992).
15. U.S. General Accounting Office, *Report to the Chairman, Subcommittee on Agriculture, Rural Development, and Related Agencies, Senate Committee on Appropriations: The Department of Agriculture's Animal Welfare Program* (1985). For a discussion of this report, see Gary L. Francione, *Animals, Property, and the Law* (Philadelphia: Temple University Press, 1995), 216–18.
16. U.S. Congress, Office of Technology Assessment, Rep. No. OTA-BA-273, *Alternatives to Animal Use in Research, Testing, and Education* (Washington, D.C.: U.S. Government Printing Office, 1986). For a discussion of this report, see Francione, *Animals, Property, and the Law*, at 216–18.
17. U.S. Department of Agriculture, Office of the Inspector General, *Enforcement of the Animal Welfare Act*, Audit Report No. 33600–1-Ch (Washington, D.C.: U.S. Department of Agriculture, 1995). All quotations are taken from the "Executive Summary of the Audit."
18. *See* Animal Welfare Institute, ed., *Beyond the Laboratory Door* (Washington, D.C.: Animal Welfare Institute, 1985). For a discussion of the AWI position, see Francione, *Animals, Property, and the Law*, at 222–24.
19. *See* Humane Society of the United States, *Petition for Changes in Reporting Procedures Under the Animal Welfare Act Before the Animal and Plant Health Inspection Service of the United States Department of Agriculture* (October 1992). For a discussion of the HSUS position, see Francione, *Animals, Property, and the Law*, 218–22.
20. Foundation for Biomedical Research, *Animal Research and Human Health: Understanding the Use of Animals in Biomedical Research* (Washington, D.C.: Foundation for Biomedical Research, 1992), 14. These statements about the federal Animal Welfare Act are accurate if they are understood to mean that under the law the experimenter will set the standards, but this is probably not how these statements were intended and probably not how they are understood by the average reader.
21. Finsen and Finsen, *The Animal Rights Movement in America*, at 141. Interestingly, Finsen and Finsen note in this regard that some companies, such as Procter & Gamble, have resisted changes regarding the use of animals for testing. Animal rights advocate Henry Spira disagrees, arguing that Procter & Gamble has reduced animal use and deserves praise. *See* Merritt Clifton, "In League with the Devil," *Animal People*, June 1995, at 1. Clifton supports Spira's views.
22. *See* James M. Jasper and Dorothy Nelkin, *The Animal Rights Crusade* (New York: Free Press, 1992), 108–9.
23. Garner, *Animals, Politics, and Morality*, at 187.
24. *Id*. at 188 (emphasis in original). Nevertheless, the animal movement has made *some* progress in the areas of fur and cosmetics testing, at least as far as educating consumers. It is important to note, however, that in these two areas more than any others,

animal advocates have consistently taken an *absolutist* approach. That is, animal advocates who object to fur do not usually urge that fur be produced more "humanely"; rather, animal advocates have argued that people should stop wearing fur immediately. Similarly, although some animal advocates, such as Henry Spira, have urged incremental reduction of animal use in cosmetics testing, many other advocates have criticized Spira for this "welfarist" approach and have pushed for the abolition of cosmetics testing. So, despite the advice that only gradual reforms work, it appears that if any approach has been successful, it is the more absolutist approach embodied in the fur and cosmetics campaigns.

25. Finsen and Finsen, *The Animal Rights Movement in America*, at 109, 116, 117.

26. *See id*. at 118.

27. *Id*. at 159.

28. Ironically, even motion pictures that purport to have an animal rights message involve the abuse of animals. For example, in the 1980s, a major studio produced *Project X*, which showed the illegal rescue of a group of chimpanzees by a military officer who became aware that the animals were being used in nuclear radiation experiments. Television personality Bob Barker discovered that at least some of the chimpanzees used in the film had been beaten and otherwise abused in order to get them to perform properly. Barker caused charges to be filed with the Los Angeles District Attorney's office, which referred the matter to the Los Angeles Department of Animal Regulation. It was determined that animals had been abused in the making of *Project X*. Don Barnes, educational director of the National Anti-Vivisection Society (NAVS), had acted as science advisor for the film. *Project X* was defended as an "outstanding motion picture" by the Ark Trust, a self-described animal rights group led by Gretchen Wyler, who formerly associated with the Fund for Animals, and Michael Giannelli. (Statement of Michael Giannelli, dated January 2, 1996; copy on file with the author.) Ark Trust supports the use of animals in entertainment and routinely defends the motion picture industry against claims that the use of animals in films and television constitutes abuse and exploitation. The author was counsel to Bob Barker in the *Project X* matter.

29. *See, e.g.*, Patrick W. Concannon, "Animal Use, Animal Rights, and Animal Legislation," in *Animal Research, Animal Rights, Animal Legislation*, ed. Patrick W. Concannon (Champaign, Ill.: Society for the Study of Reproduction, 1990). Concannon argues that animal rights advocates are "not bound by any moral requirement to be truthful about their ultimate goals and intentions. Rather, they find it easy to deny these goals and to work on multiple fronts against the easiest target as far as acceptance by the public is concerned."

30. *See, e.g.*, Hans Ruesch, *Slaughter of the Innocent* (New York: Civitas, 1983). Ruesch takes the view that the issue of vivisection is not whether the practice is immoral but whether it is valid from a scientific point of view, which Ruesch denies. Robert Sharpe, on the other hand, argues that vivisection is both immoral and unscientific. *See* Robert Sharpe, *The Cruel Deception* (Wellingborough, Northamptonshire: Thorsons Publishing Group, 1988).

31. Garner, *Animals, Politics, and Morality*, at 7.

32. Henry Spira, "Fighting to Win," in *In Defense of Animals*, ed. Peter Singer (Oxford: Basil Blackwell, 1985), 196–97.

33. Andrew N. Rowan, *Of Mice, Models, and Men* (Albany: State University of New York Press, 1984), 24 (emphasis added).

34. *See. e.g.*, Susan Sperling, *Animal Liberators* (Berkeley and Los Angeles: University of California Press, 1988).

35. *Id*. at 77.

36. Andrew N. Rowan et al., *The Animal Research Controversy* (Boston: Tufts University School of Veterinary Medicine, 1994), 15. Ironically, the study was funded by the Pew Charitable Trusts, which, at the time, was under the direction of Thomas Langfitt, who, with Thomas Gennarelli, was principal experimenter at the University of Pennsylvania head-injury lab.

37. *See* Andrew N. Rowan, "Laboratory Animal Numbers: Good News or Bad?" *Animal People*, December 1994, at 5. In this essay, Rowan expresses bewilderment at critics of his study: "Why are [animal rights] activists not then overjoyed that their campaigns are achieving a measure of success?"

38. Rowan et al., *The Animal Research Controversy*, at 14.

39. *Id.* at 15. For a general discussion of reporting requirements under the federal Animal Welfare Act, see Francione, *Animals, Property, and the Law*, at 218–24.

40. *The Use of Animals in Medical Research and Testing: Hearings Before the Subcommittee on Science, Research, and Technology of the Committee on Science and Technology*, 97th Cong., 1st Sess. 305 (1981) (statement of Andrew Rowan).

41. Rowan's other sources of data include voluntary reports from pharmaceutical companies that claim a decrease in drug testing, and an unpublished doctoral thesis that claims that animal use by the Department of Defense has decreased.

42. Rowan et al., *The Animal Research Controversy*, at 15.

43. Rowan, *Of Mice, Models, and Men*, at 68–69.

44. *See* Andrew N. Rowan et al., *The Animal Research Controversy* (Boston: Tufts University School of Veterinary Medicine, 1995). Interestingly, although the second version has a 1995 imprint date on the cover page and spine of the volume, each page has a 1994 date at the bottom. There is no explanation for this, just as there is no explanation of the circumstances that occasioned a 1995 version of the original 1994 study.

45. *Id.* at 17.

46. Private e-mail correspondence between Andrew N. Rowan and Gary L. Francione, dated June 29, 1995 (copy on file with the author).

47. Rowan et al., *The Animal Research Controversy* (1995), at 17.

48. When asked about the discrepancy between his explanation of the increase and the accounts given in recent USDA reports, Rowan stated that his information came from the USDA but that he had not verified it. *See* private e-mail correspondence between Rowan and Francione, June 29, 1995. After I informed Rowan that Jerry DePoyster, the USDA official responsible for preparing the USDA reports, told me that Rowan's statement about inclusion of rats and mice in the "other" category was incorrect, Rowan replied, after speaking to Jerry DePoyster, that I was "correct that the 'other' category does not include rats or mice." He added that the "other" category does include frogs and other species (other than the six covered species, but excluding rats and mice), and concluded that "once again, [he] got the details wrong but the general principle was correct." Private e-mail correspondence between Andrew N. Rowan and Gary L. Francione, dated July 16, 1995 (copy on file with the author).

49. Letter from Merritt Clifton to Gary L. Francione, July 15, 1995 (copy on file with the author).

50. Garner, *Animals, Politics, and Morality*, at 6. Garner clearly is correct to note that there are many similarities between the American and British animal movements. These similarities are due to myriad socioeconomic and political factors, including, but not limited to, the fact that some of the more prominent animal advocates in the United States were born and raised in Britain and were deeply involved in the British movement. The main points of similarity are, in my view, related to the economics of animal exploitation, which are similar in both countries.

It should be noted, however, that Garner makes a number of comparative statements that are open to question. For example, he states that "in America generally, the animal protection movement has used the legal system more effectively than in Britain." *Id.* at 189. Throughout Garner's analysis, he makes other assumptions about the relatively easier access to public information and political systems in the United States. Although Garner's observations are interesting, many of them seem quite anecdotal and not based on any empirical evidence, or at least on none that Garner shares with his reader. It is clear that a systematic comparative study of the British and American movements remains to be done. Since current scholarship on this relationship is lacking, and since statements based on informal observation and anecdote have therefore been aired, I offer mine: for *whatever* reasons, the British animal protection movement is far more progressive than the American movement has ever been. This comment should, however, be given no greater credence than that accorded similarly anecdotal comments in Garner's book. Recent accounts, however, appear to support my view that the British movement is more progressive. *See* "People and Animals," *The Economist,* August 19–25, 1995, at 11.

51. Garner, *Animals, Politics, and Morality,* at 234.

52. *Id.* at 34, 35.

53. For a more complete discussion of the structural problems in animal welfare laws, given the property status of nonhumans, including a discussion of anticruelty laws, see Francione, *Animals, Property, and the Law.*

54. Garner, *Animals, Politics, and Morality,* at 17.

55. *Id.* at 18.

56. *Id.* at 246.

57. *Id.* at 147. These "radicals" also sought to prohibit psychological experiments and drug-addiction studies involving animals.

58. *Id.*

59. *Id.* (emphasis in original).

60. *Id.* at 7.

61. *Id.* at 247.

62. *Id.* at 7.

63. *See* John Locke, *Two Treatises of Government,* 2d ed., ed. Peter Laslett (Cambridge: Cambridge University Press, 1967), 303–20; A. John Simmons, *The Lockean Theory of Rights* (Princeton, N.J.: Princeton University Press, 1992).

64. Simmons, *The Lockean Theory of Rights,* at 224–25.

65. Locke, *Two Treatises of Government,* at 308, 307.

66. *Id.* at 289.

67. 2 William Blackstone, *Commentaries on the Laws of England* (Chicago: Callaghan & Co., 1872), *1–2.

68. *Id.* at *2–3.

69. 1 *id.* at *139.

70. For a discussion of the measure of damages in veterinary malpractice cases, see Francione, *Animals, Property, and the Law,* at 54–63.

71. 54 Fed. Reg. 6486 (emphasis added). The original quote used "in" rather than the "of" that I placed in brackets, but "in" appears to be a mistake.

72. Wayne Pacelle, "Wayne Pacelle, Unplugged," *Animals' Agenda,* vol. 14, no. 6 (1994), at 28.

73. For an extended discussion of anticruelty statutes, see Francione, *Animals, Property, and the Law,* at 119–65.

74. Ingrid Newkirk, "Total Victory, Like Checkmate, Cannot Be Achieved in One Move," *Animals Agenda,* January / February 1992, at 45.

75. John H. Ingham, *The Law of Animals* (Philadelphia: T. & J. W. Johnson, 1900), 529.

76. *People ex rel. Walker v. Court of New York*, 4 N.Y. Sup. Ct. 441 (App. Div. 1875).

77. *State v. Jones*, 625 P.2d 503 (Kan. 1981).

78. *Commonwealth v. Vonderheid*, 28 Pa. D. & C. 101, 106 (Columbia County Ct. 1962)

79. Justinian, *Justinian's "Institutes,"* trans. Peter Birks and Grant McLeod (Ithaca, N.Y.: Cornell University Press, 1987), 41.

80. *See, e.g., State v. Fowler*, 205 S.E.2d 749, 751 (N.C. Ct. App. 1974).

81. *See, e.g.,* Alaska Stat. § 11.61.140(b)(1)–(3) (1989).

82. *See, e.g., Commonwealth v. Lufkin*, 89 Mass. (7 Allen) 579, 582–83 (1863).

83. Garner, *Animals, Politics, and Morality*, at 18.

84. *Id.* at 3, 103, 234, 211, 235.

85. There have been many fine books written that describe the heinous conditions of intensive agriculture. *See, e.g.,* Mark Gold, *Assault and Battery* (London: Pluto Press, 1983); Jim Mason and Peter Singer, *Animal Factories*, rev. ed. (New York: Harmony Books, 1990); Singer, *Animal Liberation*.

86. *See* Garner, *Animals, Politics, and Morality*, at 34–35.

87. *See* Kim W. Stallwood, "Utopian Visions and Pragmatic Politics: The Challenges of the Animal Rights Movement" (paper presented at the National Alliance for Animals conference, June 24, 1995).

88. Garner, *Animals, Politics, and Morality*, at 207, 147.

89. *Id.* at 207.

90. Andrew N. Rowan, "Animal Rights Versus Animal Welfare: A False Dichotomy?" 7 *Animal Policy Report* 1, 2 (1993).

91. This is equivalent to saying that animals cannot have respect-based rights but can have policy-based, or utility-based, rights. *See* Jeffrie G. Murphy and Jules L. Coleman, *The Philosophy of Law* (Totowa, N.J.: Rowman & Littlefield, 1984), 91. For a discussion of this distinction, see Francione, *Animals, Property, and the Law*, at 107–10.

92. Joel Feinberg, "Human Duties and Animal Rights," in Joel Feinberg, *Rights, Justice, and the Bounds of Liberty: Essays in Social Philosophy* (Princeton, N.J.: Princeton University Press, 1980), 185, 187.

93. Newkirk, "Total Victory," at 44.

Chapter Six

1. Ingrid Newkirk, "Total Victory, Like Checkmate, Cannot Be Achieved in One Move," *Animals' Agenda*, January / February 1992, at 44.

2. Mark Harris, "The Threat from Within," *Vegetarian Times*, February 1995, at 70 (quoting Henry Spira).

3. Bernard E. Rollin, *Animal Rights and Human Morality*, rev. ed. (Buffalo, N.Y.: Prometheus Books, 1992), 12, 137, 140.

4. Robert Garner, *Animals, Politics, and Morality* (Manchester: Manchester University Press, 1993), 34 (emphasis added).

5. *See* Peter Singer, *Practical Ethics* (Cambridge: Cambridge University Press, 1979), 3.

6. *Id.* at 2.

7. These views are clearly expressed by new welfarists. *See, e.g.,* Kim W. Stallwood, "Utopian Visions and Pragmatic Politics: The Challenges of the Animal Rights Movement" (paper presented at the National Alliance for Animals conference, June 24, 1995).

8. Interestingly, it is precisely in this situation that some new welfarists claim that rights theory provides *too much* guidance. For example, Barnes claims that the rightist is being "elitist" by criticizing others for eating meat. Don Barnes, "The Dangers of Elitism," *Animals' Agenda*, vol. 15, no. 2 (1995), at 44. But that is like saying the abolitionist is

"elitist" because she thinks that owning slaves is morally wrong. Barnes's claim that rights theory is "elitist" because it *overdetermines* behavior or provides *too much* guidance is merely an *assertion* that vegetarianism is not a moral imperative. That is fair; many people disagree that vegetarianism is a moral imperative. But mere disagreement does not an argument make.

9. It is often argued that making clothing from nonanimal products, such as synthetics, may have unintended but nevertheless serious consequences for humans and animals alike. That may very well be, but in that event such manufacture would be no different from other practices that yield unintended harm. Although our use of synthetics may have completely *unintentional* environmental consequences deleterious to humans, this can in no way be equated with the *intentional* killing of beings for use in making products, such as clothing. Again, this reflects a view that "personhood" establishes certain limits, irrespective of consequential considerations.

10. That Regan's theory is concerned with institutionalized exploitation is apparent from many aspects of his theory. *See* note 29 to Chapter One.

11. Henry Shue, *Basic Rights* (Princeton, N.J.: Princeton University Press, 1980).

12. *Id.* at 20.

13. *Id.* at 19.

14. *Id.* at 20.

15. *Id.* at 21.

16. I do not wish to give the impression that Shue argues that animals ought to have basic rights, since his book does not even address the question of animal rights.

17. For example, Andrew Rowan argues that there has been a significant reduction in the use of animals partially as the result of welfarist legal reform and political pressure; others disagree, citing the unreliability of the data used and of the analysis of that data and the lack of empirical evidence that would establish any sort of causal link between the decline (if there is one in fact) and welfarist reform. Indeed, Frey and Singer are both utilitarians, and they disagree over the consequences of abolishing factory farming.

18. Peter Singer, *Animal Liberation*, 2d ed. (New York: New York Review of Books, 1990), at 15.

19. Some scholars have accused Regan of the same problem, based on his discussion of the following hypothetical: Five survivors—four normal adults and one normal dog—are on a lifeboat. There is room in the boat only for four, and one of the occupants must be thrown overboard. Regan maintains that his rights theory provides an answer to the problem. Although death is a harm for the dog, Regan argues, death would be a qualitatively greater loss—and, accordingly, a greater harm—for any of the humans: "To throw any one of the humans overboard, to face certain death, would be to make that individual worse-off (would cause *that* individual a greater harm) than the harm that would be done to the dog if the animal was thrown overboard." Tom Regan, *The Case for Animal Rights* (Berkeley and Los Angeles: University of California Press, 1983), 324. It would, on Regan's view, be morally obligatory to kill the dog. Further, Regan claims, even if the choice is between a million dogs and one person, it would still be obligatory under rights theory to throw the dogs overboard.

For criticisms of this view, see S. F. Sapontzis, *Morals, Reason, and Animals* (Philadelphia: Temple University Press, 1987), 219. *See also* Peter Carruthers, *The Animals Issue* (Cambridge: Cambridge University Press, 1992), 9. Ironically, one of Regan's most vocal critics on this point is Singer, who claims that a "theory that tells us that all subjects-of-a-life (including dogs) have equal inherent value [cannot] be reconciled with the intuition that it is the dog that must be sacrificed." Peter Singer, "Ten Years of Animal Liberation," *New York Review of Books*, January 17, 1985, at 49.

To the extent that Regan allows for the resolution of this hypothetical problem by appealing to certain characteristics of the dog that he disallowed when he argued that all subjects-of-a-life have equal inherent value, his resolution is inconsistent with his general theory. But Regan's discussion of the lifeboat example is *irrelevant* to his general theory that animals ought not to be regarded exclusively as means to human ends, and even if Regan is incorrect, the error does not affect his general theory. The lifeboat example explicitly assumes the *absence* of any institutionalized exploitation, and the example cannot, therefore, be used to support the view that rights theory *could* provide support for using animals, say, to find a cure for cancer. Moreover, the lifeboat hypothetical deals explicitly with a "post-rights" situation; that is, the hypothetical concerns the content of rights that animals would have were they no longer regarded as the property of humans. As such, the hypothetical does not concern Regan's theory of basic rights. *See* Gary L. Francione, "Comparable Harm and Equal Inherent Value: The Problem of the Dog in the Lifeboat," *Between the Species* (forthcoming, 1996).

20. Singer, *Animal Liberation*, at 20.

21. *Id*. at 229.

22. *Id*. It is odd that the new welfarists seem not to comprehend the rather blatant elitism and human chauvinism embedded in Singer's observation that animals such as cows do not have a concept of their own life.

23. Lawrence Finsen and Susan Finsen, *The Animal Rights Movement in America: From Compassion to Respect* (New York: Twayne Publishers, 1994), 186.

24. *See* Garner, *Animals, Politics, and Morality*, at 229. I doubt that the British Raj regarded Gandhi as engaging in action that was tantamount to screaming until he (Gandhi) became sick.

25. Violence against persons is to be distinguished from violence against property when the property takes the form of animals that are removed from labs or other situations in which they will be exploited. Indeed, as Garner correctly observes, Regan does not regard animals as property and must be committed to the notion that animals *cannot* be stolen. *See* Garner, *Animals, Politics, and Morality*, at 229.

26. *Id*. at 193.

27. *Id*. at 207–8.

28. *Id*. at 211.

29. Deborah Blum, *The Monkey Wars* (New York: Oxford University Press, 1994), 116.

30. Finsen and Finsen, *The Animal Rights Movement in the United States*, at 80.

31. Various responses to attempted intramovement discussion of these issues have suggested that such discussion is " 'tedious' " and " 'a waste of time and energy' " (Harris, "The Threat from Within," at 69 [quoting Ingrid Newkirk]); "elitist" (Barnes, "The Dangers of Elitism," at 44–45); and "divisive" (Kim W. Stallwood, "Utopian Visions and Pragmatic Politics: The Challenges of the Animal Rights Movement" [paper presented at the National Alliance for Animals conference, June 24, 1995]).

32. Garner, *Animals, Politics, and Morality*, at 194.

33. *Id*. at 208.

34. *Id*. at 193.

35. By "property," I simply mean that which is regarded exclusively as a means to an end for someone designated as an "owner." It does not matter whether the owner is the state or a private individual for purposes of my argument that animal property will always lose in any conflict with the owners of animal property.

36. Garner, *Animals, Politics, and Morality*, at 204.

37. *Id*. at 206 (quoting the negotiating position of a coalition of animal welfare groups).

38. *Id*. at 207.

39. *See* Andrew N. Rowan, *Of Mice, Models, and Men* (Albany: State University of New York Press, 1984), 3.

40. H.R. 556, 97th Cong., 1st Sess. (1981).

41. Rowan, *Of Mice, Models, and Men*, at 3.

42. *See The Use of Animals in Medical Research and Testing: Hearings Before the Subcommittee on Science, Research, and Technology of the Committee on Science and Technology*, 97th Cong., 1st Sess. (1981).

43. Rowan, *Of Mice, Models, and Men*, at 3–4.

44. It is possible that animal users may regard a regulation as cost-effective and not object to it.

45. Some commentators claim that personality conflicts in the movement result in disunity among animal advocates. *See* Garner, *Animals, Politics, and Morality*, at 204. Even if these observations are correct (and they certainly are to some degree), it is my view that the disunity would still result from the structural problems of animal welfare and from the logical and moral incompatibility of animal rights theory and animal welfare.

46. Garner, *Animals, Politics, and Morality*, at 210.

47. Gary L. Francione, *Animals, Property, and the Law* (Philadelphia: Temple University Press, 1995), 260.

48. Shue, *Basic Rights*, at 20.

49. Harris, "The Threat from Within," at 70 (quoting Henry Spira).

50. This is not to say that Regan explicitly recognized that he was really talking about a single, basic right in *The Case for Animal Rights*. Indeed, it appears that he did not. *See* Francione, "Comparable Harm and Equal Inherent Value."

51. A. Leon Higgenbotham Jr., *In the Matter of Color* (New York: Oxford University Press, 1978), 36. For discussions of slavery, see Andrew Fede, *People Without Rights* (New York: Garland Publishers, 1992); Robert B. Shaw, *A Legal History of Slavery in the United States* (Potsdam, N.Y.: Northern Press, 1991).

52. Neil MacCormick, "Children's Rights: A Test Case," in *Legal Rights and Social Democracy* (Oxford: Clarendon Press, 1982), 159.

53. It is important to distinguish the assumptions of animal welfare theory generally from the assumptions made by any particular welfarist. That is, a welfarist may regard the property status of animals to be morally wrong, but may believe, for example, that welfarist reform will eradicate that status. The reform itself, however, rests on the status of the animal as property.

54. Again, the extent to which the new welfarist claims that rights theory provides *too much* guidance on the macro level is merely the extent to which the new welfarist disagrees with the rights view; disagreement does not constitute an argument.

Chapter Seven

1. Legal theorist Wesley Hohfeld argued that "the term 'rights' tends to be used indiscriminately to cover what in a given case may be a privilege, power, or an immunity, rather than a right in the strictest sense." Wesley N. Hohfeld, *Fundamental Legal Conceptions*, ed. Walter Cook (New Haven: Yale University Press, 1923), 36. According to Hohfeld, a right, strictly speaking, is really a *claim* that has a duty as its correlative. An example of a claim right is given in the text. But there are other senses of "right" as well. For example, to say that I have a right may mean that I have a *privilege* to do something, or it may mean that I have the legal *power* to affect a change in relationship, or I may have an *immunity*, in that some aspect of my status cannot be affected.

2. Claim rights can exist *in personam*, in that the correlative duty binds a particular

person or persons, or it can exist *in rem* and bind everyone unless the rightholder further refines that class. For example, under the law, the dogs who live with me are regarded as my property, and I have property rights *in rem* in my dogs, which means, among other things, that *everyone* has a duty not to interfere with my ownership of my dogs. I can, of course, allow people to do things with my dogs (including, under the law, to kill them), and everyone except those I, as property owner, designate is bound not to interfere with my exercise of rights over my dogs.

3. 444 A.2d 855 (R.I. 1982).

4. *See, e.g.*, Richard D. Ryder, *Victims of Science*, rev. ed. (London: National Anti-Vivisection Society, 1983); Animal Welfare Institute, ed., *Beyond the Laboratory Door* (Washington, D.C.: Animal Welfare Institute, 1985).

5. For example, the dispute between animal advocates and animal exploiters over the implementation by the USDA of the 1985 congressional amendments to the federal Animal Welfare Act is in fact a dispute over the cost-justification of the standards urged by the animal advocates. *See* Gary L. Francione, *Animals, Property, and the Law* (Philadelphia: Temple University Press, 1995), 211–13. Those in the research community who opposed these rules argued that they were getting perfectly valid data from animals used in laboratories without the more definite "engineering" standards and that these standards would require treatment beyond that required under the more traditionally welfarist "performance" standards. If the engineering standards did, indeed, establish standards with correlative duties, then they might be said to contain prohibitions (i.e., "it is prohibited to walk a dog for fewer than thirty minutes a day") that would *not* be contingent on the attending veterinarian's judgment to provide the amount of walking "necessary" to efficient exploitation of the dog.

6. I am reminded of an ad campaign several years ago in which Frank Perdue claimed that his chickens, which he refers to as his "girls," were fed cookies for dessert.

7. *See* Francione, *Animals, Property, and the Law*, at 99–100.

8. Foundation for Biomedical Research, *Animal Research and Human Health: Caring for Laboratory Animals* (Washington, D.C.: Foundation for Biomedical Research, 1992), 1.

9. Temple Grandin, *Recommended Animal Handling Guidelines for Meat Packers* (Washington, D.C.: American Meat Institute, 1991), 1.

10. Kim W. Stallwood, "A Conversation with Peter Singer," *Animals' Agenda*, vol. 14, no. 2 (1994), at 27.

11. Robert Garner, *Animals, Politics, and Morality* (Manchester: Manchester University Press, 1993), 103.

12. The property owner may, of course, try to pass along such costs to consumers. The problem is that the demand for just about any food is elastic and will change as the price changes. So, for example, if the costs of regulation added $3 per pound to the price of hamburger, many people would shift to another food.

13. For example, Roger Caras of the American Society for the Prevention of Cruelty to Animals (ASPCA) stated that Santeria is a "voodoo-like religion" that is "not legitimate in the context of modern America." Laurie Asseo, "Court Upholds Harsher Terms for Hate Crimes," *Los Angeles Times*, June 13, 1993, at A1 (quoting Roger Caras). The author was counsel to the ASPCA for a 1984 case involving Santeria sacrifices, but took the position that these uses of animals were qualitatively different from the slaughter of animals for food, although both were morally unacceptable. At that time, the ASPCA was directed by John Kullberg, who was subsequently forced from the ASPCA for endorsing positions that were identified with the animal rights movement.

14. *Church of the Lukumi Babalu Aye, Inc. v. City of Hialeah*, 113 S. Ct. 2217 (1993).

15. Regan has used this expression in conversation concerning these issues.

16. For a discussion of the legal doctrine of standing in the context of animal issues, see Francione, *Animals, Property, and the Law*, at 65–90.

17. Christopher Stone, "Should Trees Have Standing? Toward Legal Rights for Natural Objects," 45 *Southern California Law Review* 450, 464–67 (1972). Stone argues that "each time there is a movement to confer rights onto some new 'entity,' the proposal is bound to sound odd or frightening." *Id.* at 455. Stone observes that the law recognizes as "persons" corporations, joint ventures, municipalities, certain partnerships, and nations, and that it is necessary to recognize that animals have inherent value. Stone also argues that ecosystems and other parts of the environment have inherent value that should be recognized.

18. I do not think that I am being unfair by claiming that the new welfarist will support this measure. After all, there has never been such a progressive piece of legislation introduced in Congress, and new welfarists have supported legislation that is far less progressive.

19. *See* Peter Singer and Paola Cavalieri, eds., *The Great Ape Project* (New York: St. Martin's Press, 1993).

20. Scott Allen, "Apes on Edge; Air Force Pioneers' Future Unclear," *Boston Globe* November 7, 1994, at 1 (quoting Peter Singer).

21. Robert Garner, "A Strategy for Animal Rights," *The Vegan*, summer 1993, at 7.

22. Jonathan Bennett, "Whatever the Consequences," 26 *Analysis* 83, 86 (1966). *See also* Jonathan Bennett, *The Act Itself* (Oxford: Clarendon Press, 1995).

23. There is one sense in which Garner's distinction between the incremental eradication of vivisection and the incremental abolition of animal agriculture has greater explanatory force. If all the experiments that make up vivisection were incrementally prohibited, then vivisection would cease to exist as an activity. If all the incidents of modern intensive agriculture were eliminated, an animal agriculture that used "humanely" raised animals, which is all that the welfarists want anyway, might still remain. The incremental eradication of the practices constitutive of intensive farming will not be based solely on a concern for the pain and suffering of the animal, but on the interest of the animals in not being property in the first place. To the extent that this interest is recognized as primary, the goal of the rights advocate is to end up, not with "happy" animal slaves, but with the abolition of the institutionalized exploitation that causes the suffering in the first place and that justifies the imposition of pain and suffering based solely on the aggregation of consequences.

24. "People and Animals," *The Economist*, August 19–25, 1995, at 19.

25. Some measures, such as those that would require that certain types of animals not be used in any institutionalized exploitation, would achieve the basic right not to be regarded as property for some but not all animals.

Conclusion

1. "People and Animals," *The Economist*, August 19–25, 1995, at 11.

2. Wayne Pacelle, "Wayne Pacelle, Unplugged," *Animals' Agenda*, vol. 14, no. 6 (1994), at 28.

3. Richard D. Ryder, Book Review, *Animals' Agenda*, vol. 14, no. 2 (1994).

4. Andrew C. Revkin, "Chimp Research Laboratory Is Taken Over by Foundation," *New York Times*, August 10, 1995, at B5, col. 1.

5. Deborah Blum, *The Monkey Wars* (New York: Oxford University Press, 1994), 271 (quoting Alex Pacheco).

6. Richard Delgado, "Our Better Natures: A Revisionist View of Joe Sax's Public Trust

Theory of Environmental Protection, and Some Dark Thoughts on the Possibility of Law Reform," 44 *Vanderbilt Law Review* 1209 (1991).

Postscript

1. *See HSUS Statements of Policy*, at 3–4, 30, 31. HSUS is the subject of allegations concerning financial improprieties, the payment of huge salaries to HSUS executives, and allegations by female employees of sexual harassment. *See* Edward T. Pound, "One Nonprofit's Woes," *U.S. News & World Report*, October 2, 1995, at 42. Interestingly, HSUS has become one of the major financial supporters of *Animals' Agenda*. *Agenda* has increased coverage of HSUS personnel and campaigns.

2. This policy statement of Psychologists for the Ethical Treatment of Animals appears on the inside cover of its journal, *Humane Innovations and Alternatives*.

3. *AV Magazine*, September / October 1995, at 20.

4. *The Downed Animal Protection Act; Humane Methods of Poultry Slaughter Act; the Meat and Poultry Products Inspection Amendments of 1993; Hearing on H.R. 559, H.R. 649, H.R. 3646 Before the Subcommittee on Livestock of the Committee on Agriculture*, 103d Cong., 2d Sess. 192, 202 (1994) (statement of Lowell L. Wilson on behalf of the Farm Animal Welfare Coalition).

5. The National Anti-Vivisection Society (NAVS) is a principal funder of the International Foundation for Ethical Research (IFER), and Mary Margaret Cunniff, executive director of NAVS, is a director of IFER. In *IFER News*, Summer 1995, IFER advisory board member Martin Fettman described an experiment in which rats aboard the Columbia shuttle were "euthanized by decapitation, and dissected." Fettman acknowledged that "the rodents did not volunteer for the studies," but he assured animal advocates that the vivisection by NASA aboard Columbia represented "minimal and responsible animal use" for which NASA owed no apology. *See IFER News*, Summer 1995, at 6, 7.

6. For a discussion of these issues, see Chapter Four.

7. I discuss these issues in detail in Chapter Three.

8. After protest by animal advocates, NAA claimed to have removed Frederick's from its list of sponsors, asserting that Frederick's had been included as the result of a "sincere desire to promote the fact that the company had made the just and compassionate decision to abolish the use of fur in the production of its products." Statement of Liz Clancy Lyons of the National Alliance for Animals, March 24, 1996 (copy on file with the author).

9. *See* Carl Sagan, "In the Valley of the Shadow," *Parade*, Sunday, March 10, 1996, at 18, 20.

10. *See* Jane Goodall, "A Plea for the Chimps," *New York Times Magazine*, May 17, 1987, section 6, at 108.

11. Goodall has supported xenografts in a variety of contexts, including an interview on the "Larry King Show" in which she praised the use of pigs' heart valves in humans.

12. *See* Deborah Blum, *The Monkey Wars* (New York: Oxford University Press, 1994), 26–29.

13. Mark Harris, "The Threat from Within," *Vegetarian Times*, February 1995, at 64.

14. *See* Jack Rosenberger, "The Ugly Secret of the Black Beauty Ranch," *Village Voice*, December 18, 1990, at 39.

15. The Genesis Awards presentation was reported in "Genesis Awards Honors Media's Pro-Animal Coverage," *Animals' Agenda*, vol. 16, no. 1 (1996).

16. *See* Memorandum from Michael Giannelli, Executive Director, Ark Trust (January 2, 1996) (copy on file with the author).

17. Peter Singer, *Animal Liberation*, 2d ed. (New York: New York Review of Books, 1990), 8.

18. Wayne Pacelle, "Wayne Pacelle, Unplugged," *Animals' Agenda*, vol. 14, no. 6 (1994), at 28.

19. Kenneth J. Shapiro and Peter B. Field, "A New Invasiveness Scale: Its Role in Reducing Animal Distress," 2 *Humane Innovations and Alternatives in Animal Experimentation* 43 (1988).

20. Kim W. Stallwood, "Utopian Visions and Pragmatic Politics: The Challenges of the Animal Rights Movement" (paper presented at the National Alliance for Animals conference, June 24, 1995).

21. Zoe Weil, *AV Magazine*, September/October 1995, at 20. The American Anti-Vivisection Society also promotes the *Journal of Applied Animal Welfare Science*.

22. It appears that different types of promotional materials were geared toward different audiences. Many of the promotional materials do not mention "rights" at all.

23. *See* Tom Regan, "Why We Will Not Be Marching," December 7, 1995 (copy on file with the author).

24. In a November 1995 document circulated by Regan, he states that Peter Gerard invited him " 'to present [the] coveted Opening Address' at the World Congress." He also stated that Gerard had solicited Regan's "interest in serving on the International Advisory Board and the Steering Committee" (copy on file with the author).

25. Letter from Tom Regan to Peter Gerard, March 2, 1996 (copy on file with the author). Similarly, an organization called Animal Rights America (ARA) called for a boycott of the march but then rescinded the boycott. This action followed assurance by NAA director Peter Gerard that the 1996 march was really going to be a "rights" march after all, despite financial support from leading welfarists and the role of welfarists as keynote speakers.

26. Regan, "Why We Will Not Be Marching."

Index

This book primarily concerns the theorists and activists who are involved in a particular social protest movement; accordingly, the index centers more on individuals and groups than on concepts that are discussed throughout the text. The endnotes, which are extensive, are not internally indexed; the material therein can be accessed through the numbered references in the indexed text.